Gardening
with Perennials

Creating Beautiful Flower Gardens for Every Part of Your Yard

Edited by Fern Marshall Bradley

Contributors:
Sally Jean Cunningham,
Barbara W. Ellis,
Barbara Kaczorowski,
Terry Krautwurst,
Jean M. A. Nick,
Nancy J. Ondra,
Lynne Schwartz-Barker

RODALE

RODALE

WE **INSPIRE** AND **ENABLE** PEOPLE TO IMPROVE
THEIR LIVES AND THE WORLD AROUND THEM

We're always happy to hear from you. For questions or comments concerning the editorial content of this book, please write to:

Rodale Book Readers' Service
33 East Minor Street
Emmaus, PA 18098

Look for other Rodale books wherever books are sold. Or call us at (800) 848-4735.

For more information about Rodale and the books and magazines we publish, visit our World Wide Web site at:

www.rodale.com

Gardening with Perennials Editorial Staff

Editor: *Fern Marshall Bradley*
Interior Designer: *Karen Coughlin*
Cover Designer: *Brian Goddard*
Interior Illustrators: *Louise Smith (color), Debbie Smith (black and white), Randall Sauchuck (technical), Frank Fretz (pests and diseases)*
Cover Photographer: *Rob Cardillo*
Photography Editor: *Heidi A. Stonehill*
Studio Manager: *Leslie Keefe*
Copy Editor: *Sarah Dunn*
Manufacturing Coordinator: *Patrick Smith*
Editorial Assistance: *Stephanie Snyder, Gloria Krupa Andrew*

Rodale Organic Gardening Books

Managing Editor: *Fern Marshall Bradley*
Executive Creative Director: *Christin Gangi*
Associate Art Director: *Patricia Field*
Production Manager: *Robert V. Anderson Jr.*
Studio Manager: *Leslie M. Keefe*
Associate Copy Manager: *Jennifer Hornsby*
Manufacturing Manager: *Mark Krahforst*

Library of Congress Cataloging-in-Publication Data

Gardening with perennials : creating beautiful flower gardens for every part of your yard / Fern Marshall Bradley, editor : contributors, Sally Jean Cunningham ... [et al.].
   p. cm.
  Includes bibliographical references and index
  ISBN 0–87596–703–5 (hardcover : alk. paper)
  1. Perennials. 2. Landscape gardening. 3. Gardens—Design.
I. Bradley, Fern Marshall. II. Cunningham, Sally Jean.
SB434.L36 1996
635.9'32—dc20   95–39854

ISBN 0-87596-844-9 (paperback)

Distributed in the book trade by St. Martin's Press

2 4 6 8 10 9 7 5 3   hardcover
2 4 6 8 10 9 7 5 3 1 paperback

CONTENTS

CREDITS

Writers

Sally Jean Cunningham plants her perennial gardens in East Aurora, New York, where she shares Wonderland Farm with her daughter Alice, husband Brendan, 6 cats, 2 dogs, horses, and a large population of beneficial insects. At Cornell Cooperative Extension of Erie County, Sally helps home gardeners solve their gardening problems and coordinates the activities of 140 Master Gardeners.

Barbara W. Ellis has designed and planted a perennial landscape around her stone farmhouse on Walnut Hill Farm in Berks County, Pennsylvania. Barbara is a freelance writer and editor who specializes in gardening and crafts. She has also worked as managing editor of Rodale Garden Books and as publications director for *American Horticulturist* magazine.

Barbara Kaczorowski and her husband Michael live and breathe perennials at Accent Gardens in Cicero, Indiana. Accent Gardens is their perennial nursery and landscape design and installation firm. Barbara and Michael have installed large perennial display gardens, an herb garden, a huge annual garden for cutting flowers, and a vegetable and fruit garden at Accent Gardens. Barbara's newest project is a terraced rose garden.

Terry Krautwurst makes his home and gardens in the Blue Ridge Mountains of western North Carolina, where he contends with a local climate that features the heat and humidity of the Deep South, unpredictable thaws, surprise frosts, and the occasional month of constant rain. When he's not dealing with a weather crisis, Terry works as a freelance nature and garden writer. He favors "out-of-the-mainstream" perennials for his garden, including pasque flower (*Anemone pulsatilla*) and plumbago (*Ceratostigma plumbaginoides*).

Jean M. A. Nick plants and propagates perennials on a sunny hillside surrounding her home in Bucks County, Pennsylvania. She works as an information analyst for Rodale Press, but her passion is her gardens, which include an acre of small fruits. Jean has worked as an associate editor for Rodale Garden Books and has extensive experience in the commercial greenhouse industry.

Nancy J. Ondra grows unusual perennials at her specialty nursery, Pendragon Perennials, in Emmaus, Pennsylvania. Nancy serves on the board of directors of the Hardy Plant Society, Mid-Atlantic Division. She is coauthor of *Rodale's Successful Gardening: Annuals and Bulbs.* Nancy also works as a freelance garden writer and editor, and has worked as an editor for Rodale Garden Books.

Lynne Schwartz-Barker is a native New Yorker who has been gardening on 76 acres in West Virginia since 1977. Lynne and her husband Jerry own Flowerscape, a residential landscape design and contracting company. Gardeners across West Virginia enjoy reading Lynne's gardening advice and anecdotes in her weekly column for the *Charleston Gazette.*

Designers

C. Colston Burrell owns Native Landscapes, a Minnesota-based design business that specializes in landscape restoration and the innovative use of native plants and perennials in garden design. He is the coauthor of *Rodale's Illustrated Encyclopedia of Perennials.*

Stephanie Cohen is the co-designer of the perennial border at River Farm in Virginia, headquarters of the American Horticultural Society, and the designer of the herb garden at Temple University. She teaches courses in herbaceous plants at Temple University and the Barnes Arboretum.

Karen Coughlin is a book designer for Rodale Press. She has worked previously as a graphic designer in New York City designing trade book covers, brochures, and logos. With the help of her father-in-law, Karen is learning gardening skills and experimenting with home canning.

Special Thanks

I would like to thank Joanne Kostecky, owner of Joanne Kostecky Garden Design in Bethlehem, Pennsylvania, and Pat and James Agger for the use of Joanne's design for the Aggers' property. Her design is the prototype for illustrations of a perennial landscape in Part 3.

INTRODUCTION

Have you caught perennial fever? If you have, you know how fun and enjoyable gardening with perennials can be. You're ready for new challenges and ideas, ready to make perennials a part of your whole landscape. Or perhaps you're new to the world of perennials. In that case, you may be feeling a little lost or apprehensive. These plants just don't behave like familiar annual bedding plants. It can be hard to know which perennials will look best as bedfellows and how to anticipate what kind of care they'll need.

Whatever your level of perennial expertise, you'll find the how-to information you need—plus a terrific dose of inspiration and ideas—in *Gardening with Perennials*. The book has four distinct sections, each of which offers a unique way for you to approach the adventure of landscaping your yard with perennials.

In Part 1, "Perennial Gardens for Every Part of Your Yard," we've put together an instructive collection of garden designs, photographs, tables, and tips about how to use perennials to create theme gardens, to landscape special sites, and to solve landscape problems. You can browse through this section at random or zero in on your special area of interest, whether it's butterfly gardening, finding a solution for a hard-to-mow slope, or choosing the right perennials to plant on a hot, dry site.

Throughout Part 1, you'll find full-color illustrations of perennial gardens. These gardens were created by professional garden designers especially for you. All the plants they've chosen are readily available through either garden centers or retail mail-order catalogs, and all of the designs are simple enough for a backyard gardener to successfully plant and maintain.

Use these designs as a starting point. You may want to plant just a part of one design, or choose just a few of the plants and group them in different combinations. The perennials our designers selected will make wonderful companions even if you change the shape of the garden or add in a few of your favorites to suit your yard.

In Part 2, "Classic Perennials and Perennial Combinations," you'll find practical portraits of 75 easy-to-grow, versatile perennials. This section allows to you experiment with using perennials in your landscape without making or adapting a full-blown garden plan. For each perennial, you'll find a photograph of the plant in combination with other perennials (and occasionally with a companionable annual or shrub). The text suggests additional good companions and landscape uses.

Part 3, "Creating Garden and Landscape Designs," introduces you to the world of perennial landscape and garden design. Don't worry—creating your own designs doesn't have to be complicated. In fact, it can be a lot of fun! Chapter 5 helps you start working with your garden fantasies and dreams to create a list of gardens and features you'd like to include in your yard. In Chapter 6, we explain a simple system for sorting your ideas and transferring them to a map of your property to show you how to change your dreams into a finished landscape plan.

Chapter 7 takes a fresh approach to the subject of garden design. It explains garden design principles in everyday terms, using photographs of perennial combinations as examples. Chapter 8 shows how to choose plants that will give your garden season-long interest and how to group them to create a beautiful garden picture.

Part 4, "Carrying Out Your Landscape Plan," explains the organic techniques and gives step-by-step instructions that will guarantee your garden's success. Chapter 9 guides you through the all-important process of preparing your site for planting. It shows you how to install hardscape features like edgings and pathways. You'll also find helpful tips for making newly planted perennial gardens look lush and lovely. Chapter 10 provides money-saving ideas for creating your own "mini-nursery" where you can propagate your own supply of new perennials to fill your beds and borders. Chapter 11 gives you seasonal illustrated timelines highlighting important maintenance chores that will keep your beds looking their best. Plus, it includes a problem-solving section to help you identify pests and diseases that may trouble your perennials, and provides the easiest, most effective organic solutions.

So, go ahead and dig into *Gardening with Perennials* and into new perennial gardens! With this book, you're starting a great adventure: filling your yard with perennials and putting your house in the center of a beautiful garden.

1 Perennial Gardens for Every Part of Your Yard

by Barbara Kaczorowski, Sally Jean Cunningham, Terry Krautwurst, and Lynne Schwartz-Barker

Ask a hundred gardeners why they grow perennials and you'll undoubtedly get at least a hundred answers. That's because perennials play *many* roles in the garden. In this gallery of garden ideas and garden designs, you're sure to find new and exciting ways to use perennials in your home landscape. Perhaps you'll decide to plant a perennial garden to celebrate your passion for hot colors. Maybe you'll decide to create a secluded woodland garden. There are perennial gardens for many themes: color, butterflies, herbs, cut flowers, and more! You'll also find perennial solutions to tough landscape problems like poor soil, slopes, and deep shade. No matter what size yard you have or what region of the country you live in, there are perennials that will thrive in your gardens.

Chapter 1

Special Themes for Special Gardens

Color Theme Gardens • Easy-Does-It Gardens • Four-Season Landscaping •

Attracting Butterflies and Birds • Woodland, Meadow, and Wetland Gardens

• A Perennial Herb Garden • A Fragrant Garden • An Evening Garden •

Perennials for Cutting and Drying

A Color Theme Garden

Designing a single-color garden is one of the easiest ways to get a handle on orchestrating a perennial garden. Making decisions about color combinations can seem overwhelming, especially when you're new to perennial gardening. So set aside your worries about which colors "go" together. Sticking to a single color liberates you to tune in to aspects like bloom time, plant height, and texture.

Color theme gardens have been favorites of some of the most distinguished gardeners in history. The style and sophistication of these special gardens is easy to bring into your own backyard. You can even design a color theme garden to complement your interior color scheme!

Does a color theme garden really have only a single color? Unless it's composed of a single plant, the answer is a resounding "no." No matter what your chosen theme color, you'll quickly find that variations in hue and shade among perennial flowers are almost unlimited. Take advantage of your color's full range. Using a mixture of colors enlivens your composition. If, for instance, your theme is blue, choose some plants that are blue-violet or even purple. Likewise, you may find that a splash of white or pale yellow adds immeasurably to the beauty of the combination.

Use different flower forms to add contrast in a color theme garden. For example, try pairing bold white daylilies with the delicate floral sprays of baby's-breath.

The interplay of foliage colors and textures is the background music for the greater drama of the flowers in your color theme garden. For example, contrasts between ferny foliage, like that of fringed bleeding heart (*Dicentra eximia*), and bold-textured leaves, like those of a white-blooming hosta, can lend excitement to a white border. Foliage tints reinforce a color theme. Plants with blue-green leaves will echo the flower tones in a blue border. Gold-variegated foliage works well in a yellow border, and white or cream variegation in a white garden. Foliage color can also provide contrast in a color theme garden. For instance, the cool notes of gray or silvery leaves could set off the warm tones of the flowers in a yellow border to create a garden of silver and gold.

In a white garden, the foliage of sea holly (*Eryngium* sp.) and annual dusty miller can offer a silvery variation on the color theme. ➤

A Garden with the Blues

This blue border isn't just a bunch of blue flowers. Designer Barbara Kaczorowski mixed flowers of many shades and used foliage color and plant form to enliven the design. Shown here in late spring, the blue false indigo, speedwell, and Rocky Mountain columbine have "true blue" flowers. Other blossom colors range from the deep blue-violet of the cranesbill to the pale blue milky bellflower. Blue oat grass foliage is a fine-textured fountain of blue-gray leaves, and the leaves of bluebeard and Russian sage are gray-green. The flowers of threadleaf coreopsis are not blue at all, but a luminous lemon yellow, which serves to intensify the blues that surround it.

All plants in this design will thrive in Zones 4–8, except for the bluebeard, which is hardy only to Zone 5.

Bluebeard (*Caryopteris × clandonensis* 'Longwood Blue'). 3'–5' tall; flat clusters of smoky blue flowers midsummer–frost.

Blue false indigo (*Baptisia australis*). 2'–4' tall; attractive black seedpods and long-lasting foliage; blooms late spring–early summer.

Balloon flower (*Platycodon grandiflorum* var. *mariesii*). 3' tall; balloonlike buds open to 2", violet-blue, star-shaped flowers midsummer–fall.

Cranesbill (*Geranium* 'Johnson's Blue'). 18" tall; flowers late spring. Reblooms in late summer if scrupulously deadheaded.

Speedwell (*Veronica* 'Sunny Border Blue'). 2' tall; 4"–6" spikes of medium blue flowers on stout stems early summer–frost.

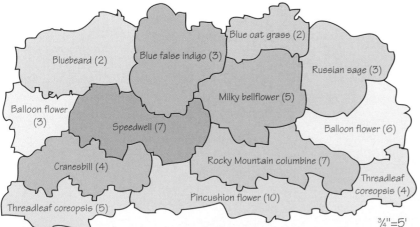

Bluebeard (2)

Blue false indigo (3)

Blue oat grass (2)

Russian sage (3)

Balloon flower (3)

Speedwell (7)

Milky bellflower (5)

Balloon flower (6)

Cranesbill (4)

Rocky Mountain columbine (7)

Threadleaf coreopsis (4)

Threadleaf coreopsis (5)

Pincushion flower (10)

¾"=5'

Numbers in parentheses indicate quantities to plant

Blue oat grass (*Helictotrichon sempervirens*). 2' tall; oatlike flowers in early summer; semi-evergreen. Requires moderately well-drained soil.

Milky bellflower (*Campanula lactiflora*). 3' tall; flowers can also be white or pink; early summer bloom. Reblooms late summer and fall if deadheaded.

Russian sage (*Perovskia atriplicifolia*). Shrubby perennial to 3' tall; forms clouds of blue flower spikes midsummer–frost. Leave skeleton in place for winter interest.

Threadleaf coreopsis (*Coreopsis verticillata* 'Moonbeam'). 18" tall; luminous, pale yellow, single flowers with pink centers early summer–frost.

Pincushion flower (*Scabiosa caucasica* 'Butterfly Blue'). 18" tall; flowers spring–frost. Requires good drainage, otherwise tolerant of most soil types.

Rocky Mountain columbine (*Aquilegia caerulea*). 1'–2' tall; blooms for 4–6 weeks late spring–early summer. Grows best in cool soil.

A Hot-Color Garden

Incandescent, high-voltage colors electrify a garden. Crimson, scarlet, oranges, yellows, and even fuschia (hot pink!) are the powerful palette that crank up the heat—and the excitement—in your border. Bright colors add exuberance that soft pastels just can't convey. Hot-color borders like this garden designed by Barbara Kaczorowski, shown here in summer, will seem closer to the eye of the viewer than a garden of cool hues. It's a good choice for a site that you'll view from a distance (such as inside your house).

All plants in this border for full sun will grow well in Zones 5–8. If you're a Zone 4 gardener, you may want to substitute a hardier choice for the common torch lily and montbretia.

Cardinal flower (*Lobelia cardinalis*). 4' tall; flowers mid- to late summer. Best with steady moisture but takes drought with reduced flowering.

Bee balm (*Monarda didyma* 'Purple Mildew Resistant'). 3'–4' tall; flowers in summer. Best with steady moisture; requires frequent division.

Golden marguerite (*Anthemis tinctoria* 'Moonlight'). Sprawling plant 2'–3' tall; flowers summer–fall. Drought-tolerant; self-sows.

Blood-red cranesbill (*Geranium sanguineum* 'New Hampshire Purple'). Mounded plant to 12"; flowers in summer.

Speedwell (*Veronica* 'Sunny Border Blue'). 2' tall; flowers early summer–frost.

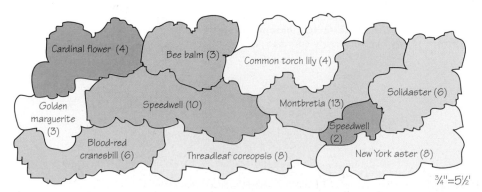

Cardinal flower (4)

Bee balm (3)

Common torch lily (4)

Golden marguerite (3)

Speedwell (10)

Montbretia (13)

Solidaster (6)

Speedwell (2)

Blood-red cranesbill (6)

Threadleaf coreopsis (8)

New York aster (8)

¾"=5½'

Numbers in parentheses indicate quantities to plant

Common torch lily (*Kniphofia uvaria* 'Primrose Beauty'). 3' tall; flowers in summer.

Montbretia (*Crocosmia* 'Lucifer'). 3' tall; flowers in midsummer. Provide good drainage and mulch in northern zones; grows from a corm.

Solidaster (✕ *Solidaster luteus*). 2' tall; flowers late summer–early fall. More drought-tolerant than asters; good cut flower.

New York aster (*Aster novi-belgii* 'Alert'). 18" tall; deep crimson flowers in fall.

Threadleaf coreopsis (*Coreopsis verticillata* 'Moonbeam'). 18" tall; flowers early summer–frost. Plants late to emerge in spring.

Don't Overheat Your Garden

Combining too many hot colors can be jarring and chaotic. To avoid a garden that's too hot to handle, try some simple tricks to keep the colors under control.

- Surround a hot color like scarlet with related shades like orange and yellow, together with white.

- Use a complementary color like cool blue to quench an overly fiery combination.

- Buffer clashing colors, such as red and lavender, by separating them with silver.

- Soothe jarring combinations by softening one color to pastel. For instance, pair bright red with a pale lemon yellow.

A Cool-Color Garden

Blues, violets, gray, silver, pastel pinks, mauve, and white impart serenity and calm to the garden. Cool colors are easy to work with: No matter how you mix them up, the compatible tones of cool colors rarely clash.

The cool-color border evokes an illusion of distance. A cool-color garden at the edge of a small yard will seem to enlarge it. In this garden, designer Barbara Kaczorowski used bright pink common beardtongue to add spice to the cool palate. Contrasts in texture—like the dark, hairy leaves and spiky flowers of the strawberry foxglove—also add drama.

All the plants in this border, shown here in late summer, will grow well in Zones 5–8, in sun to light shade.

Catmint (*Nepeta* × *faassenii*). 1½'–2' tall; flowers early summer and late summer–fall. Very drought-tolerant; moderately spreading.

Common beardtongue (*Penstemon barbatus* 'Elfin Pink'). 18" tall; flowers in early summer. May rebloom in late summer.

Thick leaf phlox (*Phlox carolina* 'Miss Lingard'). 2'–3' tall; flowers in summer. Mildew-resistant.

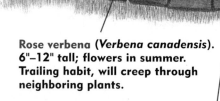

Rose verbena (*Verbena canadensis*). 6"–12" tall; flowers in summer. Trailing habit, will creep through neighboring plants.

Frikart's aster (*Aster* × *frikartii* 'Monch'). 3' tall; flowers late summer–fall.

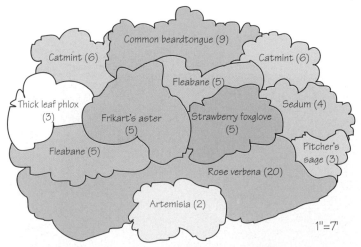

Catmint (6)

Common beardtongue (9)

Catmint (6)

Fleabane (5)

Thick leaf phlox (3)

Frikart's aster (5)

Strawberry foxglove (5)

Sedum (4)

Fleabane (5)

Pitcher's sage (3)

Rose verbena (20)

Artemisia (2)

1"=7'

Numbers in parentheses indicate quantities to plant

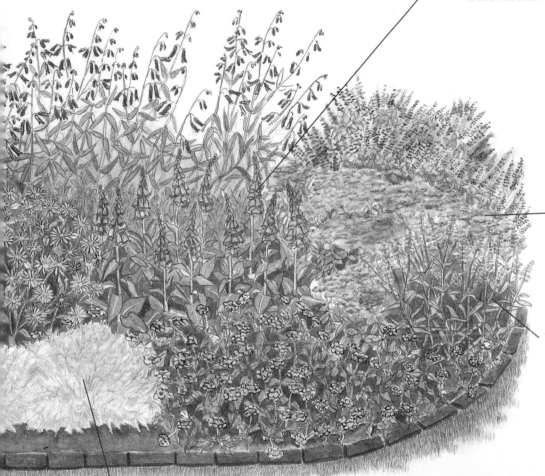

Fleabane (*Erigeron* 'Azure Fairy'). 18" tall; 2" violet-blue, daisylike flowers in early summer. Cut back after blooms fade (not visible in illustration).

Strawberry foxglove (*Digitalis* X *mertonensis*). 3' tall; flowers in early summer. Reblooms later if deadheaded.

Sedum (*Sedum* 'Autumn Joy'). 2' tall; flowers late summer–frost. Tough, drought-resistant plant; flowers dry and provide winter interest in the garden.

Pitcher's sage (*Salvia azurea* var. *grandiflora*). 3' tall; flowers in fall. One of the purest blues in the plant world.

Artemisia (*Artemisia* 'Powis Castle'). 2'–3' tall; aromatic leaves. Doesn't bloom; cut back by one-half every year to maintain form.

Cool Characters

There are hundreds of cool-color cultivars and species of perennials for home gardens. If you're thinking blue, try delphinium species and hybrids (*Delphinium grandiflorum*, *D.* Pacific Hybrids), `Fama' pincushion flower (*Scabiosa caucasica* 'Fama'), plumbago (*Ceratostigma plumbaginoides*), and willow blue star (*Amsonia tabernaemontana*). For a touch of pink, use columbine meadow rue (*Thalictrum aquilegifolium*) and `Minuet' spike speedwell (*Veronica spicata* 'Minuet'). Add violet shades with `Purple Rain' lilac sage (*Salvia verticillata* 'Purple Rain'), purple lobelia (*Lobelia* X *gerardii*), and Siberian statice (*Limonium gmelinii*).

Easy-Does-It Gardens

So you want a colorful perennial garden, but don't want—or have the time—to work for it? Well, you're in luck! Many terrific perennials thrive on benign neglect.

The most important rule to remember for easy-care perennial gardens is to *match the plant to your growing conditions.* And that means more than checking whether a plant is hardy in your zone. Most plants are best adapted to a certain soil type, as well as moisture and light supply. If your soil is dry or sandy, don't fight your site! Pick plants that do well in the soil you have. For some specific matches of plants to soil types, see "Perennials for a Hot, Dry Site" on page 69 and "Perennials for Soggy Situations" on page 41. "Tough, Easy-Care Perennials" on the opposite page features plants that tolerate sandy or heavy clay soils.

Another rule is to match a plant's growing style to your purpose. If you have a large area that you want to fill quickly, a rampantly spreading or avidly self-sowing plant could be just the ticket. But if your objective is to have a mixed perennial garden, such aggressive plants would be a maintenance nightmare. For tips on managing aggressive perennials, see "Perennial Crowd Control" on page 13.

For an easy-care garden, stick with perennials that seldom or never need dividing. Taprooted plants, like gasplant (*Dictamnus albus*) and baptisias (*Baptisia* spp.), prefer never to be disturbed at all. Daylilies need dividing only about every five years. But stay away from plants like snow-in-summer (*Cerastium tomentosum*), which tend to die out in the middle and need frequent division to keep them vigorous.

Choose plants that are disease- and insect-resistant. While occasional insect problems can appear on almost any plant, certain perennials are distinctly more disease-prone than others. Mildew often disfigures garden phlox, for example. If you want to grow phlox, choose mildew-resistant cultivars like 'David'.

Select long-blooming, "self-cleaning" perennials that don't need deadheading. Leave the dead tops in place over the winter. They provide winter interest, help protect the crowns from injury, and provide food for birds.

Mass plantings of tough perennials make easy-care gardens. 'Blue Hill' salvia (*Salvia* 'Blue Hill') backed by 'Mary Todd' daylilies form a simple but dramatic border.

Tough, Easy-Care Perennials

Common and Botanical Name	Hardiness and Exposure	Bloom Time and Color	Description
Lead plant *Amorpha canescens*	Zones 4–9 Sun	Early–midsummer Amethyst	2' mound; gray-green leaves with silvery, felted undersides; 4"–6" spikes of small flowers that attract bees. Likes sandy soil.
Butterfly weed *Asclepias tuberosa*	Zones 3–9 Sun to light shade	Midsummer Orange, yellow, or red	Upright, 1'–3' stems; lance-shaped, leathery leaves; flat clusters of waxy, star-like flowers that attract butterflies. Tolerates sandy soils.
Astilbes *Astilbe* spp.	Zones 3–9 Sun to shade	Summer White, pink, or red	1'–3' stems; glossy, fernlike leaves; plume- or spire-shaped flowers. Needs constant moisture; can grow well in heavy clay soils.
Red valerian *Centranthus ruber*	Zones 4–8 Sun	Early summer–fall Cerise, white, or dusty pink	1'–3' mound; gray-green, pointed leaves; 3"–4" dome-shaped heads of tiny flowers. Tolerates sandy soil. Deadhead to prolong bloom.
Pinks *Dianthus* spp.	Zones 3–9 Sun to light shade	Late spring–summer Red, pink, white, or salmon	6"–18" clumps or mats; narrow leaves; masses of fringed, single or double, often fragrant flowers. Likes sandy soil, won't grow in wet soil.
Flowering spurge *Euphorbia corollata*	Zones 3–8 Sun to partial shade	Late summer White	Graceful, 1'–3' stems; light gray-green leaves; airy clusters of flowers over a long period. Tolerates drought and sandy soil.
Sunflower heliopsis *Heliopsis helianthoides*	Zones 3–9 Sun to light shade	Summer Bright yellow	3'–6' bushy plant; wedge-shaped leaves; 3"–4" single or double flowers. Tolerates heavy clay soil. Choose short cultivars to avoid staking.
Daylilies *Hemerocallis* spp. and hybrids	Zones 2–9 Sun to partial shade	Late spring–summer Red, yellow, orange, or pink	1'–4' grasslike foliage; 2"–6" lily-shaped flowers, sometimes fragrant. Tolerates heavy clay soil. Some rebloom throughout summer.
Sea lavender *Limonium latifolium*	Zones 3–9 Sun to light shade	Late summer Lavender-blue	Masses of tiny flowers on 2' wiry stems rising above large, oval leaves. Adaptable to sandy and salty soils. Use in fresh or dry arrangements.
Showy evening primrose *Oenothera speciosa*	Zones 5–8 Sun	Summer–fall Pink	Wiry stems to 1'; wavy-edged, red-tinged leaves; 2"–4" flowers. Grows well in heavy clay soil. Can become highly invasive.

An Island in the Sun

If you love the idea of a perennial garden but just don't think you have the time for one, this island bed is for you. Designer Stephanie Cohen chose perennials for their disease and insect resistance, drought tolerance, and self-supporting growth (no staking!). Be sure to mulch the garden when you plant it, and renew the mulch yearly to hold in moisture and help keep down weeds.

Most of these plants, shown here in summer, will thrive in average garden soil in Zones 4–8. (Threadleaf coreopsis and Japanese silver grass are reliably hardy only to Zone 5.) Many of the flowers also make excellent cut flowers. So instead of spending time caring for this garden, you can dabble in creating lovely arrangements for your living room.

'White Swan' coneflower (*Echinacea purpurea* 'White Swan'). 2'–3' tall; flowers summer–fall. Heat- and drought-tolerant.

Longleaf speedwell (*Veronica longifolia* 'Icicle'). 2'–4' tall; flowers early summer–fall. Long-lasting foliage.

Yarrow (*Achillea* 'Apple Blossom'). 3' tall; flowers in summer. Prefers well-drained soil.

Daylily (*Hemerocallis* 'Stella de Oro'). 12"–18" tall; flowers late spring–frost.

Perennial candytuft (*Iberis sempervirens* 'Autumn Beauty'). Mat-forming, 8" plants; covered with white flowers spring and fall; foliage evergreen.

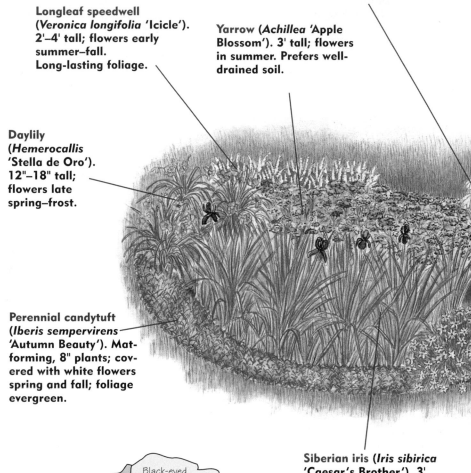

Siberian iris (*Iris sibirica* 'Caesar's Brother'). 3' tall; violet flowers late spring–early summer. Prefers moist, slightly acidic soil.

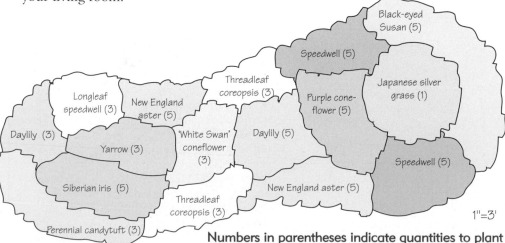

Daylily (3)
Longleaf speedwell (3)
New England aster (5)
Yarrow (3)
Siberian iris (5)
Perennial candytuft (3)
Threadleaf coreopsis (3)
'White Swan' coneflower (3)
Daylily (5)
New England aster (5)
Threadleaf coreopsis (3)
Speedwell (5)
Black-eyed Susan (5)
Purple coneflower (5)
Japanese silver grass (1)
Speedwell (5)

1"=3'

Numbers in parentheses indicate quantities to plant

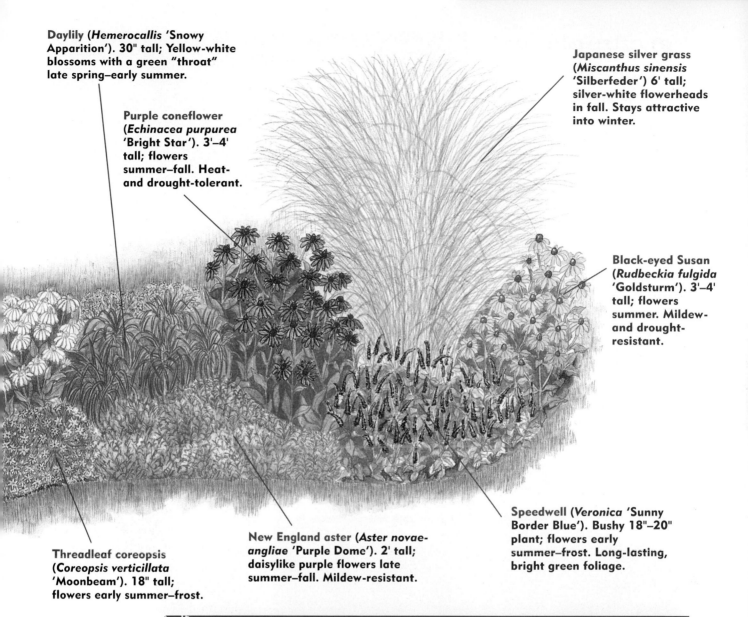

Daylily (*Hemerocallis* 'Snowy Apparition'). 30" tall; Yellow-white blossoms with a green "throat" late spring–early summer.

Purple coneflower (*Echinacea purpurea* 'Bright Star'). 3'–4' tall; flowers summer–fall. Heat- and drought-tolerant.

Japanese silver grass (*Miscanthus sinensis* 'Silberfeder') 6' tall; silver-white flowerheads in fall. Stays attractive into winter.

Black-eyed Susan (*Rudbeckia fulgida* 'Goldsturm'). 3'–4' tall; flowers summer. Mildew- and drought-resistant.

Threadleaf coreopsis (*Coreopsis verticillata* 'Moonbeam'). 18" tall; flowers early summer–frost.

New England aster (*Aster novae-angliae* 'Purple Dome'). 2' tall; daisylike purple flowers late summer–fall. Mildew-resistant.

Speedwell (*Veronica* 'Sunny Border Blue'). Bushy 18"–20" plant; flowers early summer–frost. Long-lasting, bright green foliage.

Perennial Crowd Control

Perennials that grow aggressively spread quickly and generally need little water or fertilizing. But aggressive plants can be a headache if they overgrow their bounds. Here are some tips for preventing them from crowding out other plants.

- Keep wet-soil denizens like hardy ageratum (*Eupatorium coelestinum*) and bee balms (*Monarda* spp.) dry.

- Surround aggressive spreaders like obedient plant (*Physostegia virginiana*) with a 6-inch-high rigid plastic or metal barrier buried to within 1/4 inch of the soil surface.

- Fertilize minimally or not at all.

- Use them for groundcover-style plantings of a single species.

Perennials for a Four-Season Landscape

Perennial gardens look great in June, when most "classic" perennials are at their peak of bloom. But what about the remaining 11 months of the year? Do the dog days of July and August find you sitting in the shade, trying not to look at a perennial garden that looks as worn out by the heat as you feel? When autumn arrives, do you rely on a few pots of mums to give your garden color?

Imagine a winter garden where snow highlights the forms

Choose plants with different bloom periods and long-lasting features to make the most of your garden. Artemisia foliage stays silvery bright all season, while the towering dusty rose flowerheads of Joe-Pye weed (*Eupatorium fistulosum*) bring a border back to life in late summer. Japanese silver grass (*Miscanthus sinensis*) has lovely summer foliage and reddish flowers that emerge in October.

Perennials That Go the Distance

These perennials really bloom *all* summer and into fall. (Be sure to ask for the specific cultivar named here.) Plant name is followed by flower color.

Gaura (*Gaura lindheimeri*); white, aging to pink; Zones 5–9.

Grayleaf cranesbill (*Geranium cinereum* 'Ballerina'); pink; Zones 5–8.

Knautia macedonica; maroon; Zones 4–8.

'Moonbeam' coreopsis (*Coreopsis verticillata* 'Moonbeam'); pale yellow; Zones 3–9.

Pincushion flower (*Scabiosa caucasica* 'Pink Mist' and 'Butterfly Blue'); pink and periwinkle blue; Zones 3–7.

Red valerian (*Centranthus ruber*); cerise, mauve, or white; Zones 4–8.

'Stella de Oro' daylily (*Hemerocallis* 'Stella de Oro'); yellow; Zones 4–9.

Rose verbena (*Verbena canadensis* 'Homestead Purple'); rich purple; Zones 4–10.

Speedwell (*Veronica* 'Sunny Border Blue'); medium blue; Zones 4–8.

and textures of perennial seedheads and stems, while birds flit about harvesting seeds. Dream about strolling through your yard on a winter day admiring evergreen leaves—and even flowers in the snow. When you engage the wider world of four-season perennials, your garden can shine year-round.

Summer

In June, perennial gardens are bursting with flowers of every hue. But there's more to summer gardening than June bloomers. Enhance your summer garden by planting late summer bloomers among or near early bloomers. The late bloomers will scarcely be noticeable in June, but as the early bloomers fade and begin to look ratty, the burgeoning late-comers will hide them, creating areas of nonstop bloom.

Also, include some true all-summer bloomers in your beds and borders. See "Perennials That Go the Distance" on the opposite page for suggestions.

Fall

Many of the year's final flowers, like asters and Japanese anemone (*Anemone* × *hybrida*), are true fall bloomers. Others, like Russian sage (*Perovskia atrip-*

licifolia), are merely continuing the show they began in July.

Add to the show by encouraging some of your perennials that bloomed during summer to rebloom late in the season. Here's how to encourage rebloom.

- Deadhead plants that can re-bloom promptly after the first flowering, long before they begin to set seed.
- Work bonemeal into the soil around perennials annually. Bonemeal supplies phosphorus, which encourages flowering.
- Water your perennials evenly

and deeply throughout the summer.

- Feed reblooming perennials with manure tea, fish emulsion, or seaweed in mid- to late summer.

Fall gardens can be filled with color. Pinkish sedum flowerheads contrast with delicate white Japanese aster (*Kalimeris pinnatifida* 'Hortensis'), bright yellow European goldenrod (*Solidago virgaurea* 'Crown of Rays'), violet Frikart's aster (*Aster* × *frikartii* 'Monch'), and purple annual perilla.

Late Bloomers

These perennials will light up a border long after most plants have quit the scene. Plant name is followed by flower color.

'Autumn Joy' sedum (*Sedum* 'Autumn Joy'); icy pink to deep rose and russet; Zones 3–9.

Boltonias (*Boltonia asteroides* 'Snowbank' and 'Pink Beauty'); white and pink; Zones 3–9.

Hardy ageratum (*Eupatorium coelestinum*); periwinkle blue; Zones 6–10.

'Herrenhausen' oregano (*Origanum* 'Herrenhausen'); pink; Zones 5–9.

Japanese anemone (*Anemone tomentosa* 'Robustissima'); pink; Zones 3–8.

Mint shrub (*Elsholtzia stauntonii*); pink; Zones 5–9.

'Monch' Frikart's aster (*Aster* × *frikartii* 'Monch'); light blue; Zones 5–8.

Pitcher's sage (*Salvia azurea* var; *grandiflora*); brilliant blue; Zones 5–9.

Plumbago (*Ceratostigma plumbaginoides*); clear blue; Zones 5–9.

Left: Chrysanthemums are a great source of fall color, but don't forget other sources of fall interest: bright red berries, oak leaves, dry astilbe flower-stalks, and ornamental grasses.

Below: Before you launch a fall cleanup frenzy, pause to consider whether your perennials offer late-season interest. Spike gayfeathers (*Liatris spicata*) turn rich bronze only after temperatures dip several degrees below freezing.

Perennial gardens can also offer a host of more subtle autumn beauty. For example, many perennials have leaves that color as brilliantly as any maple. Among these are balloon flower (*Platycodon grandiflorus*), bigroot cranesbill (*Geranium macrorrhizum*), cushion spurge (*Euphorbia epithymoides*), heartleaved bergenia (*Bergenia cordifolia*), hostas, obedient plant (*Physostegia virginiana*), and plumbago (*Ceratostigma plumbaginoides*).

Warm–season ornamental grasses are at their peak of beauty in September and October. Flowering and fruiting shrubs planted in or near your perennial borders add another layer of warm autumnal tones. Use purple beautyberry (*Callicarpa dichotoma*), with its clusters of metallic purple berries and

yellow leaves, to create a gorgeous echo for violet asters. Red chokeberry (*Aronia arbutifolia* 'Brilliantissima') burnishes the garden with wine red fruits and long-lasting flaming foliage.

Winter

The landscape in winter has an austere beauty. When you plan for winter appeal, consider the unique interaction of winter with plants. First of all, the winter sun is low in the sky; the pronounced angle of winter sunlight accentuates textures as well as patterns of light and shadow. Frost and snow italicize plant forms and textures as well.

Plant skeletons, seedheads, and old foliage gilded by frost or iced with snow are much more appealing than uniform blocks of shorn stubble. As you plan your plantings with an eye to winter, be sure to include some perennials with evergreen foliage, as well as those with attractive seedheads or dried foliage and stems. Choose some ornamental grasses, which will dry to lovely shades of buff and russet and retain their plumelike flowers until spring. An added bonus is the graceful motion of these grasses in winter winds.

Choose plants with interesting forms for winter. Think about the woody muscle of tree trunks, the patterns of branches against a flaming winter sunset, and the sculptural twining of bare vines. Include a tree or shrub with horizontal branching, like pagoda dogwood (*Cornus alternifolia*) or an unpruned burning bush (*Euonymus alata*).

Observe the beauty of buds, such as the fat, gray-green velvety ones of magnolias, or the plump, round ones punctuating the zigzagging stems of Ural false spirea (*Sorbaria sorbifolia*). American smoketree (*Cotinus obovatus*) has striking plated bark resembling giant fish scales. Amur chokecherry (*Prunus maackii*), an incredibly fast-growing tree, has shiny bark of burnished copper.

Shrubs can offer bursts of color with the brilliant coral stems of red-osier dogwood (*Cornus sericea* 'Cardinal'), the bright yellow bark of variegated golden twig dogwood (*Cornus sericea* 'Silver and Gold'), and the slender lime green stems of Japanese kerria (*Kerria japonica*). Trees and shrubs with winter-persistent fruits add sparkles of

10 Perennials for Winter Interest

These perennials look good even in winter. Plant name is followed by winter features.

Blackberry lily (*Belamcanda chinensis*); seedpods split open, revealing shiny black seeds that look like blackberries; Zones 4–10.

Blue false indigo (*Baptisia australis*); handsome black seedpods; Zones 3–9.

Cottage pinks (*Dianthus plumarius*); dense mounds of stiff, silver-gray, grasslike foliage; Zones 3–9.

European wild ginger (*Asarum europaeum*); highly glossy, heart-shaped leaves; Zones 4–8.

Heartleaf bergenia (*Bergenia cordifolia*); 6", glossy, fleshy, upright leaves turn red or purplish in cold weather; Zones 3–9.

Lenten rose (*Helleborus orientalis*); 6"–10", glossy, palmate leaves; Zones 4–9.

Orange coneflower (*Rudbeckia fulgida*); myriad conelike flower centers; Zones 3–9.

Partridgeberry (*Mitchella repens*); prostrate, glossy, white-veined, paired round leaves and bright red berries; Zones 3–8.

Purple coneflower (*Echinacea purpurea*); conelike seedheads look pretty and attract birds; Zones 3–8.

Showy stonecrop (*Sedum spectabile*); large, flat, russet seedheads especially handsome with snow; Zones 3–9.

Deep red seedheads of sedum and dried ornamental grasses are a lovely combination in summer and continue to offer subtle beauty against a snowy background.

color and attract birds to the winter garden. Crabapple (*Malus* 'Donald Wyman'), green hawthorn (*Crataegus viridis* 'Winter King'), possum haw (*Ilex decidua* 'Warren Red'), and winterberry (*Ilex verticillata* 'Winter Red') are some of the best.

Spring

February finds most of us chafing at the bit for spring. We know the daffodils, tulips, and familiar spring blossoms of trees and shrubs will delight us in April and May. But you don't have to wait for April if you plant perennials and bulbs that flower in late winter and the first moments of spring, such as the ones listed in "Winter Bloomers" on the opposite page.

In addition to the familiar spring-flowering bulbs, a good number of perennials flower in early spring before the rest of the perennial garden stirs a leaf. Three of the best are pasque flower (*Anemone pulsatilla*) and rock cresses (*Arabis* spp. and *Aubrieta deltoidea*).

Pasque flower bears cupped flowers in white, pink, magenta, and blue. *Arabis caucasica* forms an evergreen mat with upright clusters of white or pink flowers; *A. procurrens* has creeping stems and white flowers. *Aubretia deltoidea* forms evergreen mats and has white, rose, or purple flowers.

Winter Bloomers

A handful of special plants offer us a tantalizing taste of spring by flowering while everything else remains in winter's grip. For earliest flowering, situate these plants in a sheltered spot out of the wind, with plenty of winter sun.

Shrubs

Fragrant winter hazel (*Corylopsis glabrescens*); fragrant, pale yellow flowers; Zones 5–8.

Vernal witch hazel (*Hamamelis vernalis*); highly fragrant yellow or bronze flowers; Zones 4–8.

Wintersweet (*Chimonanthus praecox*); fragrant, pale yellow-and-purple flowers; Zones 6–8.

Witch hazel (*Hamamelis × intermedia*); fragrant yellow or red flowers; Zones 5–8.

Perennials

Christmas rose (*Helleborus niger*); waxy white flowers; Zones 3–8.

Lenten rose (*Helleborus orientalis*); waxy white or rose-pink flowers spotted with maroon; Zones 4–9.

Polyanthus primrose (*Primula × polyantha*); wide range of flower colors; Zones 3–8.

Sweet violet (*Viola odorata*); violet flowers; Zones 5–9.

Bulbs

Crocuses (*Crocus biflorus, C. imperati, C. korolkowii, C. tommasinianus*); wide range of flower colors; Zones 5–9. *C. imperati* Zones 7–9.

'February Gold' Daffodil (*Narcissus* 'February Gold'); bright yellow blossoms; Zones 3–9.

Irises (*Iris bakeriana, I. danfordiae, I. reticulata*); yellow, white, or blue flowers; Zones 5–9.

Snowdrop (*Galanthus nivalis*); white flowers; Zones 4–9.

Winter aconite (*Eranthis hyemalis*); bright yellow blossoms; Zones 4–9.

Purple glory-of-the-snow (*Chionodoxa luciliae*) and Lenten rose (*Helleborus orientalis*) make wonderful early spring companions for a lightly shaded spot under trees.

Two spring favorites—daffodils and forsythia—look even better when planted together.

A Garden through Four Seasons

The photos on these pages show the changes of plant forms, colors, and textures along a front yard walkway that was planted to provide four-season interest. The garden features many native plants, such as prairie dropseed and wild quinine. Spring bulbs supply early spring color, while dried grasses and perennials give strollers a pleasing view even in winter. All of the plants in this garden will thrive in Zones 5–9 and grow best in full sun.

In early spring daffodils bloom, with glory-of-the-snow (*Chionodoxa luciliae*) providing spots of blue. Position daffodils near the back of your beds—as ornamental grasses and other perennials emerge, they will hide the ripening daffodil foliage.

Summer interest along the walkway comes from native wildflowers and grasses. Soft, feathery green clumps of prairie dropseed (*Sporobolus heterolepis*) line the path, while white-flowered wild quinine (*Parthenium integrifolium*) and orange coneflowers (*Rudbeckia fulgida*) add spots of color.

As fall unfolds, there's no mistaking the colors that signal the return of cold weather. Billowing clumps of orange coneflowers spill onto the path, and the ripening seedheads of prairie dropseed, which smell like buttered popcorn, are a fluffy low cloud. Clumps of goldenrods promise more color as the season progresses: Tall goldenrod (*Solidago altissima*) is on the left; stiff goldenrod (*S. rigida*) on the right.

In winter, the feathery tan clumps of prairie dropseed add appealing texture and movement. A wet snow will probably push them to the ground, but each of the coneflower seedheads will undoubtedly wear a crown of white. In late winter, the garden can be cut to the ground to repeat the cycle anew.

Gardens for Butterflies

If you grow flowers, you can't help but attract some butterflies. But if you'd like to attract them in droves, you'll need to make sure that your garden provides special butterfly accommodations.

Choose a sunny spot sheltered from wind for your butterfly garden. If all your property is open, you can plant a windbreak of trees like cherries, hawthorns (*Crataegus* spp.), poplars (*Populus* spp.), and willows. These trees also serve as important food sources for cater-

Unable to drink from open water, butterflies need to sip from the surface of moist earth or stones. To make a drinking puddle in a low spot in your garden, sink a plastic basin or bucket into the soil and fill it with wet sand.

Flat-topped flower clusters like those of sedums are easy for butterflies to feed from, and they make convenient landing platforms, too.

pillars—the immature life stage of butterflies.

Lay out your beds and prepare the soil as for any permanent flower garden. Plant a profusion of perennials and annuals and allow some weeds to grow. Successful butterfly gardens often look slightly messy and jumbled. Don't cut plants back after flowering, as you may unwittingly remove egg masses or young larvae.

Providing water. If you have a low spot in your garden where water tends to puddle, then you have a natural watering hole for butterflies. Butterfly "drinking clubs"—a dozen or more butterflies of a single species—sometimes gather at these low spots. You can make a butterfly watering hole in your garden using a shallow container.

Food sources. Many butterfly species love to feast on rotting fruit and even dung, urine, and carrion. Positioning your compost pile near your butterfly garden is a great way to establish an informal butterfly restaurant. Viceroys, mourning cloaks, red and white admirals, and others will likely arrive to feast on your leftovers.

Surround your garden with some flowering shrubs and trellised vines favored by butterflies for larval food and nectar. Trees and shrubs nearby will offer butterflies shelter at night and in bad weather.

If your butterfly garden can be near a woods or wild meadow—or even a weed patch—so much the better. The diversity of wild plants in these spots will help support a wider butterfly population.

One thing *not* to include in your butterfly garden is a bird feeder. While it will be impossible to keep birds out of the butterfly garden, don't encourage them: They are major predators of butterflies and their larvae.

Hibiscus (*Hibiscus* spp.), milkweeds (*Asclepias* spp.), and parsley are important food plants for larvae, as well as a source of nectar for butterflies. These may

The Life of a Butterfly

The butterfly life cycle has four stages: egg, larva, pupa, and adult. After mating, the female butterfly lays eggs on a specific plant or group of plants that will provide food for the emerging larvae, or caterpillars. For the monarch caterpillar shown here, milkweed is the primary food source.

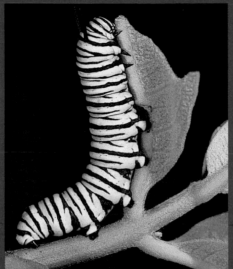

The larva progresses through stages of growth called instars, molting its skin as it goes. When it is fully grown, it becomes dormant. This is called the pupal stage, and the shell containing the pupa is called a chrysalis. After anywhere from a few weeks to several months, the adult butterfly emerges from the chrysalis. It pumps fluid from its body into its crumpled wings and flies off to feed on flower nectar.

grow in a wild, weedy area on your property. If not, then plant some in your butterfly garden.

Consult a local guide to determine what butterflies you can expect to attract in your area, and what their favored food and nectar sources are. Use this information to fine-tune your plant selection.

A Butterfly Border

Butterflies are attracted to fragrance and to certain colors. In general, they prefer tubular flowers arranged around a central head, like the purple coneflowers in this garden. They also like clusters of small flowers, such as butterfly weeds (*Asclepias* spp.) and Joe-Pye weed. When you have a choice, always choose single-flower forms rather than double selections. Choose both very early- and late-flowering plants to ensure a nonstop smorgasbord for the butterfly season. Many annual flowers and flowering shrubs also attract butterflies.

Purple is the favorite color of butterflies, with yellow in second place. But color preferences vary from species to species.

All the plants in this butterfly garden designed by Barbara Kaczorowski, shown here in summer, will thrive in Zones 4–8, and many will even survive winters in Zone 3.

Orange-eye butterfly bush (*Buddleia davidii* 'Nanho Blue'). 3' tall; sweetly fragrant flowers summer–fall. Requires good drainage and regular moisture.

Purple cone-flower (*Echinacea purpurea* 'Magnus'). 2'–3' tall; flowers summer–fall. Soil- and moisture-tolerant.

Rose verbena (*Verbena canadensis*). 6"–12" tall; fragrant flowers spring–frost. Drought-tolerant; self-sows.

Perennial candytuft (*Iberis sempervirens* 'Snowflake'). Mat-forming, 8" plants; covered with white flowers spring and fall. Foliage semi-evergreen.

Spike gayfeather (*Liatris spicata* 'Kobold'). 2'–3' tall; flowers in summer. Needs moist, well-drained soil.

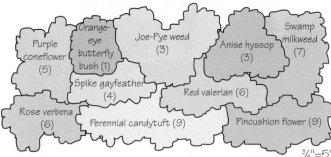

Purple coneflower (5)

Orange-eye butterfly bush (1)

Joe-Pye weed (3)

Anise hyssop (3)

Swamp milkweed (7)

Spike gayfeather (4)

Red valerian (6)

Rose verbena (6)

Perennial candytuft (9)

Pincushion flower (9)

¾"=5'

Numbers in parentheses indicate quantities to plant

Joe-Pye weed (*Eupatorium pur-pureum*). 5' tall; vanilla-scented, fuzzy flowers late summer–fall. Soil- and moisture-tolerant.

Anise hyssop (*Agastache* 'Fragrant Delight'). 2'–3' tall; sweetly scented foliage; fragrant flowers summer–fall.

Swamp milkweed (*Asclepias incarnata*). 3'–4' tall; flowers in summer. Moisture-tolerant.

Pincushion flower (*Scabiosa caucasica* 'Butterfly Blue'). 18" tall; flowers spring–frost. Needs good drainage.

Red valerian (*Centranthus ruber* var. *coccineus*). 3' tall; blue-green foliage; flowers early summer–frost. Drought tolerant; self-sows.

More Plants for Butterflies

Butterflies also love annuals and shrubs that have tubular flowers. Good annual flowers for butterflies include Brazilian vervain (*Verbena bonariensis*), nasturtium (*Tropaeolum majus*), heliotrope (*Heliotropium arborescens*), and sweet alyssum (*Lobularia maritima*). Some of the best butterfly-attracting shrubs are beautybush (*Kolkwitzia amabilis*), glosssy abelia (*Abelia grandiflora*), and spicebush (*Lindera benzoin*).

Hummingbirds in the Garden

It's a bee! It's a bird! It's a hummingbird! The arrival of these special birds flitting like high-speed hovercraft among the flowers is cause for excitement in any garden. With their tiny bodies, blur of wings, and dainty habit of sipping flower nectar, hummers are the fairies of the bird world.

Hummingbirds are migratory visitors in most of the United States, heading north from Central America and ap-pearing in Zone 5 as early as April. Those of us east of the Mississippi enjoy only one species, the familiar ruby-throated hummingbird. The exception to this is the rufous hummingbird, which frequents the southernmost part of the Gulf states (except for Florida).

Several species are native to Mexico and appear only in the southernmost part of the Southwest. But in California, especially southern California, gardeners get to enjoy the buzzing, busy presence of a wide variety of hummers.

Hummingbirds are attracted to bright colors, especially red and orange. However, flower form is the true quality that determines whether a hummingbird will feed, and tubular flowers are their requirement.

Plants for hummers. Many perennial vines are great hummingbird favorites, so if you can, plant your garden near a vine-covered fence or include some on trellises. Trumpet vine (*Campsis radicans*) is the classic hummingbird attractor. But hummers also favor clematis and honeysuckle. Hummingbirds eat

Hummingbirds feed from tubular flowers. Many perennial flowers that don't look tubular actually are, such as delphinium, phlox, and columbine.

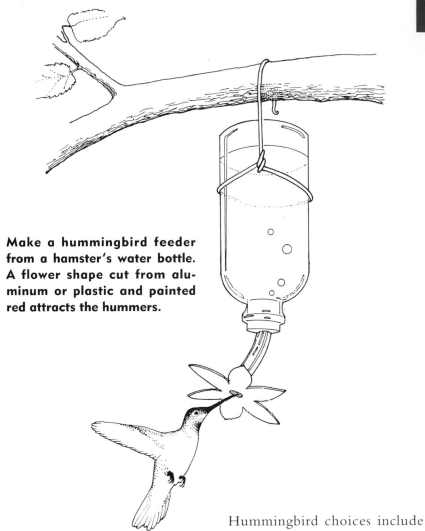

Make a hummingbird feeder from a hamster's water bottle. A flower shape cut from aluminum or plastic and painted red attracts the hummers.

Red cardinal flower (*Lobelia cardinalis*) and great blue lobelia (*L. siphilitica*) are hummingbird favorites. They grow best in rich, moist soil.

a wide variety of small insects like aphids and gnats, and honeysuckle attracts aphids. 'Dropmore Scarlet' honeysuckle (*Lonicera × brownii* 'Dropmore Scarlet') ranks with trumpet vine in the hummer's heart and certainly outblooms it, flowering from June through October.

Make sure to include some annuals in your hummingbird garden. Their nonstop bloom will ensure that hungry hummers never run short of food.

Hummingbird choices include flowering tobacco (*Nicotiana alata*), larkspur (*Consolida* spp.), nasturtiums, petunias, red-flowered salvias (*Salvia* spp.), and snapdragons.

Hummingbird feeders. Hummingbirds have fantastically high metabolisms and must feed almost nonstop every waking hour. You can make your own hummingbird feeder to supplement the nectar in your hummingbird garden, as shown on this page. Although the benefits of providing sugar solution in hummingbird feeders has been long contested, hummingbird experts

have concluded that feeding does help hummingbird populations deal with diminished feeding grounds as well as freak natural occurances like late freezes that temporarily kill off their food sources. To make a feeding solution, mix 1 part sugar and 4 parts water, then boil the mixture for 2 minutes.

A Garden to Attract Hummingbirds

Attracting tiny whirring visitors can be as simple as dispersing a few favorite hummingbird plants throughout your perennial garden or yard. Be sure to group at least three plants of a particular type to effectively attract the hummers' attention. Even hanging planters of fuschia or a potted hibiscus (*Hibiscus* spp.) on a sunny patio can entice hummingbirds.

This garden designed by Barbara Kaczorowski, shown here in summer, is full of hummingbird favorites. Most of the plants in this garden will grow well in Zones 3–7 (some will also thrive in Zones 8 and 9). The bee balm is hardy only to Zone 4, and the montbretia and common torch lily are hardy only to Zone 5.

Belladonna delphinium (*Delphinium* × *belladonna* 'Bellamosum'). 4' tall; flowers in early summer. Reblooms in fall if deadheaded.

Montbretia (*Crocosmia* 'Lucifer'). 3' tall; flowers in midsummer. Provide good drainage and mulch in northern zones.

Bee balm (*Monarda didyma* 'Gardenview Scarlet'). 3' tall; aromatic foliage; flowers in early summer.

Wild columbine (*Aquilegia canadensis*). 2' tall; crimson flowers in late spring. Drought-tolerant.

Carpathian harebell (*Campanula carpatica* 'Blue Clips'). 8"–12" tall; flowers early summer–fall. Prefers good drainage.

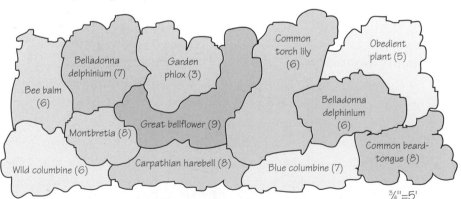

Bee balm (6)

Belladonna delphinium (7)

Garden phlox (3)

Common torch lily (6)

Obedient plant (5)

Montbretia (8)

Great bellflower (9)

Belladonna delphinium (6)

Wild columbine (6)

Carpathian harebell (8)

Blue columbine (7)

Common beard-tongue (8)

¾"=5'

Numbers in parentheses indicate quantities to plant

Garden phlox (*Phlox panicu-lata* 'Eva Cullum'). 2½' tall; fragrant flowers in summer.

Great bellflower (*Campanula latifolia* var. *macrantha*). 3' tall; flowers in summer. Provide rich, well-drained soil.

Common torch lily (*Kniphofia uvaria*). 3' tall; flowers in summer. Drought-tolerant.

Obedient plant (*Physostegia virginiana* 'Variegata'). 3' tall; flowers late summer–early fall.

Common beard-tongue (*Penstemon barbatus* 'Prairie Fire'). 2' tall; flowers early summer–fall. Provide excellent drainage.

Blue columbine (*Aquilegia caerulea*). 1'–2' tall; deep blue-and-white flowers late spring–early summer.

Make a Hummer Haven

- Plant annual and perennial tubular flowers. Include plenty of reds and oranges.

- Choose a warm, sunny, sheltered site for your garden.

- Plant shrubs and trees with dense foliage to provide nesting sites and protection from bad weather.

- Hang a hummingbird feeder in your garden. Keep the feeding solution fresh.

- Position a mist nozzle over a perching plant for a hummingbird-size shower.

- Remove large spiderwebs that can trap hummers.

29

Birds in the Garden

If you're a bird lover, make your garden bird heaven. With wild bird habitats shrinking daily, your seemingly small efforts will be a big help to your local bird population. By providing a wide variety of food sources, as well as shelter, nesting sites, and water, your bird garden will likely attract species you've never even seen before.

Most of the gardens described in this book will attract birds; many birds feast on insects, which are attracted to flowers in general. A good approach is to include plants that are especially attractive to birds in your regular perennial garden. But be sure to

Your perennial gardens will attract beetles and flies, which in turn will attract birds like Eastern phoebes (*below*), and song sparrows (*left*), which may nest in shrubs nearby.

provide other bird-friendly plants nearby: trees and shrubs to provide cover, nesting sites, perches, and even food in the form of fruits. And to be effective for bird watching, your garden should be visible from a major window.

Providing shelter. Birds need their moments of privacy, with some species being notoriously shy. Trees and shrubs provide private spots as well as safe haven from inclement weather and predators. Birds use woody plants as nesting sites, song posts, and perches.

Food sources. Trees and shrubs supply a bounty of food, especially during the barren winter months. In addition to pines and spruces, alders (*Alnus* spp.), American holly (*Ilex opaca*), beeches (*Betula* spp.), small-fruited crabapples (*Malus* spp.), hawthorns (*Crataegus* spp.), mountain ash (*Sorbus* spp.), and oaks (*Quercus* spp.) all provide a bounty of food.

For bird-attracting shrubs, choose from hip-bearing shrub roses, privets (*Ligustrum* spp.), serviceberries (*Amelanchier* spp.),

A feeder and insects among the flowers provide food for birds; shrubs and trees offer shelter and nesting sites.

winterberry (*Ilex verticillata*), and yews (*Taxus* spp.). In fact, just about any fruit-bearing shrub will attract birds.

Vines are a great addition to the bird garden as well. The flowers of mature ivy attract hosts of insects. Birds also relish the fruits, and its woody vines provide good nesting spots. Honeysuckles also provide berries for birds. And the fruits of native bittersweet are devoured by bluebirds as they return north in late winter.

Providing water. Adding water to your garden can often do as much to attract birds as planting food plants. Even a sprinkler or mist nozzle in the garden will attract avian bathers.

Providing birds with water in winter is something that novice birdwatchers often ne-

A concrete or terra-cotta saucer in the garden can supply water for birds. Reflections on the water add a pleasing design touch as well.

glect. The challenge in most areas of the country is to keep the water from freezing. During cold months, place saucers of warm water in the warmest outdoor spot you can find. Near a furnace or dryer vent—or even on a sunny windowsill where heat from your home radiates through the glass—are all good spots. Provide fresh, unfrozen water as often as possible.

Perennials for a Bird Smorgasbord

These perennials attract insects, which in turn attract birds. Many also produce seeds that birds favor. All these perennials will do well in a sunny site.

Artichoke (*Cynara scolymus*); large blue thistlelike flowers develop heads of plump seeds; Zones 5–9.

Button gayfeather (*Liatris aspera*); spikes of bright pink, buttonlike flowers; Zones 4–8.

Compass plant (*Silphium laciniatum*); Golden yellow blossoms; Zones 3–8.

Downy sunflower (*Helianthus mollis*); profuse, butter-yellow single flowers; Zones 3–8.

Globe thistle (*Echinops ritro*); globe-shaped, blue flowerheads; Zones 3–8.

Gray-headed coneflower (*Ratibida pinnata*); tiny yellow sombrero-like flowers; Zones 3–9.

Lance-leaved coreopsis (*Coreopsis lanceolata*); brilliant yellow flowers with jagged-edged petals; Zones 3–8.

New England aster (*Aster novae-angliae*); blue, violet, or pink flowers with yellow centers; Zones 3–8.

Orange coneflower (*Rudbeckia fulgida*); golden yellow flowers with dark brown centers; Zones 3–8.

Perennial sunflower (*Helianthus* × *multiflorus*); large, golden yellow flowers; Zones 3–8.

Purple coneflower (*Echinacea purpurea*); pink daisies with iridescent, conelike centers; Zones 3–8.

A Cool Woodland Garden

If you have a wooded yard or a lawn that's shaded by mature trees, you may have poor luck growing flowering shrubs, perennials, or lawn grass. Forget your frustrations—plant a woodland garden and you'll learn to love your trees.

Planting a woodland garden is distinctly different from any other kind of gardening. Instead of planting an empty bed, you'll be working plants into a site that already has some very large occupants: mature trees. And if you're about to tackle gardening in an existing wild woodland, you'll encounter a dense understory of smaller trees and shade-tolerant shrubs, weeds, and wildflowers in your way.

The key to successful woodland gardening is to consider all these other tenants of your woodland at every step of the way. Although you may be able to eradicate the less desirable ones, at the very least the trees will stay. You must garden with the trees rather than against them. This means modifying your usual soil-preparation protocol. The woodland soil will be chock-full of roots and probably impossible to dig up or till in the manner to which you're accustomed. And perhaps most important, you must rely on plants which are adapted to shade and to growing under trees.

Planning your garden. What are your goals for your woodland garden? They may be as modest as converting a small area around some mature shade-trees from grass to shade perennials. In this case, you simply need get rid of the sod, outline some curving beds around the

Pair red cardinal flower (*Lobelia cardinalis*) and the white flower spikes of black snakeroot (*Cimicifuga racemosa*) to create summer color in your woodland garden.

If you want to retreat and be alone with nature, plant a woodland garden. Two western natives for woodland gardens are pink-flowered western bleeding-hearts (*Dicentra formosa*) and fringe-cup (*Tellima grandiflora*).

trees, and plant interlocking drifts of shade-loving plants.

If your project is overhauling a neglected woodland on your property, start by setting limits on the area you plan to improve. You might want to carve out an area to provide a pleasant view from your house, with future plans to expand the "improved" areas, perhaps including a path and a rustic seat.

Take an inventory of the existing plants, identifying desirable species and marking them. Don't shrink from cutting undesirable trees such as box elder (*Acer negundo*), whose innate agenda is to colonize the entire area. Try to inventory existing plants in spring, when spring ephemeral wildflowers will be in full evidence.

Preparing and planting. Planting perennials under trees can be a tricky job. You want to ensure that your perennials will establish well, yet you don't want to butcher the roots of your trees. See "Planting under Trees" on page 61 for more information. If you're creating your woodland garden in an area that's in lawn, you will have to strip off the sod first. If your area is an existing woodland, it may have a layer of leafmold that you can dig individual planting holes in.

Due to the intense root competition, the soil under mature trees is very dry. Most woodland plantings profit greatly from regular watering at least until they're established—or better, from the installation of drip irrigation. Top off all your woodland plantings with a generous layer of shredded bark or leaf mulch to keep down weeds and conserve moisture.

An Evergreen Woodland Garden

Evergreen woodlands are deeply shady all year long and have acidic soil. Designer C. Colston Burrell has created a shade-loving perennial and wildflower garden under a grove of pine trees, shown here in spring. The soil in this garden is rich and humusy. The plants are adapted to the acidic soil conditions caused by the slow decay of pine needles.

Because many home landscapes include both deciduous and evergreen trees, Burrell designed this garden to flow naturally into a deciduous area (see pages 36–37).

All the plants in this garden will grow well in Zones 4–8, except for the autumn fern, which is hardy only to Zone 5. Many will survive Zone 3 winters.

Wild cranesbill (*Geranium maculatum*). 1'–2' tall; flowers in late spring. Afternoon shade will preserve foliage.

Wintergreen (*Gaultheria procumbens*). 2"–8" tall; nodding white flowers in summer followed by red berries; evergreen leaves.

Partridgeberry (*Mitchella repens*). Spreading, 2"–4" plants; fragrant white flowers in summer followed by red berries.

Western bleeding heart (*Dicentra formosa*). 10"–12" tall; flowers spring–early summer.

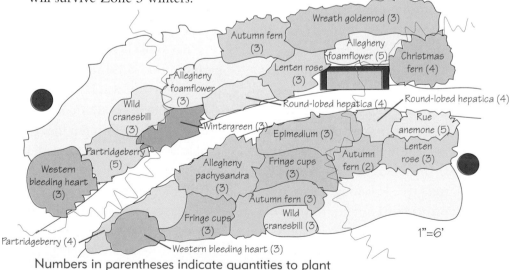

Wreath goldenrod (3)

Autumn fern (3)

Allegheny foamflower (5)

Lenten rose (3)

Christmas fern (4)

Allegheny foamflower (3)

Round-lobed hepatica (4)

Round-lobed hepatica (4)

Wild cranesbill (3)

Wintergreen (3)

Epimedium (3)

Rue anemone (5)

Partridgeberry (5)

Allegheny pachysandra (3)

Fringe cups (3)

Autumn fern (2)

Lenten rose (3)

Western bleeding heart (3)

Autumn fern (3)

Wild cranesbill (3)

Partridgeberry (4)

Fringe cups (3)

Western bleeding heart (3)

1"=6'

Numbers in parentheses indicate quantities to plant

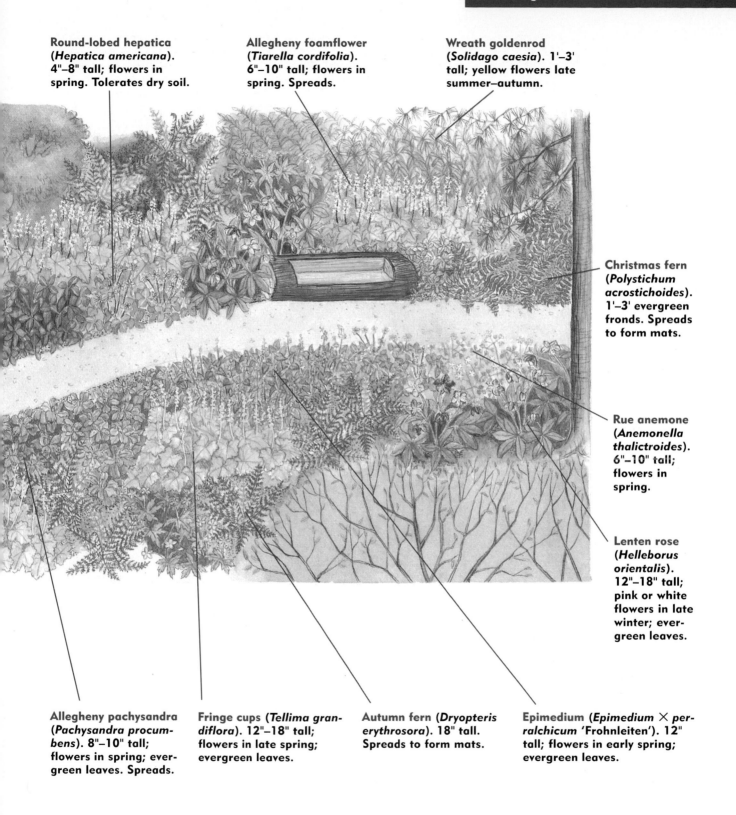

Round-lobed hepatica (*Hepatica americana*). 4"–8" tall; flowers in spring. Tolerates dry soil.

Allegheny foamflower (*Tiarella cordifolia*). 6"–10" tall; flowers in spring. Spreads.

Wreath goldenrod (*Solidago caesia*). 1'–3' tall; yellow flowers late summer–autumn.

Christmas fern (*Polystichum acrostichoides*). 1'–3' evergreen fronds. Spreads to form mats.

Rue anemone (*Anemonella thalictroides*). 6"–10" tall; flowers in spring.

Lenten rose (*Helleborus orientalis*). 12"–18" tall; pink or white flowers in late winter; evergreen leaves.

Allegheny pachysandra (*Pachysandra procumbens*). 8"–10" tall; flowers in spring; evergreen leaves. Spreads.

Fringe cups (*Tellima grandiflora*). 12"–18" tall; flowers in late spring; evergreen leaves.

Autumn fern (*Dryopteris erythrosora*). 18" tall. Spreads to form mats.

Epimedium (*Epimedium* × *perralchicum* 'Frohnleiten'). 12" tall; flowers in early spring; evergreen leaves.

A Deciduous Woodland Garden

In deciduous woods, you'll find large hardwood trees, small trees, shade-tolerant shrubs, ferns, wildflowers. Soils in deciduous woodlands range from slightly acidic to slightly alkaline.

C. Colston Burrell has designed this garden, shown here in spring, to grow in a wooded area shaded by oaks and maples. It includes spring-flowering perennials, some of which go dormant after they flower. Others produce lush foliage throughout the summer months. In early fall a fresh flush of flowers begins, and many showy berries appear.

Burrell planned this garden to be a companion to an evergreen woodland garden (see pages 34–35). All of the plants in this garden will grow well in Zones 4–8, and many will survive Zone 3 winters.

Common witch hazel (*Hamamelis virginiana*). To 30' tall; yellow flowers in winter; leaves yellow in fall.

Christmas fern (*Polystichum acrostichoides*). 1'–3' tall evergreen fronds. Spreads to form mats.

Variegated Japanese Solomon's seal (*Polygonatum odoratum thunbergii* 'Variegatum') 2'–3' tall; flowers in spring.

Lenten rose (*Helleborus orientalis*). 12"–18" tall; pink or white flowers in late winter; evergreen leaves.

Lungwort (*Pulmonaria longifolia* 'Bertram Anderson'). 4"–8" tall; flowers in early spring. May go dormant in drought.

Canada wild ginger (*Asarum canadense*). 6"–12" tall; red, jug-shaped flowers hide under the leaves in spring.

Virginia bluebell (*Mertensia virginica*). 1'–2' tall; flowers in spring. Plants disappear after flowering.

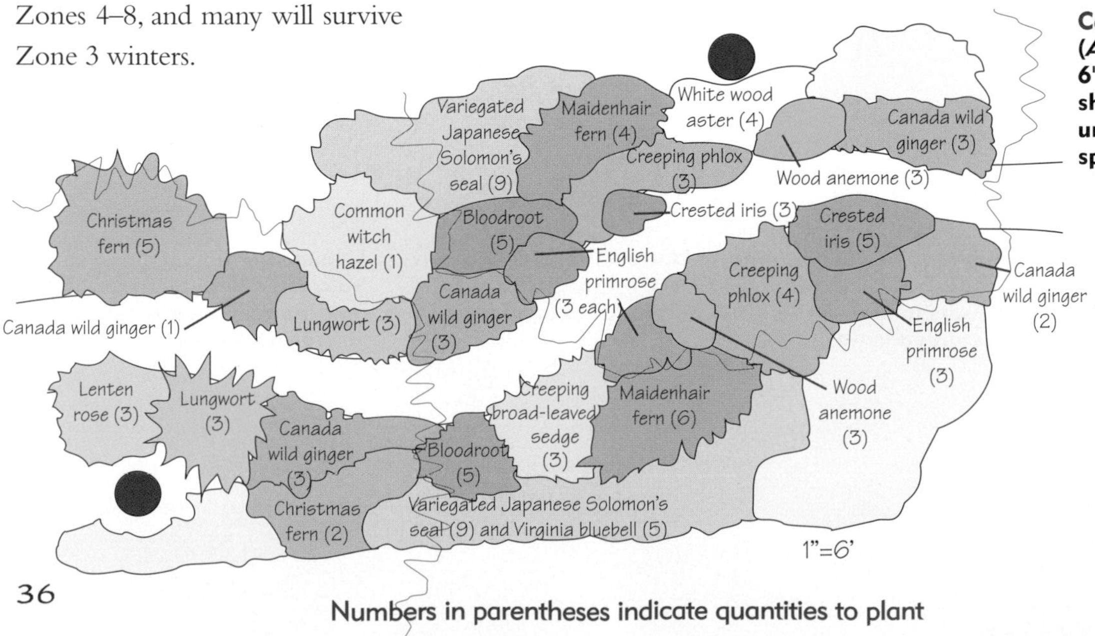

Christmas fern (5)
Canada wild ginger (1)
Common witch hazel (1)
Lungwort (3)
Variegated Japanese Solomon's seal (9)
Bloodroot (5)
Canada wild ginger (3)
Maidenhair fern (4)
White wood aster (4)
Creeping phlox (3)
Crested iris (3)
Canada wild ginger (3)
Wood anemone (3)
English primrose (3 each)
Crested iris (5)
Creeping phlox (4)
Canada wild ginger (2)
English primrose (3)
Lenten rose (3)
Lungwort (3)
Canada wild ginger (3)
Bloodroot (5)
Creeping broad-leaved sedge (3)
Maidenhair fern (6)
Wood anemone (3)
Christmas fern (2)
Variegated Japanese Solomon's seal (9) and Virginia bluebell (5)

1"=6'

Numbers in parentheses indicate quantities to plant

English primrose (*Primula vulgaris*). 6"–10" tall; flowers in spring. Mulch in northern zones.

Maidenhair fern (*Adiantum pedatum*). 1'–3' tall. Plants go dormant under drought conditions.

White wood aster (*Aster divaricatus*). 12"–18" tall; small white flowers in late summer.

Crested iris (*Iris cristata*). 4"–10" tall; flowers in late spring. Spreads to forms mats.

Creeping phlox (*Phlox stolonifera* 'Blue Ridge'). 8"–12" tall; flowers in late spring.

Bloodroot (*Sanguinaria canadensis*). 4"–6" tall; flowers in early spring. May go dormant in drought; needs summer shade.

Creeping broad-leaved sedge (*Carex siderostricta* 'Variegata'). 12"–18" tall; flowers not showy. Spreads to form mats.

Wood anemone (*Anemone nemorosa*). 4"–10" tall; flowers in spring. Plants disappear after flowering.

37

A Backyard Meadow Garden

Brightly colored wildflowers and graceful grasses blowing in the wind fill wild meadows. They are alive with birds and butterflies, and plants grow in natural abandon. In a meadow garden, you can create a similar wild community artificially by preparing the soil and introducing plants or seeds of desired wildflowers and grasses.

Do you have an area that is difficult to mow because it's either along a fenceline, on a slope, or in a wet area? A meadow garden can turn all these liabilities into lower-maintenance assets. Or perhaps you want to plant *all* the theme gardens in this chapter, but you don't have enough garden space or enough time to do so. A meadow garden combines many themes in a single garden: Your meadow can include plants for butterflies, flowers for cutting and drying, *and* fragrant plants!

Choosing a Site

Meadow gardens need sun. A little-used side yard can make a great spot for a meadow. You can even create a "pocket meadow" as a small island bed within your lawn. Meadow plantings contrast beautifully with neatly mowed lawn. Your use of the meadow will also influence its location. If you want to observe its birds and butterflies from your windows, keep it relatively near the house. If you appreciate its impressionistic blurs of color, place it near the limits of your property.

The size of your meadow depends on the constraints of your lot, as well as the time you want to devote to it. After the initial preparation, planting, and watering, you can maintain a 2,000-square-foot meadow with just a half-hour of hand weeding per week and an annual mowing. Smaller gardens require even less maintenance time.

Step-by-Step Meadow Making

You can start a meadow from seed, transplants, or a combination of the two. Starting with transplants is more expensive but

Natural meadows generally contain more grasses than wildflowers, but in "human" meadows, gardeners choose to make flowers like daisies and coreopsis (*Coreopsis* spp.) predominate.

gives you more control over plant placement, yields quicker results, and requires less early maintenance. Initial weeding of a seed-grown meadow can be a real headache, especially if you're new to seedling recognition. With transplants, it's easy to recognize the "good" plants, and you can mulch around them to minimize weeding and watering.

If you want to start from seed, choose your seed carefully. Check seed packet labels for non-native species. While some of these can contribute to a meadow's beauty, others are aggressive and invasive, and will eventually crowd out more desirable native species. Follow this ten-step guide to a successful seed-grown meadow:

1. Dig out perennial weeds by hand and till the site 6 to 8 inches deep. Eradicate weeds by successive shallow tillings at three-week intervals. Water between tillings if necessary to speed weed germination.

2. Rake the area smooth and dig out the remaining perennial weeds, roots and all.

3. Choose your seed mix carefully, making sure it contains plants adapted to your area and your local soil and moisture conditions, and is free of invasive species. Buy from a reputable dealer.

4. Thoroughly mix equal parts seed and sand, and scatter it evenly over the entire site.

5. Tamp the area down by walking over it or using a lawn roller. Good seed-to-soil contact greatly aids germination of most species.

6. Mulch very lightly with straw or sawdust, much as you would grass seed.

7. Water thoroughly at regular intervals as needed until plants are established.

8. Weed out unwanted grasses and plants that will, without a doubt, appear.

9. Mow your meadow in late winter or earliest spring to scatter seed and open the plantings to more light and air. Early spring mowing allows birds and wildlife to enjoy the seeds that remain over winter.

10. Enjoy your meadow!

Purple coneflowers (*Echinacea purpurea*) are natives of our wild prairies. Beware of invasive non-native species when planning a meadow garden.

Prickly rattlesnake master (*Eryngium yuccifolium*), spike gayfeather (*Liatris spicata*), and grasses make a great meadow mix. To get the best meadow from seed, buy seeds individually and mix them yourself, or plant them in drifts.

A Wetland Garden

Problems caused by poor drainage are almost never cheap or easy to correct. They usually require tiresome, disruptive solutions like regrading your yard or installing perforated drain tile. It's much easier to go with the flow and grow some of the host of lovely plants adapted to living with wet feet. And if your garden is high and dry, you may want to create a mini-bog, like the one shown on this page.

When selecting wet-tolerant plants, take your cues from the plants themselves. Plants adapted to boggy conditions often have large or abundant leaves, such as ligularias (*Ligularia* spp.) and ornamental rhubarb (*Rheum palmatum*). Wetland plants usually have a mass of shallow, fibrous roots that spread out in the uppermost soil layer, avoiding the

For a wetland effect, edge a small water garden or fill a homemade bog with water-loving plants like bigleaf ligularia (*Ligularia dentata*) and ferns.

waterlogged layers below. Siberian iris and daylilies are good examples. Plants like hosta, which are adapted

to normal-moisture shade conditions, can often be successfully grown in a full-sun boggy area.

Strangely enough, some wet-tolerant plants are also drought-tolerant. This is because water-logged soils contain very little oxygen, which is necessary for roots to take up water. This means that plants living in the wettest soil are actually experiencing drought! Their adaptation to this condition enables them to endure real drought conditions, as well. 'Autumn Joy' sedum is one popular example of a perennial that grows in both wet and dry soils. Unfortunately, not all wetland plants fall into this category; many, like astilbe, will quickly scorch if allowed to become dry.

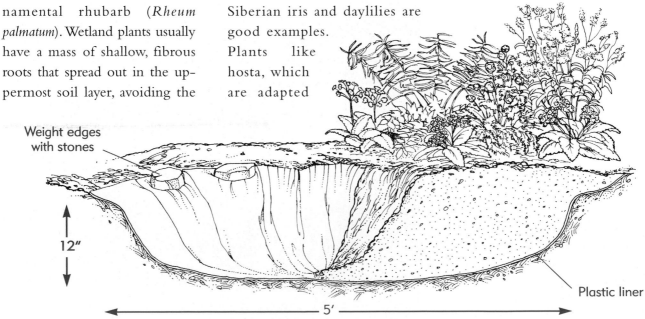

Weight edges with stones

12"

5'

Plastic liner

Create an artificial bog using a flexible PVC plastic or butyl rubber liner as a barrier to hold moisture in the soil. Fill your bog with compost-enriched soil.

Perennials for Soggy Situations

Common and Botanical Name	Hardiness and Exposure	Bloom Time and Color	Description
Common monkshood *Aconitum napellus*	Zones 3–8 Sun to partial shade	Late summer Blue-violet	3'–4' tall; deeply lobed leaves; spikes of helmetlike flowers.
Goat's beard *Aruncus dioicus*	Zones 3–7 Sun to partial shade	Late spring White	3'–5' tall; divided, compound leaves; 1' feathery flower plumes.
Masterwort *Astrantia* 'Rainbow'	Zones 4–8 Sun to shade	Spring–early fall White, aging to pink	30" tall; basal rosette of divided foliage; dome-shaped heads of tiny flowers.
Joe-Pye weed *Eupatorium purpureum*	Zones 3–8 Sun to light shade	Late summer Frosty mauve	4'–6' tall; bold whorled foliage; 1' domed heads of fuzzy flowers.
Queen-of-the-prairie *Filipendula rubra* 'Venusta'	Zones 3–9 Sun to light shade	Early summer Pink	3'–5' tall; lime green, compound leaves; stout stems with fluffy flower-heads.
Common rose mallow *Hibiscus moscheutos* 'Southern Belle'	Zones 5–10 Sun to light shade	Summer–early fall White, pink, or red	4'–6' tall; shrublike proportions on tropical-looking plant; heart-shaped leaves and dinner plate–size flowers.
Cardinal flower *Lobelia cardinalis*	Zones 2–9 Sun to partial shade	Late summer Crimson	2'–4' tall; lance-shaped leaves; spires of dense flowers.
Forget-me-not *Myosotis scorpioides*	Zones 3–7 Sun to partial shade	Late spring–early fall Sky blue	6"–8" tall; prostrate, creeping plant with narrowly oval leaves; pink buds open to sky blue flowers.
Primroses *Primula* spp.	Zones 2–8 Sun to partial shade	Spring–early summer Wide range of colors	6"–24" tall; wide leaves in basal rosette; flowers vary by species.
Bethlehem sage *Pulmonaria saccharata*	Zones 3–8 Sun to shade	Spring–early summer Blue, pink, or white	1' tall; big, lance-shaped leaves are dark green and spotted with silver; clusters of nodding flowers.
Fingerleaf rodgersia *Rodgersia aesculifolia*	Zones 4–7 Partial to full shade	Spring–early summer Creamy white	4'–6' tall; huge, crinkled leaves tinged bronze; 2' fluffy flower clusters.
Fleeceflower *Tovara virginiana* 'Painter's Palette'	Zones 4–8 Sun to shade	Midsummer Red	2' tall; stems clothed with broad leaves splashed with cream and pink; wispy flowers.
Chinese globeflower *Trollius chinensis*	Zones 3–6 Sun to partial shade	Spring Golden yellow	2'–3' tall; five-part leaves in basal rosette; 1"–2" double, rounded flowers.

A Perennial Herb Garden

Herb gardens lend themselves to any imaginable landscape style: formal, informal, classic, or contemporary. Loosely defined, an herb is any plant which people have used to their benefit through the ages. So an herb garden, more than any other garden, is a place to reflect and explore your special interests. Of course, not all herbs are perennials, and your gardens will most likely be an exuberant mix of perennials, biennials, and annuals.

Herb gardens lie at the intersection of people and plants. Are you a history buff? Plant a garden of herbs used during a specific historic era. If you enjoy crafting, an herb garden can supply you with a fantastic palette of inspiring materials. And no passionate cook wants to be without the most sumptuous herb garden possible, offering hosts of exotic flavors right outside the kitchen door.

An herb garden is a fragrant garden. Herb blossoms are attractive to honeybees, butterflies, and even hummingbirds. And although most herbs don't have showy flowers, their blossoms are lovely in a subtle, old-fashioned

Many formal herb gardens are beyond the home scale, but a small-scale formal garden can have appeal. Each bed in a formal layout can be devoted to herbs of a certain theme.

Herb Garden Themes

Here's a sampling of the fascinating twists you can give to an herb garden.

A Shakespearian Herb Garden

Common wormwood (*Artemisia absinthium*)
English daisy (*Bellis perennis*)
English primrose (*Primula vulgaris*)
Hyssop (*Hyssopus officinalis*)
Lavender (*Lavandula angustifolia*)
Rue (*Ruta graveolens*)
Spearmint (*Mentha spicata*)
Sweet violet (*Viola odorata*)

A Biblical Herb Garden

Boxwood (*Buxus sempervirens*)
Chicory (*Cichorium intybus*)
Costmary (*Chrysanthemum balsamita*)
Horseradish (*Armoracia rusticana*)
Lady's-mantle (*Alchemilla mollis*)
Saffron crocus (*Crocus sativus*)
Sage (*Salvia officinalis*)
Sorrel (*Rumex acetosa*)

A Native American Herb Garden

Boneset (*Eupatorium perfoliatum*)
Common camass (*Camassia quamash*)
Fireweed (*Epilobium angustifolium*)
Indian paintbrush (*Castilleja coccinea*)
Joe-Pye weed (*Eupatorium purpureum*)
Pale coneflower (*Echinacea pallida*)
Swamp milkweed (*Asclepias incarnata*)

way. Herbs also offer many beautiful foliage textures and colors. So don't hide your herb garden away. Put it out where you can see its warm colors, smell its fragrance, and hear the sleepy drone of busy honeybees.

The possibilities of herb garden layouts are almost unlimited. Historically, herb gardens of the wealthy and of religious orders were formal, comprising geometric, symmetrically arranged beds with paths between. Folks of more modest means were likely to intersperse useful herbs with flowers and even vegetables in a dooryard or cottage garden.

Informal Herb Gardens

You can transform difficult sites, such as a steep hillside or even a former parking area, into an herb garden. These sites may be too dry to support classic perennials, but there are countless herbs, especially those of Mediterranean origin, that can thrive there. Adapt a hillside by installing stone-edged terraces and letting herbs cascade over their edges. On a compacted parking area, build wood- or metal-edged raised beds and fill them with improved soil. (Of course, you'll have to remove all paving material prior to installing the raised beds.) Cover the paths

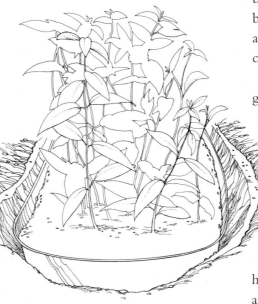

Keep bee balm and other spreading perennial herbs in bounds by surrounding their roots with a rigid plastic barrier at least 6 inches deep.

between the beds with gravel, or brick or stone pavers set in sand, and plant leaf thyme and other creeping herbs in the crevices.

Laying out an informal herb garden is similar to creating a standard perennial bed. Outline a curvilinear bed with a length of garden hose or rope before digging. Double-check that all parts of the bed are easily accessible because you'll probably want to harvest parts of all your herbs for cooking, crafts, or arrangements. An island bed can be up to 5 feet wide, but a border against a fence or house should not exceed 3 feet. Deeper beds should have stepping-stones or walkways to allow easy access.

An unruly mix of common chives, peppermint (*Mentha* × *piperita*), and golden oregano (*Origanum vulgare* 'Aureum') makes an exuberant grouping for a bed by a sunny front entry.

An Ornamental Herb Garden

Designer Stephanie Cohen mixed traditional herbs and ornamental perennials in this garden. This design, shown here in summer, provides color from late spring to early fall.

Choose the sunniest possible site for your herb garden. Strong sunlight intensifies the perfume, flavor, and potency of almost all herbs. Many familiar herbs grow best in well-drained soil. Gardeners with poorly drained, heavy clay soils can either make raised beds, lighten the soil with plenty of sharp sand and organic matter, or both.

Most of the plants in the garden will grow well in Zones 4–8. The lavender, rose, and creeping thyme are hardy only to Zone 5.

Rose (*Rosa* 'The Fairy'). 3' tall; flowers in summer. Mildew- and black spot–resistant.

Artemisia (*Artemisia ludoviciana* 'Silver Queen'). 2'–2½' tall; inconspicuous flowers in late summer; aromatic foliage.

Lamb's-ears (*Stachys byzantina*). 6"–15" tall; flowers in summer. Do not overwater; remove flowerstalks to prevent self-seeding.

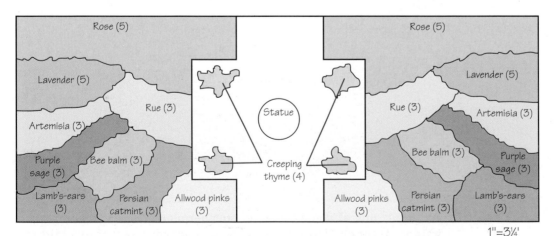

1"=3¼'

Numbers in parentheses indicate quantities to plant

Creeping thyme (**Thymus praecox** subsp. **arcticus**). 1"–4" tall; flowers in summer. Creeping; can be grown in paving joints.

Rue (**Ruta graveolens**). 18" tall; yellow flowers in late summer. Some people get a rash from touching rue, so handle with care.

Lavender (**Lavandula angustifolia** 'Munstead'). 12"–15" tall; fragrant flowers late spring–early summer. Fresh or dried cut flower.

Bee balm (**Monarda didyma** 'Marshall's Delight'). 3'–4' tall; flowers in summer; fragrant foliage. Mildew resistant.

Purple sage (**Salvia officinalis** 'Purpurea'). 1½'–2' tall; flowers in summer. Culinary herb.

Allwood pinks (**Dianthus** × **allwoodii** 'Aqua'). 10"–12" tall; fragrant flowers late spring–summer.

Persian catmint (**Nepeta** × **mussinii** 'Blue Wonder'). 15"–18" tall; flowers in summer. Cut back after flowering for later rebloom.

A Tea Garden

Try these perennials for making your own fragrant and healthful herbal teas.

Agrimony (*Agrimonia eupatoria*)

Anise hyssop (*Agastache foeniculum*)

Chamomile (*Chamoemelum nobile*)

Chocolate mint (*Mentha* × *piperita* 'Chocolate Mint')

Ginger mint (*Mentha* × *gentilis* 'Variegata')

Horehound (*Marrubium vulgare*)

Hyssop (*Hyssopus officinalis*)

Lemon balm (*Melissa officinalis*)

Spearmint (*Mentha spicata*)

45

Fragrant Perennials

After 50 years of being ignored by plant breeders, fragrant plants are enjoying a renaissance. Today's gardeners are rediscovering the fragrances that, through the ages, inspired gardeners and poets alike.

Site is all-important for peak enjoyment of fragrant plants. Choosing a spot near a patio or deck where you enjoy spending time outdoors will allow you to effortlessly experience their bouquet. Or, situate some fragrant plants near a screened porch or open window, where their perfume can waft your way. A site in full sun is best for most fragrant plants and will allow the sun's warmth to amplify their scents.

One approach to laying out a fragrant garden is to group fragrant plants together, creating an island of scent. But if you don't like the idea of different perfumes getting mixed and muddled, you can string aromatic plants out along a path or throughout a larger perennial bed, where their scents will remain separate.

Since many plants have fragrant foliage that must be rubbed to be appreciated, you may want to plant your fragrance garden in raised beds to facilitate touching them. This arrangement also makes it easier to plunge your nose into flowers like peonies that don't usually waft their fragrance.

Accent on Fragrance

Try these tips for accentuating fragrance in the garden.

- Choose a sheltered location. Fragrance is more noticeable in a still, enclosed area.
- Pick the sunniest, warmest spot you can find. The sun's heat intensifies all plant fragrances.
- Mass plants of a particular perfume together. For example, a row of lavender along a walkway will perfume the air, while a single plant may go unnoticed.
- Bring cool-weather fragrant bloomers indoors to intensify their perfume. Tulips or witch hazel may have little fragrance outdoors. But indoors, they will perfume an entire room.

Many peonies and other fragrant perennials are heirloom plants. They date from times before mail-order catalogs, when people visited nurseries throughout the growing season to test fragrances before deciding what to buy.

Fabulously Fragrant Perennials

Common and Botanical Name	Hardiness and Exposure	Bloom Time and Color	Fragrance Notes
Golden columbine *Aquilegia chrysantha*	Zones 3–9 Sun	Spring Golden yellow	Delicate, violetlike. Sniff close up to detect fragrance.
Calamint *Calamintha grandiflora*	Zones 4–9 Sun to partial shade	Early summer Pink	Foliage has delightfully fruity scent. Rub leaves for fragrance.
Lily-of-the-valley *Convallaria majalis*	Zones 2–8 Sun or shade	Spring White	Heavy, sweet. Wafts its fragrance into the air.
Cottage pinks *Dianthus plumarius*	Zones 3–9 Sun to light shade	Early summer White, pink, or salmon	Aromatic, clovelike. Sniff close up to detect fragrance.
Joe-Pye weed *Eupatorium purpureum*	Zones 3–8 Sun to light shade	Early fall Purple	Aromatic, vanillalike. Sniff close up to detect fragrance.
Daylily *Hemerocallis* 'Hyperion'	Zones 3–9 Sun to partial shade	Early–midsummer Lemon yellow	Lemony. Sniff close up to detect fragrance.
Lavender *Lavandula angustifolia*	Zones 5–9 Sun to light shade	Midsummer–early fall Lavender-blue	Aromatic, spicy clean. Wafts its fragrance into the air.
Goldband lily *Lilium auratum*	Zones 4–9 Sun to partial shade	Summer White and yellow	Heavy, sweet. Wafts its fragrance into the air.
Creeping phlox *Phlox stolonifera*	Zones 3–8 Sun to shade	Spring Lavender, white, or pink	Aromatic, spicy. Sniff close up to detect fragrance.
Primroses *Primula auricula; P. × polyantha; P. vulgaris*	Zones 4–8 Sun to partial shade	Spring–early summer Many colors	Delicate, honeylike. Sniff close up to detect fragrance.
False Solomon's seal *Smilacina racemosa*	Zones 3–8 Light to full shade	Early summer White	Lemony. Wafts its fragrance into the air.
Allegheny foamflower *Tiarella cordifolia*	Zones 3–8 Partial to full shade	Spring White	Honeylike. Wafts its fragrance into the air.
Sweet violet *Viola odorata*	Zones 6–9 Sun to shade	Spring White, blue, or purple	Intensely violetlike. Sniff close up to detect fragrance.

A Scented Garden Retreat

The perception of fragrance varies greatly: What smells delightful to one person may smell unappealing to another. It's best to buy fragrant plants at a nursery or garden center where you can sniff before you buy.

Include plants that bloom at different times of the year and also plants with fragrant foliage. In this garden, shown here in early summer, designer Barbara Kaczorowski included peonies and rose verbena for early color and fragrance, and the butterfly bush for late-season bloom.

All of the plants in this garden will thrive in Zones 4–8, except the rugosa rose, which may not grow well in Zone 8 areas with hot, humid summers.

Gas plant (*Dictamnus albus* 'Purpureus'). 2'–3' tall; lemon-scented flowers in early summer. Do not transplant once established.

Rugosa rose (*Rosa rugosa* 'Blanc Double de Coubert'). 5'–6' tall; fragrant double white flowers all summer followed by large red hips; leaves orange in fall.

Cheddar pinks (*Dianthus gratianopolitanus*). 10" tall; clove-scented flowers late spring–early summer.

Lily (*Lilium* 'Black Dragon'). 4'–6' tall; fragrant flowers in summer. Plant 8"–10" deep; provide good drainage.

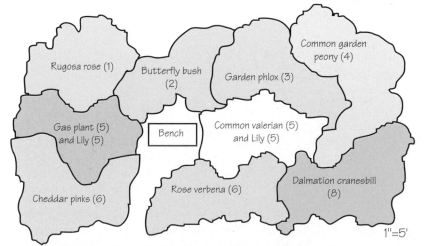

Rugosa rose (1)   Butterfly bush (2)   Garden phlox (3)   Common garden peony (4)

Gas plant (5) and Lily (5)   Bench   Common valerian (5) and Lily (5)

Cheddar pinks (6)   Rose verbena (6)   Dalmation cranesbill (8)

1"=5'

Numbers in parentheses indicate quantities to plant

Butterfly bush (*Buddleia* 'Lochinch'). 6' tall; lavender, vanilla-scented flowers summer–frost. Requires regular moisture.

Garden phlox (*Phlox paniculata* 'David'). 3' tall; rounded heads of white, spicy-scented flowers in summer. Highly mildew-resistant.

Common garden peony (*Paeonia lactiflora* 'Sarah Bernhardt'). 3' tall; spicy-scented flowers in early summer; foliage turns wine-red in fall.

Common valerian (*Valeriana officinalis*). 3' tall; musky-scented flowers in early summer. Likes moist soil.

Dalmation cranesbill (*Geranium dalmaticum* 'Biokovo'). 12" tall; flowers in early summer; leaves apple scented; leaves red autumn–winter.

Rose verbena (*Verbena canadensis*). 6"–12" tall; spicy-scented flowers spring–frost. Provide good drainage; self sows.

Fragrant Companions

Don't limit a fragrant garden to perennials. Many annuals and shrubs have pleasant perfumes to offer. Try using annual chocolate flower (*Berlandiera lyrata*), heliotrope (*Heliotropium arborescens*), mignonette (*Reseda odorata*), stock (*Matthiola incana*), sweet pea (*Lathyrus odoratus*), and sweet scabious (*Scabiosa atropurpurea*). Fragrant shrubs include bottlebrush buckeye (*Aesculus parviflora*), Carolina allspice (*Calycanthus floridus*), clove currant (*Ribes odoratum*), 'Northern Lights' azalea (*Rhododendron* 'Northern Lights'), and summersweet (*Clethra alnifolia*).

49

An Evening Garden

An evening garden is a midsummer night's dream. It's a garden filled with plants that bloom in the late afternoon or at night. The evening garden also features plants with luminous white flowers and silvery foliage, and blossoms that release their sweet fragrances especially at night. A well-planned evening garden can be a place of magic and mystery.

Some of the best white-flowered species and cultivars for evening enjoyment are Clark's geranium (*Geranium clarkei* 'Kashmir White'), Japanese aster (*Kalimeris pinnatifida* 'Hortensis', also known as *Asteromoea mongolica*), pincushion flower (*Scabiosa caucasica* 'Alba'), and prairie wild indigo (*Baptisia leucantha*).

Although it seems like an oxymoron, there are hosts of night-blooming daylilies which can light up the evening perennial garden. Ask your supplier for cultivars that open in the evening and have a pleasant fragrance.

Pick a sunny spot for your evening garden since most of the plants in it require full sun during the daylight hours. And a spot that is sunny by day will be well-moonlit by night. A dark background of evergreens is ideal to set off the pale flowers of this garden. Keep the location relatively near your house so that you can reach it easily in the dark, but not so close that lights in the house are a distraction. To preserve the mysterious air of the evening garden, make sure that your line of view toward it is directed away from the house.

Lighting for an evening garden should be minimal. A handsome light post with a low-wattage bulb toward one end of the garden is sufficient for viewing on moonless nights. On moonlit nights, the less ambient light, the better. Too much electric light will be harsh and blinding, destroying the softly luminous mystery of the garden, and will attract large numbers of unwanted insects besides.

The evening garden should be enjoyed at close range. Keep the scale of the garden small and intimate, unless you have decided to devote all your gardening efforts to this theme. Lay it out in a curved or irregular shape that allows placement of a bench very close to the plants. Or, site the garden at the edge of a patio or terrace—or even poolside—anywhere it would be pleasant to stroll and sit in the evening.

White Madonna lily (*Lilium candidum*) glows in the moonlight. White-flowered perennials are an especially good choice for evening gardens.

Stars of the Evening Garden

Common and Botanical Name	Hardiness and Exposure	Bloom Time and Color	Description
Night-Fragrant Perennials			
Gas plant *Dictamnus albus*	Zones 3–8 Sun to light shade	Late spring–early summer White or pink	Glossy, leathery, aromatic leaves; spikes of fragrant flowers to 2'. Drought-resistant, long-lived plant. Taprooted; resents transplanting.
August lily *Hosta plantaginea* 'Royal Standard'	Zones 3–8 Light to full shade	Late summer White	Large, fresh, green, heart-shaped leaves remain attractive all season; 2' spikes of waxy tubular flowers. Competes well with tree roots. Divide every 4–5 years.
Regal lily *Lilium regale*	Zones 3–8 Sun to partial shade	Summer Violet and brown	Thick stalks with narrow, glossy leaves to 4'–6'; terminal clusters of 6" trumpet-shaped flowers. Plant bulb 8"–10" deep with good drainage.
Tufted evening primrose *Oenothera caespitosa*	Zones 4–7 Sun	Summer White	Creeping 6" plant; 3" luminous fragrant flowers open in evening. Very drought-resistant and tolerant of heavy "gumbo" soils.
Bouncing bet *Saponaria officinalis*	Zones 2–8 Sun to light shade	Summer Pale pink, rose, or white	Oval leaves on 30" plant; 1" flowers look ragged by day, but fresh, lovely, and fragrant by night. Somewhat lax habit. Widely naturalized.
Yuccas *Yucca filamentosa, Y. flaccida*	Zones 3–9 Sun to light shade	Early summer White	2" spiky, flat, evergreen leaves similar to agave; 3'–5' spikes of waxy, bell-shaped flowers; flowers release sweet fragrance at night. Very tough, drought-resistant plant.
Silver-Leaved Perennials			
White sage *Artemisia ludoviciana* 'Valerie Finnis'	Zones 3–9 Sun	Summer–fall Insignificant	Felty, white, jagged leaves on 2' plant.
Silver sage *Salvia argentea*	Zones 5–9 Sun to light shade	Summer Yellow	Basal rosette of soft, felty, silvery leaves. Remove the flowers before they open. Often biennial.
Lavender cotton *Santolina chamaecyparissus*	Zones 6–8 Sun	Summer Yellow	Feathery gray, aromatic leaves on 18" shrublet; buttonlike flowers. Takes shearing well. Provide good drainage.

A Moonlight Patio Garden

In order to experience some of the most delectable perfumes of the night, you need to include some annuals in your evening garden. In this garden, designer Barbara Kaczorowski has used annual evening stock. This unassuming plant will add an inimitable sensual dimension to your summer nights. In the evening, stock flowers exhale an ethereal jasminelike scent that carries 50 feet or more.

All of the plants in this design, shown here in summer, have fragrant flowers, except for the white sage, which is included for its soft, silvery foliage. All of the plants in the garden will grow well in Zones 4–8, except for the citron daylily, which is hardy only to Zone 5.

Gas plant (*Dictamnus albus*). 2' tall; white lemon-scented flowers in early summer; aromatic leaves. Drought-tolerant, long-lived, taprooted, and resents transplanting.

Flowering tobacco (*Nicotiana alata* 'Grandiflora'). 3'–4' tall; fragrant flowers summer–frost. Tender perennial grown as an annual.

Daylily (*Hemerocallis* 'Master Blend'). 25" tall; flowers in early summer with later rebloom. Soil- and moisture-tolerant.

Evening stock (*Matthiola longipetala* subsp. *bicornis*). 18" tall; powerfully jasmine-scented flowers summer–frost. Annual.

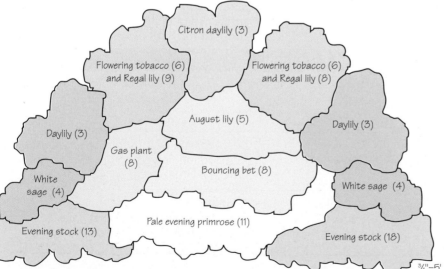

Citron daylily (3)

Flowering tobacco (6) and Regal lily (9)

Flowering tobacco (6) and Regal lily (8)

August lily (5)

Daylily (3)

Daylily (3)

Gas plant (8)

Bouncing bet (8)

White sage (4)

White sage (4)

Evening stock (13)

Pale evening primrose (11)

Evening stock (18)

¾"=5'

Numbers in parentheses indicate quantities to plant

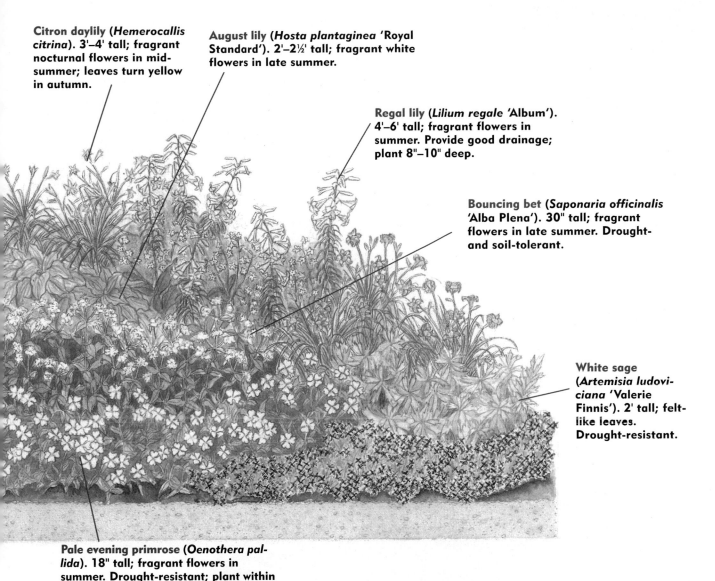

Citron daylily (*Hemerocallis citrina*). 3'–4' tall; fragrant nocturnal flowers in mid-summer; leaves turn yellow in autumn.

August lily (*Hosta plantaginea* 'Royal Standard'). 2'–2½' tall; fragrant white flowers in late summer.

Regal lily (*Lilium regale* 'Album'). 4'–6' tall; fragrant flowers in summer. Provide good drainage; plant 8"–10" deep.

Bouncing bet (*Saponaria officinalis* 'Alba Plena'). 30" tall; fragrant flowers in late summer. Drought- and soil-tolerant.

White sage (*Artemisia ludoviciana* 'Valerie Finnis'). 2' tall; felt-like leaves. Drought-resistant.

Pale evening primrose (*Oenothera pallida*). 18" tall; fragrant flowers in summer. Drought-resistant; plant within a 6" deep barrier to prevent spreading.

More Elegant Evening Plants

Many night-blooming plants are annuals or are only adapted to tropical conditions. Fragrant evening annuals include moonflower (*Ipomoea alba*), four-o'clock (*Mirabilis jalapa*), and heirloom seed strains of flowering tobacco (*Nicotiana alata* and *N. sylvestris*). Gardeners in tropical areas can grow tender perennial plants with powerful night fragrance, such as night jessamine (*Cestrum nocturnum*), peacock orchid (*Acidanthera bicolor*), and tuberose (*Polianthes tuberosa*). Gardeners north of Zone 10 can try growing tropical night-bloomers in containers.

Perennials for Cut Flowers

With a perennial garden, the luxury of cut flowers is yours for the snipping. All you need is a sharp pair of scissors and a bucket of water, and any foray into the flower garden can lead to bouquets and arrangements far more unique than anything you could order at the florist.

Cutting materials. What often sets great floral designers apart from the rest is their ability to see the beauty in unusual materials and to use them to advantage in arrangements. But this knack needn't be the province of elite arrangers only. Everyone can open their eyes to the beauty of offbeat materials, like bare branches, seed-pods, unusual foliage, and mosses and lichens. Even vegetable gardens can lend beautiful materials, including sculptural foliage like the metallic-hued outer leaves of a purple cabbage or the jagged silver of cardoon. These off-the-beaten-path materials supply texture and sculptural forms that define an arrangement and elevate it above the mundane.

When you venture out for cutting materials, search fields, forests, and roadsides as well as your perennial garden. These wild areas can often supply uniquely seasonal notes for your arrangements. Just don't bring home any poison ivy, oak, or sumac, all of which produce ornamental berries in fall!

Cutting and conditioning. Early morning is the best time for cutting flowers, with evening being second-best. Flowers cut at midday, when plant tissues are most water-depleted, will have a short vase life. If the ground is extremely dry, thoroughly water the flowers the night before you plan to cut them.

Always carry a bucket of water with you into the garden and plunge your flowers directly into it as you cut them. Place the bucket in a cool, dark place for several hours to condition the flowers before arranging. As you work with your flowers, recut them underwater to keep air bubbles from entering their stems.

◄ **Cutting and arranging perennials from your own garden lets you express your personality and style. Yarrow, iris, daylilies, and oxeye daisies are just a few of the many cutting perennials you can grow.**

Perennials for Cutting

We all have favorite perennials for flower arrangements. But here are some perennials you may not have thought of growing for cut flowers. Plant name is followed by flower color.

Spring Bloomers

Columbines (*Aquilegia* spp.); various colors; Zones 3–8.

Gas plant (*Dictamnus albus*); pink or white; Zones 3–8.

Heartleaf bergenia (*Bergenia cordifolia*); pink to rose red; Zones 3–9.

Lady's-mantle (*Alchemilla mollis*); chartreuse; Zones 3–8.

Lenten rose (*Helleborus orientalis*); white or pink, spotted with purple; Zones 4-9.

Mountain bluet (*Centaurea montana*); cobalt blue; Zones 3–8.

Summer Bloomers

Astilbes (*Astilbe* spp. and cvs.); white, pink, rose, or red; Zones 3–8.

Bellflowers (*Campanula* spp., tall species and cultivars only); white or blue; Zones 3–8.

Golden marguerite (*Anthemis tinctoria*); yellow; Zones 3–8.

Patrinia (*Patrinia scabiosifolia*); yellow; Zones 4–9.

Penstemons (*Penstemon* spp. and cvs.); pink, white, red, blue, or violet; Zones 4–9.

Pincushion flower (*Scabiosa caucasica*); blue, lavender, or white; Zones 3-7.

Purple coneflower (*Echinacea purpurea*); pink, with iridescent, conelike centers; Zones 3–8.

Red valerian (*Centranthus ruber*); white, mauve-pink, or rose-red; Zones 4–8.

Russian sage (*Perovskia atriplicifolia*); amethyst flowers and silvery foliage; Zones 4–9.

Salvias (*Salvia* spp.); blue, violet, or rose; Zones 3–10.

Speedwells (*Veronica* spp. and cvs.); purple, blue, or pink; Zones 3–8.

Sunray flower (*Inula orientalis*); gold; Zones 4–8.

Fall Bloomers

Asters (*Aster* spp. and cvs.); white, blue, violet, pink, or red; Zones 3–9.

Boltonias (*Boltonia asteroides* cvs.); white or pale pink; Zones 3–9.

'Clara Curtis' chrysanthemum (*Chrysanthemum zawadskii* var. *latilobum* 'Clara Curtis'); pink; Zones 4–9.

Common sneezeweed (*Helenium autumnale* cvs.); bronze or yellow; Zones 3–8.

'Herrenhausen' oregano (*Origanum* 'Herrenhausen'); cerise and purple; Zones 4–9.

Mist flower (*Eupatorium coelestinum*); periwinkle; Zones 4–10.

Perennials for Dried Flowers

Drying flowers for indoor arrangements is a wonderful way to preserve your garden's beauty for off-season enjoyment. While you can buy bundles or arrangements of dried flowers, they're expensive and can never compare with the abundance and variety of flowers you can dry from your own garden. Crafted into wreaths or bouquets, your home-grown dried flowers will make unique and (for you) inexpensive gifts that anyone would be thrilled to receive.

Choosing flowers for drying. It may surprise you to learn that you can dry most flowers successfully in one way or another. You needn't limit yourself to the flowers known as "everlastings," which have papery bracts or petals, although these certainly dry wonderfully and most easily. Countless common garden perennials, like asters, astilbes, catmints (*Nepeta* spp.), delphiniums, gayfeathers (*Liatris* spp.), pinks (*Dianthus* spp.), and yarrows, will air-dry beautifully. Just hang them upside down in small bundles in a well-ventilated shady spot for a few days. If you don't have any exposed rafters or beams from which to hang flowers, suspend a section of chicken wire from the ceiling in the well-ventilated area. You can then tie the bundles of flowers to the wire.

Certain perennials lend themselves especially well to drying. Foremost among these are German statice (*Limonium tataricum*), sea lavender (*L. latifolium*), and Siberian statice (*L. gmelinii*), whose clouds of papery silver, dark blue, and lavender flowers dry effortlessly. Use them as "filler" and to create a delicate foil for big, dramatic blossoms. Baby's-breath falls in this category. Globe thistle (*Echinops ritro*) and amethyst sea holly (*Eryngium amethystinum*) both have metallic blue flowerheads that are naturals for drying. And Chinese lantern (*Physalis alkekengi*) is a perennial bearing bright orange papery fruits valued for their unusual and brilliant color in dried arrange-

While you can create a special garden for growing flowers for cutting and drying, you may prefer just to mix perennials for drying into your existing beds and borders.

'Herrenhausen' oregano (*Origanum* 'Herrenhausen') has beautiful purple-tinted bracts surrounding tiny pink flowers that dry wonderfully. The yellow, buttonlike flowers of common tansy (*Tanacetum vulgare*) are another natural for drying, but mind this invasive plant doesn't take over your garden! Tall artemisias make for premier drying materials because the gray-green color and silvery highlights of their foliage complement dried flowers so handsomely.

Cut flowers for drying in the morning just after the dew dries off. As a general rule, you'll want to cut them less than fully open, as they will continue to mature while they're hanging up to dry. If they are fully open, many flowers will just turn to puffs of seed. After they're dry, flowers may be sprayed with a special fixative to help preserve their colors and to prevent them from reabsorbing moisture or from shattering when humidity is low.

You can leave dried flowers hanging in place until you're ready to use them, or you can store them in boxes. Line the boxes with tissue paper, and place the flowers loosely in layers with more tissue paper between each layer. Store the boxes on shelves or in a closet, but keep them away from humid locations.

It's easy and fun to make your own dried arrangements using perennial and annual flowers and herbs. Try a simple swag using dried yellow yarrow and tansy, lavender, sage, and brilliant red annual cockscomb.

ments. Don't dry Chinese lanterns in bunches. Instead, make a "clothesline" in your drying area and individually hook each stem right side up to the line.

Herbs for drying. Perennial herbs offer a wealth of cutting material to the dried flower crafter. Lavender is wonderful for both its flowers and foliage.

Chapter 2

Solving Landscape Problems with Perennials

Success with Shady Sites • Dealing with Soil Problems •

Improving the View • Solutions for Slopes • Solving Mowing Woes •

Managing High-Traffic Areas • Renovating an Overgrown Garden •

Transforming Weedy Corners

Success with Shady Sites

Great gardening opportunities await you if your yard has shade. That's right—shady sites don't have to be a landscape problem. Once you learn to select shade-tolerant plants, those shady corners may become your favorite gardens. Some of the loveliest perennials around thrive in shade, including lungworts (*Pulmonaria* spp.), Solomon's seals (*Polygonatum* spp.), and a host of woodland wildflowers.

You can plant shade-tolerant perennials under trees to create cool, forestlike nooks. Perennials can lighten up the often drab, sheltered north sides of buildings. And shade-loving groundcovers make a beautiful understory of flowers and foliage beneath existing shrubs.

Light shade. Lightly shaded sites receive spotty shade cast by a few high branches or leaves throughout the day. Or, the site may be fully shaded for a couple of hours during hot summer afternoons, but otherwise receive strong sun. Many perennials that favor full sun also grow well in light shade.

Partial shade. Partially shaded sites have alternating periods of sun and shade, with a total of three to five hours of shade each day. Most shade plants will grow well in partial shade, although delicate cool-weather wildflowers such as trilliums (*Trillium* spp.) may not survive in a partially shaded spot for more than a few seasons.

Full shade. This is day-long shade, typically created by the spreading branches of mature trees. Ferns, ivies, hostas, and many groundcovers thrive in full shade. A smattering of flowering perennials, such as astilbes and violets, will grow and bloom well in full shade. See "Perennials That Survive Deep Shade" on page 63 and "Great Perennial Groundcovers" on page 85 for planting ideas for these very shady sites.

Light requirements for a given plant can differ from region to region. For example, avens (*Geum* spp.) grow well in full sun, but in the South they often do better in partial shade where they're protected from the worst of the afternoon sun.

High shade cast by tall trees is a wonderful setting for perennial gardens. Some morning and late afternoon sun will reach the plants. Plus, air circulation is good, which helps prevent plant disease problems. ➤

Shade gardens are anything but boring. A partially shaded site is perfect for many well-loved perennials, including bleeding heart (*Dicentra* sp.), cranesbill (*Geranium* sp.), alliums (*Allium* spp.), iris, and hostas.

Shade Basics

Shade plants suffer few pest problems and generally don't need to be watered as often as plants in a sunny border. Most do best in soil that's well drained and rich in organic matter.

One problem gardeners often face in planting perennials on shady sites is tree roots. You can plant in pockets between roots or prepare beds above the roots. This does require some care. See "Planting under Trees" on the opposite page for details.

Here are a few special considerations in keeping shade gardens looking their best.

• The moist, closed-in conditions in many shady spots sometimes foster fungal diseases. To encourage good airflow, allow plenty of space between plants, and thin low-hanging branches from surrounding shrubs or trees.

• Many shade-loving perennials emerge and bloom in early spring. Remove protective winter mulch from shady beds early to allow spring sunlight to warm the beds and to keep the plants from becoming sun-starved and leggy.

• Slugs can be a menace in moist, shady gardens. If you've had slug problems, don't mulch around shade perennials because the mulch provides cover for the slugs.

• As surrounding foliage matures, a partially shaded site may become densely shaded. Trim away encroaching tree and shrub branches when necessary to get more light to your plants.

Dry Shade

Many shady sites in home gardens are next to houses or garages, where the natural topsoil was stripped during construction. Plus, the building overhang blocks rainfall. How can you make a dry, shady site like that a good home for shade-loving perennials?

The best solution is adding organic matter—lots of it. If the site isn't root-filled, dig it thoroughly and mix in plenty of compost or shredded leaves. After planting, check soil moisture frequently and water as needed.

Some perennials that tolerate dry shade include hostas, Japanese anemone (*Anemone* × *hybrida*), lady fern (*Athyrium filix-femina*), and Siberian bugloss (*Brunnera macrophylla*).

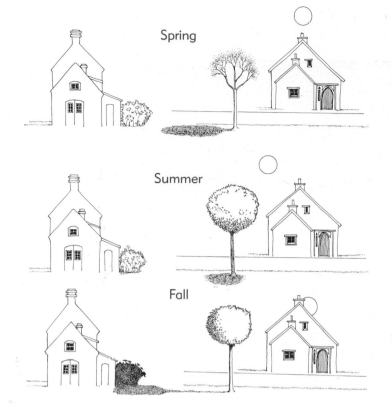

Spring

Summer

Fall

Shade isn't static. Midafternoon sun and shade patterns change with the seasons, so a sunny spring bed may be mostly shaded in fall.

Leave a ring around the tree. You can save considerable stress to a tree by leaving undisturbed soil around its base. The undisturbed area should have a ring of 6 to 8 feet; plant at the edge of the ring. Cover the unplanted area with 3 inches of composted mulch (composted shredded leaves or wood). Once your perennials grow in, the composted area won't be noticeable.

Start small. Choose perennials in 4-inch pots—smaller roots mean less digging. The small plants will be competing with tree roots, so they may need more watering than usual.

Point your plants in. Plant spreading groundcovers at the edge of the rooty area, and train their stems in toward the tree.

Make a planting bed. Spread a layer of light soil mix up

Planting under Trees

Shade gardens under trees may be either moist or dry. But when you establish a garden under trees, digging is *not* the best approach. If you disturb the trees' roots too much, you're likely to end up with a shade garden under dying and dead trees. *Never* use a rotary tiller to loosen the soil under trees.

Choose perennials that have the same moisture and pH requirements as the trees you're planting them near. One good method for planting perennials around trees is to dig individual "planting pockets," work in or-

ganic matter, and set plants in small clusters. Here are some other tips to try when planting under trees.

Ferns, hostas, astilbes, and spiderwort (*Tradescantia* sp.) make a lush grouping for a moist, shady site.

For spring color in a shady garden, try planting white Allegheny foamflower (*Tiarella cordifolia*), pale yellow wild columbine (*Aquilegia canadensis* 'Corbett'), pink creeping phlox (*Phlox stolonifera* 'Pink Ridge'), and blue Siberian bugloss (*Brunnera macrophylla*).

to 4 inches thick over the rooty area under a tree to make gently mounded raised beds. The mix should be rich in compost and pine bark, and it should contain only about 20 percent natural soil so that air can penetrate. Some experts feel that this technique can be stressful to established trees, but many landscape professionals report good success with it.

Shade around Shrubs

Shrubs can provide year-round greenery, but when planted alone, evergreen shrubs are just plain dull. Make those "same old shrubs" sparkle by planting shade-tolerant perennials around them.

Yews. With their dark green foliage, yews (*Taxus* spp.) make the perfect background for white-flowering and variegated-foliage perennials. Light up the shady spots near yews with white astilbes, white bleeding hearts (*Dicentra* spp.), variegated hostas, white Japanese anemone (*Anemone* × *hybrida*), silvery Japanese painted fern (*Athyrium goeringianum*), spotted lamium (*Lamium maculatum* 'White Nancy'), and sweet woodruff (*Galium odoratum*).

Hollies. Echo the glossy leaves of hollies (*Ilex* spp.) with hellebores (*Helleborus* spp.), Italian arum (*Arum italicum*), and variegated cultivars of periwinkle (*Vinca* spp.).

Rhododendrons and azaleas. Add to the spring show by planting spring-flowering perennials, including bleeding hearts (*Dicentra* spp.), columbines (*Aquilegia* spp.), cushion spurge (*Euphorbia epithymoides*), forget-me-nots (*Myosotis* spp.), Virginia bluebells

62

Perennials That Survive Deep Shade

Common and Botanical Name	Hardiness	Bloom Time and Color	Description
Italian arum *Arum italicum* 'Pictum'	Zones 6–9	Spring Cream	12"–20" tall; arrow-shaped leaves emerge in late summer and disappear in spring; orange berries appear before leaves in late summer.
European wild ginger *Asarum europaeum*	Zones 4–8	Spring Reddish brown	6"–8" tall; glossy rounded evergreen leaves. Flowers are insignificant. Prefers moist, rich soil.
Japanese painted fern *Athyrium goeringianum* 'Pictum'	Zones 4–9	None	18" tall; silvery green variegated fronds. Prefers moist soil.
Hardy begonia *Begonia grandis*	Zones 6–10	Late summer–fall Pink	24"–36" tall; pendulous flowers above reddish green waxy foliage. Spreads rapidly by tubers.
Siberian bugloss *Brunnera macrophylla*	Zones 3–8	Spring Light blue	12"–18" tall; sprays of tiny flowers are held above fuzzy, green, heart-shaped leaves. Prefers moist soil; will tolerate dry shade.
Leadwort *Ceratostigma plumbaginoides*	Zones 5–9	Late summer–fall Deep blue	6"–12" tall; reddish leaves emerge in mid-spring, changing to green in summer; dark red fall foliage. Rapid spreader.
Wintergreen *Gaultheria procumbens*	Zones 3–8	Spring White or pale pink	6" tall; dark green evergreen leaves turn burgundy in fall; ½" bright scarlet fruits attract birds. Prefers acid, moist soil rich in organic matter.
Yellow archangel *Lamiastrum galeobdolon*	Zones 4–9	Spring Yellow	8"–14" tall; flowers grow in whorls around stem; puckered leaves are silver and green. Long vining stems overhang walls nicely.
Mazus *Mazus reptans*	Zones 4–9	Spring–summer Rosy purple	1"–2" tall; semi-evergreen matlike foliage makes dense spreading groundcover. Tolerates dry soil.
Virginia bluebells *Mertensia virginica*	Zones 3–9	Spring Blue and pink	12"–24" tall; flowers in clusters above basal rosette of medium green leaves. Foliage dies back to ground after bloom; plants will self-sow.

(*Mertensia virginica*), and wild blue phlox (*Phlox divaricata*).

Arborvitaes. Create contrast between lacy arborvitae foliage and bold-leaved perennials. Try hardy begonias, bergenias (*Bergenia* spp.), large-leaved hostas, lungworts (*Pulmonaria* spp.), and variegated Solomon's seal (*Polygonatum odoratum* 'Variegatum').

Spring sunlight shines through the leafless branches of deciduous shrubs, making a perfect microclimate for spring-flowering bulbs. Good perennial companions include daylilies, epimediums (*Epimedium* spp.), lungworts (*Pulmonaria* spp.), Siberian bugloss (*Brunnera macrophylla*), and spiderworts (*Tradescantia* spp.).

A Deck Foundation Shade Garden

Designer Stephanie Cohen created this garden to surround a shady deck. It could also be adapted to flank a shady patio or to run along a shady foundation. The garden is shown at its flowering peak in spring. All the plants have outstanding foliage, and some, such as Lenten rose, Wherry's foamflower, and heuchera, provide foliage for winter interest. Cohen selected August lilies for their fragrant flowers. The plants in this low-maintenance garden perform well with moist, rich soil. All the plants in this garden will grow in Zones 4–8, except the heuchera and yellow archangel, which may not tolerate the heat south of Zone 7 well.

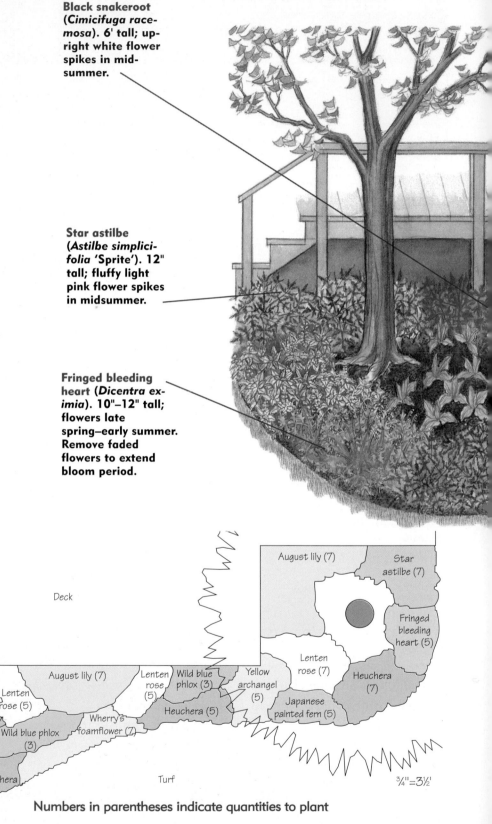

Black snakeroot (*Cimicifuga racemosa*). 6' tall; upright white flower spikes in midsummer.

Star astilbe (*Astilbe simplicifolia* 'Sprite'). 12" tall; fluffy light pink flower spikes in midsummer.

Fringed bleeding heart (*Dicentra eximia*). 10"–12" tall; flowers late spring–early summer. Remove faded flowers to extend bloom period.

Numbers in parentheses indicate quantities to plant

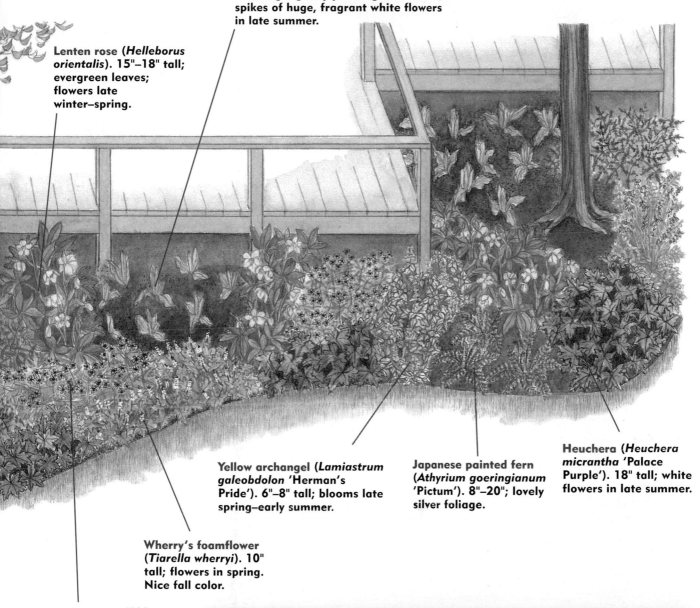

August lily (*Hosta plantaginea***). 3'–4'
tall; large, glossy yellow-green leaves;
spikes of huge, fragrant white flowers
in late summer.**

Lenten rose (*Helleborus
orientalis***). 15"–18" tall;
evergreen leaves;
flowers late
winter–spring.**

Yellow archangel (*Lamiastrum
galeobdolon* **'Herman's
Pride'). 6"–8" tall; blooms late
spring–early summer.**

**Japanese painted fern
(***Athyrium goeringianum*
**'Pictum'). 8"–20"; lovely
silver foliage.**

Heuchera (*Heuchera
micrantha* **'Palace
Purple'). 18" tall; white
flowers in late summer.**

**Wherry's foamflower
(***Tiarella wherryi***). 10"
tall; flowers in spring.
Nice fall color.**

Wild blue phlox (*Phlox
divaricata* **subsp.
*laphamii***). 18" tall;
blooms in late spring.
Remove faded flower
clusters.**

Make Your Own Shade

Stuck on a treeless lot, wishing you had a nice spot for a
shady garden? Make shade where there is none! Create
"living shade" by training a dense evergreen climbing
vine, such as English ivy, up a trellis or high fence. Or
build a simple lath screen—a crisscrossed framework of inexpensive wooden lath strips—and put plants in the dappled shade cast
by the screen.

Dealing with Soil Problems

Have you ever envied the soil on television garden shows? It always seems to be rich, dark, and full of humus. The dullest of shovels slides into it effortlessly. *That* is good soil—and it is *not* what most of us have.

"Poor" soil can be due to one of many in a grab bag of conditions. It may contain a high proportion of clay or lack fertility. Perhaps it's choked with rocks or doesn't drain well. Otherwise decent soil may become poor through compaction or a failure to replenish nutrients by adding organic matter each season. The wrong pH can mean poor soil, too. The important thing is to make sure you know *why* your soil is poor before you begin the process of improving it.

Most gardeners don't want to spend large amounts of their time or money on fixing the soil. After all, the fun of gardening is planting plants and enjoying their beauty. You may want to tackle soil problems gradually. Here are some suggestions on how to handle problem soils.

Set priorities. First, decide what areas are most important to you, or what looks so terrible that you feel embarrassed about it. That's where you'll feel most motivated to work. Also, decide early what plants you want to use in those spots. You'll need to match your soil improvements to your plant choice. Then you can begin the process of carting in and turning under the organic

Plants with a Warning

Some perennials that make good choices for poor soils may be unsuitable for rich soil. They may grow so tall that they will sprawl or flop over unless they are staked. Or they may spread so rampantly that they overrun the garden. So keep these lovely perennials in poor soil, or beware!

Sprawlers
Blanket flowers (*Gaillardia* spp.)
Coneflowers (*Rudbeckia* spp.)
Coreopsis (*Coreopsis* spp.)
Gaura (*Gaura lindheimeri*)
Obedient plant (*Physostegia virginiana*)
Rock cresses (*Arabis* spp.)
Salvias (*Salvia* spp.)
Soapworts (*Saponaria* spp.)

Spreaders
Ajugas (*Ajuga* spp.)
Bear's-breech (*Acanthus* spp.)
Bishop's weed (*Aegopodium podagraria*)
Evening primrose (*Oenothera speciosa*)
Goldenrods (*Solidago* spp.)
Spiderworts (*Tradescantia* spp.)

For sun-baked sites along sidewalks, choose plants that like dry soil, such as ornamental grasses, Russian sage (*Perovskia atriplicifolia*), and cheery yellow threadleaf coreopsis (*Coreopsis verticillata*).

matter that will ultimately create *your* rich, crumbly, humuslike soil. (See "Improving Your Soil" on page 225 for details.)

Let earthworms work for you. If you can't tackle all the poor soil in your landscape at once, use an improvement technique that doesn't require digging! Simply cover the soil with organic material—straw, grass clippings, leaves, or shredded newspaper—and top it with a more attractive mulch, such as wood chips, if you wish. Then let the earthworms do the job of working the organic matter into your soil. When you return to dig the site next season, you may be amazed to find your terrible soil is well on its way to being friable, rich, and ready to work.

Pick plants that can take it. Consider what plants will succeed in the soil you have. You'll find suggestions in "Plants with a Warning" on the opposite page. You can also ask advice from local garden centers, the extension service, and neighbors with similar soils.

Wet and Dry Soils

You can improve drainage in damp, poorly drained planting areas by installing drainage tiles or by adding an underlying layer of coarse sand or pea gravel. Likewise, a piped irrigation system can transform an excessively dry

spot. But mechanical remedies such as these can be expensive.

A better approach is to work with the existing conditions. Both wet and dry soils will benefit if you work in a 1- to 2-inch layer of compost before planting. Then choose perennials that favor the soil's existing moisture level, whether wet or dry, and work to keep those conditions constant.

After planting perennials that need moist conditions, mulch beds with pine straw, shredded bark, or other organic matter to retain soil moisture and to dis-

courage broad-leaved weeds, many of which favor damp soil. During periods of drought, water moist-soil perennials often and thoroughly to keep plant roots from drying. If the site is very wet, with soggy soil or standing water most of the season, the best alternative is to establish a bog or wetland garden, as described on page 40.

Dry-soil plants will tolerate heat and extended periods of drought, but they can become diseased if placed in overly wet or humid sites. Before planting,

Glossy-leaved umbrella plant (*Darmera peltata*) is a West Coast native that flourishes in wet soil along streams or beside ponds. Plan ahead if you plant it— its leaves can reach 18" in diameter.

Seedlings that emerge near rocks benefit from the rock's shelter, and later grow to overhang the rocks. Create this effect in your garden with woodland plants like fringed bleeding heart (*Dicentra eximia*).

be sure the site is consistently dry (but not bone-dry). When squeezed, a handful of soil should hold together but crumble into small granules under pressure. Water plants sparingly. Use crushed stone mulch to discourage weeds and provide a small amount of supplemental water. (Moisture condenses on the stone overnight, giving plants a quick sip before the next day's heat.) For information on growing perennials in arid regions, see "The Desert Southwest" on page 100.

Taking Stock of Rocks

It's a fact of gardening: We hit rocks. They dull our shovels and bend the teeth of our rakes. We can even hurt ourselves in the fight to rid our gardens of rocks. We scrape our knuckles, pinch our fingers, and can do serious damage to our backs by lifting them incorrectly.

Yes, rocks are stronger than we are, and often our best choice is to work *with* them rather than getting rid of them. One option is to try rock gardening.

Traditionally, rock gardening refers to the effort to reproduce proper conditions for growing alpine plants (small plants that grow at high elevations in mountainous areas). Alpine plants, which commonly grow among rocks, require cool summers, a short growing season, and ex-

tremely fast-draining soil (usually a sand-and-gravel combination).

However, most gardeners do not have the inclination to reproduce alpine conditions. Rather, we become "rock gardeners" because we acquire, discover, or are left with rocks on our property. If they are large rocks, the choices are to avoid them, move them with great difficulty, or use them creatively in the landscape. If small rocks are hidden throughout the soil, rake or dig and remove them, or leave them in the soil.

Rocks in the soil are not harmful to plants unless they are so large that roots cannot penetrate the soil around them. In most cases rocks help drainage and ultimately add to the mineral content of the soil.

Rocks can be focal points, centerpieces, backdrops, and windscreens, and they can provide texture or four-season interest. Rocks can be seats, stepping-stones, borders, or walls. If you have rocks, look at their shapes, colors, sizes, and textures, and consider their potential in your landscape design. Then use them consciously as part of your landscape plan, just as you would a fence, trellis, water garden, or pathway. For more ideas on using rocks in your garden, see "A Garden among the Rocks" on page 70.

Perennials for Hot, Dry Sites

Common and Botanical Name	Hardiness and Exposure	Bloom Time and Color	Description
Yarrows *Achillea* hybrids	Zones 3–9 Sun	Spring–summer Red, rose, pink, salmon, or yellow	Aromatic, fernlike foliage. Place in middle or back of border. Excellent for cutting or drying.
Artemisias *Artemisia* spp.	Zones 4–8 Sun	Summer–fall Gray-green foliage	Grown for attractive aromatic foliage. Varieties range from low mounding types, such as silvermound artemisia (*A. schmidtiana*), to taller shrublike species, such as white sage (*A. ludoviciana*).
Butterfly weed *Asclepias tuberosa*	Zones 3–9 Sun to light shade	Summer Yellow, orange, or red	Grows from taproot; do not try to move established plants.
Globe thistle *Echinops ritro*	Zones 3–8 Sun	Summer Blue	Tough, easy-care plants produce dark blue flowers atop tall spikes. Excellent for cut or dried arrangements.
Blue oat grass *Helictotrichon sempervirens*	Zones 4–9 Sun–partial shade	Early summer White, drying to golden brown	12"–18" tall and wide; foliage is a striking blue. Works well in mass plantings or as an accent plant.
Daylilies *Hemerocallis* spp. and cultivars	Zones 4–9 Sun–partial shade	Spring–summer Yellow, orange, pink, purple, or red	Wide selection of cultivars, including bicolor and tricolor. Some types require division every three to four years.
Tall gayfeather *Liatris scariosa*	Zones 4–9 Sun	Summer White or purple	Flower spikes grow 2'–3' tall. Rough gayfeather (*L. aspera*) is also good for dry soil.
Sea lavender *Limonium latifolium*	Zones 3–9 Sun–light shade	Summer Pink	Wide, misty clusters of tiny flowers above low rosettes of triangular leaves. Do not move established plants.
Switch grass *Panicum virgatum*	Zones 5–9 Sun	Summer–fall Red or blue-green foliage	Ornamental grass grows rapidly to 4' tall; taller stems support clouds of tiny blooms. Foliage golden in fall.
Oriental poppy *Papaver orientale*	Zones 2–7 Sun	Spring–summer Orange, red, pink, or white	Very showy early-summer blossoms. Foliage dies back after bloom. Hide the resulting gap by planting next to bushy or tall plants.
Goldenrods *Solidago* spp.	Zones 3–9 Sun–light shade	Summer–fall Yellow	Profuse, striking yellow flowers. Wreath goldenrod (*S. caesia*) prefers partial to full shade.
Yuccas *Yucca* spp.	Zones 3–10 Sun–light shade	Summer White	Tropical-looking but quite hardy. Huge bell-shaped flowers above broad base of sword-like leaves.

A Garden among the Rocks

Basket-of-gold (*Aurinia saxatilis*), blood-red cranesbill (*Geranium sanguineum*), candytufts (*Iberis* spp.), common thrift (*Armeria maritima*), flax (*Linum* spp.), sea lavender (*Limonium latifolium*), speedwells (*Veronica* spp.), strawberry geranium (*Saxifraga stolonifera*), and woolly yarrow (*Achillea tomentosa*) are all great choices for rocky sites.

For this rock garden, shown here in late summer, designer Sally Cunningham selected plants that would create interesting special effects when placed near rocks. The plants in the garden will all grow well in average soil in a sunny location. All are hardy from Zones 5–8, except the snow-in-summer, which won't tolerate the heat south of Zone 7.

White gaura (*Gaura lindheimeri*). 3' tall; flowers spring–summer.

Purple coneflower (*Echinacea purpurea*). 36" tall; blooms late summer–fall.

Clustered bellflower (*Campanula glomerata* 'Joan Elliot'). 18" tall; blooms all summer.

Heuchera (*Heuchera micrantha* 'Palace Purple'). 18" tall; white flowers in late summer.

Cranesbill (*Geranium* 'Johnson's Blue'). 18" tall; blooms spring–fall.

Snow-in-summer (*Cerastium tomentosum*). 7" tall; white flowers in spring; attractive foliage all year. Spreads rapidly.

Siberian iris (*Iris sibirica*). 2'–3' tall; select a deep blue cultivar with early-summer bloom.

Clustered bellflower (1)

Lady's mantle (3)

Fountain grass (1)

Lady's mantle (3)

Clustered bellflower (3)

White gaura (1)

Purple coneflower (3)

Heuchera (4)

Lady's mantle (4)

Heuchera (4)

Tricolor sage (3)

Purple coneflower (3)

Alpine sea holly (3)

Heuchera (1)

Threadleaf coreopsis (1)

Siberian iris (5)

Threadleaf coreopsis (3)

Lady's mantle (9)

Hameln fountain grass (1)

Cranesbill (3)

Siberian iris (5)

Pincushion flower (5)

Lavender (5)

Cranesbill (2)

'Hameln' fountain grass (3)

Snow-in-summer (20)

1"=5½'

Numbers in parentheses indicate quantities to plant

Fountain grass (*Pennisetum alopecuroides*). 2'–3' tall; flowers summer–fall. Remains attractive through winter.

Alpine sea holly (*Eryngium alpinum*). 36" tall; flowers in summer; fall foliage interest.

Lady's-mantle (*Alchemilla mollis*). 12" tall; yellow-green flowers in spring.

Threadleaf coreopsis (*Coreopsis verticillata* 'Moonbeam'). 1'–3' tall; flowers early summer–fall.

'Hameln' fountain grass (*Pennisetum alopecuroides* 'Hameln'). 18" tall; flowers summer–fall. Remains attractive through winter.

Lavender (*Lavandula angustifolia*). 24" tall; flowers spring–fall.

Tricolor sage (*Salvia officinalis* 'Tricolor'). 18"–24" tall; blue-purple flowers summer–fall.

Pincushion flower (*Scabiosa caucasica* 'Butterfly Blue'). 18" tall; flowers late spring–fall.

Great Garden Roles for Rocks

Once you've dug rocks out of a bed, put them to work.

Erosion control. Rocks can hold back a bank, direct water runoff, and prevent topsoil from escaping.

Water garden edging. Disguise the edges of pool liners with rocks.

Landing sites. Place some rocks in a shallow bird bath. Beneficial insects like lacewings and lady beetles will use them as a perch to avoid drowning when they drink.

Terraces. Separate growing areas on slopes with tiers of rocks.

Raised beds. Frame them with rocks.

Paths and stepping-stones. Use rocks as stepping-stones in beds.

Walls. Build rock walls to enclose a garden or direct traffic.

Waterfalls. Midsize rocks make perfect foundations and falling-off places for waterfalls.

Toad shelters. Make small rock piles for toads to hide in.

A good seat. A large rock invites visitors to rest and observe.

Improving the View

The neighbor's trash cans, the electric meter, the overgrown shrubs, the cracks in the driveway—we all have some views in our yard that are less than beautiful. Sometimes, we don't even notice them (but chances are, our neighbors do!). Wouldn't it be nicer to blot out the unsightly sights so every view is a pleasure?

To see your garden through fresh eyes, photograph it. Take pictures looking out the windows of your house, from the patio, and as you approach your house along the front walk. You don't need an expensive camera to do this—even a disposable camera will work fine. The camera forces your eye to focus on a narrow area. And the resulting pictures will show you, beyond the shadow of a doubt,

what areas need some beautification. Then, you can get to the fun and exciting task of using perennials to dress up sad-looking shrubs, add accents, and create living screens to block out the uglies.

Dressing Up Shrubs

One nearly ubiquitous feature of our home landscapes is shrubs, including lollipop-shaped forsythia, foundation yews, and

Once the vivid azalea blossoms fade in a landscape without perennials (*left*), there will be uniform greenery with no pizzazz.

In a mixed landscape of perennials, annuals, and shrubs (*right*), the yard will be dynamic and colorful throughout spring, summer, and fall.

scraggly privet hedges. All too often, they're less than lovely. Why keep them? It may be because they serve a purpose, such as blocking wind, providing privacy, or even because they're where you hang your holiday decorations. Perhaps they bloom gloriously, though briefly, in early spring. Or maybe you're just attached to them despite their homeliness.

Whatever your reasons for keeping your shrubs, you can certainly take steps to make them handsome. Some plants are inherently less beautiful than others, but a shrub may look bad because it needs some organic fertilizer or occasional watering. Perhaps it's received too little— or too much—pruning.

You can also make your shrubs look better by giving them lovely companions. Plant flowering perennials to block an unattractive side of your problem shrub. Or distract the eye of the viewer by placing some dramatic perennials nearby as a focal point.

Play up foliage colors. Play off the foliage color of your shrubs to create interesting combinations. The foliage colors of evergreen shrubs range from yellow-greens to true greens and blue-greens. For shrubs with yellowish tones like some species and cultivars of false cypress (*Chamaecyparis* spp.), try perennials with dark green foliage, or

The yellow spring blossoms of cushion spurge (*Euphorbia epithymoides*) brighten up the ground around shrubs and trees. Its red fall foliage will also add late-season interest.

with yellow, gold, dark red, or purple flowers. Some good companions include 'Stella de Oro' and 'Happy Returns' daylilies, goldenrods (*Solidago* spp.), golden variegated hakone grass (*Hakonechloa macra* 'Aureola'), 'Gold Standard' hosta, ligularias (*Ligularia* spp.), and yellow and gold Siberian irises.

With blue-green evergreens such as pines and some junipers, use blue, silver, pink, or white flowers and dark green or burgundy foliage. You might consider underplanting coral bells (*Heuchera* spp.), cranesbills (*Geranium* spp.), hostas with blue-toned leaves, white Japanese anemones (*Anemone* × *hybrida*), or lamb's ears (*Stachys byzantina*).

Broad-leaved evergreens such as rhododendrons usually blend well with many foliage and blossom colors, as long as their own bloom colors are compatible. Try them with astilbes, cinammon fern (*Osmunda cinnamomea*), coral bells (*Heuchera* spp.), cranesbills (*Geranium* spp.), and hellebores (*Helleborus* spp.).

Try mixing perennials and shrubs with contrasting shapes. For example, with vase-shaped shrubs, use sprawling and spreading perennials with horizontal lines. With tall, upright shrubs, use free-flowing, billowing masses. With mounded shrubs, try some spiky perennials for interest and contrast.

Adding Star Quality

When your landscape needs some drama, try adding *specimen* plants—plants that make a strong statement. These star-quality plants stand out whether in a border or placed alone. They're often an easy solution when you lack the budget or time for a large landscape project.

Big, bold plants. Plants said to "have architectural interest" are prime candidates for specimen planting. They are usually big, bold plants that have strong geometric features, such as vertical lines.

Try bear's-breech (*Acanthus* spp.), with its multicolored flower spikes and prickly bracts. It works well either alone or with low-growing plants such as lamb's-ears (*Stachys byzantina*). For a moist, shady spot, use rocket ligularia (*Ligularia stenocephala* 'The Rocket'), which has huge, attractive leaves and bright yellow flower spikes.

Montbretia (*Crocosmia* spp.) offers high drama with 3-foot straplike leaves that "patter" in a breeze. The brilliant orange-red

Add spice to bland views by planting dramatic perennials like yuccas (*Yucca* spp.), which make a powerful statement both in and out of bloom.

blooms of the hybrid 'Lucifer' would be stunning in clumps surrounded by lady's-mantle (*Alchemilla mollis*) or contrasting with the blue flowerstalks of speedwell (*Veronica* 'Sunny Border Blue').

Giant plants. In the truly giant category, gunnera (*Gunnera manicata*) stands alone, with 6-

foot-wide leaves on 7-foot stalks. Ornamental rhubarb (*Rheum palmatum*) is somewhat less imposing but still quite massive. In moist soils, plant rodgersias (*Rodgersia* spp.) for their impressively large leaves.

Some perennials that make spectacular specimens are potential bullies that are best planted alone, and with some caution. Plume poppy (*Macleaya cordata*), for example, can overrun the neighborhood, and its height (over 10 feet) is out of scale for most gardeners' perennial borders or beds. Yet as its own island, it offers a powerful focal point, a long season of interest, and can block anything you care to hide!

Grasses. Many large ornamental grasses, such as feather reed grass (*Calamagrostis acutiflora* 'Stricta'), maiden grass (*Miscanthus* spp.), or pampas grass (*Cortaderia* spp.), can handle solo performances in any setting that needs a "star." For maximum effectiveness, place the grasses so the sun will set behind them. The backlighting, whether for photography or viewing, is stunning, especially when a breeze makes the grass foliage dip and sway.

Trees and shrubs flanked by perennials block the view of a fence and the glaring white siding of the house next door, and create cool seclusion around a patio.

Screening the Uglies

Sometimes a single plant or shrub isn't enough to block out the view you want to hide. For example, if you live on a very busy street, you may be tired of the hubbub of cars and trucks passing. The solution is to create a screen. A solid fence makes a successful screen, of course. But a grouping of tall plants or plants with dense foliage can also shield you from unpleasant sights and sounds. And of course, blocking ugly views isn't the only use for screens. They also provide privacy, blocking the outside world from having a view *into* your yard.

Creating a Mixed Border Screen

A mixed planting of shrubs, trees, and perennials makes a screen that's effective in all four seasons. Shrubs and trees can form the background with a perennial border in front. Or, you can mix tall perennials in with shrubs and trees, or combine small shrubs with perennials.

Use visualizing tricks like those described on page 179 to determine how high, wide, and long your screen needs to be. Always make your screen taller than the object you're trying to hide. For example, if you're trying to screen a gas meter that's 2 feet off the ground, make your screen 3 feet high.

Plan the "bones" of your screen first. Position evergreens at the most critical points in your screen for year-round coverage. Smaller evergreens in the front layer will provide structure when ornamental grasses or tall perennials are cut back.

Start your screen project by

When creating a private nook, plan screens that are high enough to block views where needed but allow good air flow so you won't feel stifled in hot weather.

planting the trees and shrubs. Be sure to account for mature size when placing them. The planting probably will be sparse initially. Fill in the spaces with annuals, such as cosmos or tall zinnias. Or interplant perennials, which you can transplant later when the shrubs fill out.

Don't skimp on the width of the border. For privacy, you need to arrange layers of plants, and for pleasure, you want a steady supply of flowers in bloom. See

"Living Screens" on the opposite page for suggested plants. Place bushy plants in front of tall, leggy plants to screen them at the base.

Versatile Planting Mounds

Another screening option is to create a planting mound on a flat site. A planting mound is a mound of soil, 3 to 4 feet high at most, and wide enough to grade up and taper out gradually. To be successful, it must look natural; in

fact, once plants get established on it, it should look like Nature created it for you.

The first order of business when creating a planting mound is to decide its dimensions— length, width, and height. You don't want to create Mount Fujiyama in your garden, just a gently graded hillock. Plants will add height and screening. If you plan to include perennials over 3 feet tall, keep the mound itself less than 2 feet high. Mounds need not run in a straight line; they can curve to enclose an area.

If you're making a shallow mound, prepare the site by stripping off the sod. Then till or dig to loosen the exposed soil, as plant roots will probably reach down into it.

The mound can be a mixture of topsoil, peat moss, compost, well-rotted manure, and any other organic material available. One good mix is 6 parts topsoil, 1 part compost, and 1 part well-rotted manure. Incorporating small pine bark chips into the mix will aid drainage. Adjust the mix to suit the plants. Heavy feeders like roses and delphiniums like a richer soil, while some perennials, like lavender, do better in leaner soil.

For any sizable mound, you'll probably have to buy a load of topsoil. Use a wheelbarrow to deposit the soil on the site. When you've reached the point of putting on the top 12- to 18-inch layer, begin dumping wheelbarrows of organic matter on as well—two barrows of organic matter for every six of topsoil. Mix the organic matter and soil together with a garden rake. Try to keep from compacting the soil as you're mounding it. Don't drive any heavy equipment over it. Contour your mound with a rake until the shape pleases you.

Make the mound higher

than you ultimately want it to be. Over time, the soil in the mound will settle by as much as one-third to one-half. This is especially true if the soil mix is high in organic matter.

It's best to wait for a soaking rain to drench the mound and

help it settle before planting. The alternative is to soak it slowly and well with a hose or sprinkler. Do not step on the mound or plant it when the soil is freshly soaked—let it sit a few days first. The mound will continue to settle over time.

Living Screens

Perennials for screening should be tall or bushy, or have big, bold foliage. The good news is there are dozens of lovely perennials with those qualities, including bee balm, black-eyed Susans, delphiniums, foxgloves, hostas, and peonies. Here's a list of additional perennials and ornamental grasses that are excellent for screens.

Carolina lupine (*Thermopsis caroliniana*); 3'–5' tall; lemon yellow flowers in late spring. Zones 3–9.

Crocosmia (*Crocosmia* hybrids); 2'–3' tall; orange or red flowers in summer. Zones 5–9.

Fountain grass (*Pennisetum alopecuroides*); 2'–3' tall; bright green summer foliage fades to straw color in winter. Zones 6–9.

Globe thistle (*Echinops ritro*); 3'–4' tall; steel blue flowers in summer. Zones 3–8.

Hairy golden aster (*Chrysopsis villosa* 'Golden Sunshine'); 4'–5' tall; bright yellow flowers late summer–fall. Zones 4–9.

Hollyhock (*Alcea rosea*); 2'–8' tall; cupped yellow, white, pink, or red flowers in summer. Zones 2–9.

Japanese silver grass (*Miscanthus sinensis*); 4'–8' tall; silvery flower plumes late summer–fall. Zones 5–9.

Ravenna grass (*Erianthus ravennae*); 8'–10' tall in flower; gray-green foliage turns many shades in fall. Zones 6–10.

Sunflower heliopsis (*Heliopsis helianthoides*); 3'–6' tall; bright yellow flowers in summer. Zones 3–9.

Willow blue star (*Amsonia tabernaemontana*); 3' tall; pale blue flowers in early summer. Zones 3–9.

A Perennial Screen

Lynne Schwartz-Barker designed this garden to cover a planting mound, as described on page 76. Shown here in summer, this garden works well to create privacy or block unwanted views. The garden mixes perennials, evergreens, flowering shrubs, and annuals. Low-growing rose verbena and threadleaf coreopsis tie the taller perennials and shrubs together visually.

Most of the plants in this garden will grow well in Zones 4–9. The New England aster does not tolerate summers well in Zone 9, and the orange-eye butterfly bush and black-flowering pennisetum may not survive winters north of Zone 5.

Black-flowering pennisetum (*Pennisetum alopecuroides* 'Moudry'). 3' tall; black-purple flowers in fall. Cut to ground in early spring; self-seeds readily.

Siberian iris (*Iris sibirica* 'Cleve Dodge'). 30" tall; flowers late spring–early summer.

Rose verbena (*Verbena* 'Homestead Purple'). 8" tall; flowers spring–summer. Spreads rapidly.

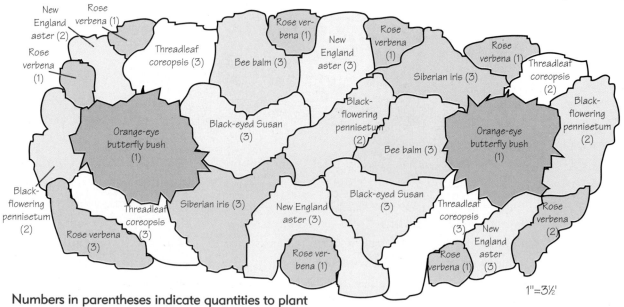

Numbers in parentheses indicate quantities to plant

1"=3½'

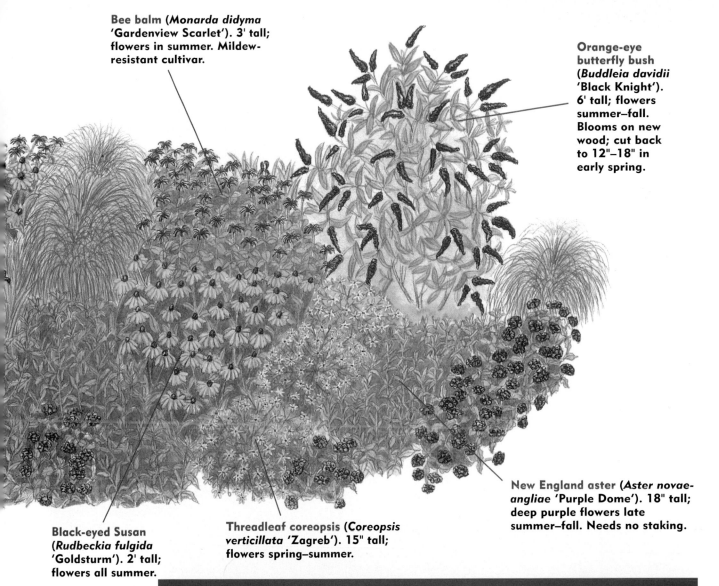

Bee balm (*Monarda didyma* 'Gardenview Scarlet'). 3' tall; flowers in summer. Mildew-resistant cultivar.

Orange-eye butterfly bush (*Buddleia davidii* 'Black Knight'). 6' tall; flowers summer–fall. Blooms on new wood; cut back to 12"–18" in early spring.

New England aster (*Aster novae-angliae* 'Purple Dome'). 18" tall; deep purple flowers late summer–fall. Needs no staking.

Black-eyed Susan (*Rudbeckia fulgida* 'Goldsturm'). 2' tall; flowers all summer.

Threadleaf coreopsis (*Coreopsis verticillata* 'Zagreb'). 15" tall; flowers spring–summer.

Fences and Hedges

Take advantage of existing fences to screen views and create private areas. Perennial vines, such as honeysuckle, wisteria, and clematis, dress up a chain-link fence and turn it into an effective screen. Try tying perennial vines or climbing roses to split-rail fences or planting an informal perennial garden whose flowers can spill through the rails.

Hedges fronted by a perennial border also make effective screens. If you choose a formal hedge of yews (*Taxus* spp.) or Lawson cypress (*Chamaecyparis lawsoniana*), you may want to plant a symmetrical border using perennials like delphinium, phlox, and iris. Or you can contrast an informal border against the hedge, placing plants more randomly and using cottage-style perennials like Shasta daisies (*Chrysanthemum* × *superbum*) and daylilies.

Solutions for Slopes

A sloping garden or lawn can be lovely to look at but murder to maintain. In hilly neighborhoods, it's not uncommon to see people hauling their lawnmowers up and down the hill on a rope, which is definitely not a recommended practice! (When is a slope too steep to mow? Well, if the slope is uncomfortable to stand on, it is too steep to safely run a lawnmower across.)

What else can you do with a slope? If you have only a small area of flat gardening space and a lot of hillside, you may want to convert the slope into flat gardening space by building terraces into it. Terracing involves creating a series of stepped flat spaces using retaining walls to hold the soil in place. You can make the walls of wood, stone, or brick. (See Chapter 9 for step-by-step instructions for making terraces).

Groundcovers

If terracing is a daunting prospect, leave the slope intact and plant it with perennial groundcovers. Groundcovers are plants that will effectively cover

Above: Don't let groundcovers be monotonous. Try combinations like heartleaved bergenia (*Bergenia cordifolia*), stinking hellebore (*Helleborus foetidus*), and alpine epimedium (*Epimedium alpinum* 'Rubrum').

Left: For quick coverage on a shady slope, combine common bugleweed (*Ajuga reptans*) with white-flowered sweet woodruff (*Galium odoratum*).

your soil and need little care; they are not necessarily ground-hugging plants, though many familiar groundcovers are under 1 foot tall. For example, you can even use a spreading shrub like butterfly bush (*Buddleia davidii*) as a groundcover on a large, sloping bank.

When choosing plants to cover slopes, be sure to pick groundcovers that are fast spreaders. You can choose a single groundcover or create a tapestry of several groundcovers.

Spacing. Space plants closely to get quick coverage. If the groundcover you choose can be planted from 6 to 12 inches apart, set plants 6 inches apart so that 100 plants will cover 25 square feet. Spaced 12 inches apart, 100 plants will cover 100 square feet, but you'll have to do a lot more weeding while your plants are growing together. (You can buy 100 plants of a common groundcover like periwinkle for about $50.)

Before you plant, clear *all* the vegetation from the site. It's a good idea to mulch the area with black plastic or thick layers of newspaper for a season to kill all the weeds.

Planting a slope. Add some organic matter to your soil before planting or as you plant. Start planting at the top and work your way down. Set plants in rows, off-setting each row of plants from the one above. Mulch well after planting to help suppress weeds. Keep your planting watered well the first year to establish roots and encourage new growth.

Don't cut back groundcovers along a retaining wall. Let them drape naturally to soften the strong edges of the wall.

Weeding. The first year's weeding is critical. Weeds will be strong competitors for water, food, and space. Be sure that weeds don't set seed in your planting, or you'll have a mainte-nance nightmare the second year weeding all the seedlings out. At a minimum, weed a new planting of groundcovers once every three weeks in spring, and then once a month in summer and fall.

If you do a good job the first year, by the second year your plants will have spread, leaving less open area for weeds to grow in. By the third year, you should have very little hand weeding. If you're careful, you can use a string trimmer and cut down any weeds that are growing up above your groundcover. This will prevent them from going to seed and give your groundcover a uniform look. Any weeds that are still noticeable after being trimmed can be pulled by hand.

Because ground-covers do require in-tensive maintenance the first year, you may wish to phase in your planting. It's better to start small and be suc-cessful than plant a large area that you don't have time to maintain.

If you've chosen a fast-growing groundcover, by the third year you may be able to di-vide it and use the divisions to expand your planting. Some groundcovers will also throw seed and start new plants for you.

A Sloping Groundcover Tapestry

Groundcovers, hostas, ferns, and shrubs create a multilevel tapestry in this sloping garden designed by Lynne Schwartz-Barker. She mixes different types of plants to create something more interesting than the typical bank of pachysandra. These plants need little attention and will cover the ground adequately to shade out weeds. When mixing groundcovers together, be sure to avoid ones that will overrun their neighbors, like those named in "Greedy Groundcovers" on the opposite page.

All the plants in this garden, shown here in spring, will grow well in shade in Zones 4–8, except for summersweet, which is hardy only to Zone 5.

Fortune's hosta (*Hosta fortunei* 'Albo-marginata'). 18" tall; large, dark green, white-edged leaves; lavender flowers in summer.

Spotted lamium (*Lamium maculatum* 'Beacon Silver'). 8" tall; flowers in spring; leaves semi-evergreen.

Common periwinkle (*Vinca minor*). 6" tall; flowers in spring; glossy leaves are evergreen. Spreads to form mats.

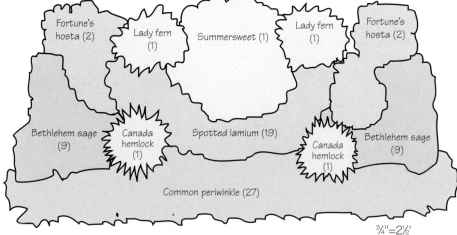

Fortune's hosta (2)

Lady fern (1)

Summersweet (1)

Lady fern (1)

Fortune's hosta (2)

Bethlehem sage (9)

Canada hemlock (1)

Spotted lamium (19)

Canada hemlock (1)

Bethlehem sage (9)

Common periwinkle (27)

¾"=2½'

Numbers in parentheses indicate quantities to plant

Summersweet (*Clethra alnifolia*). 5' shrub; fragrant white flowers mid–late summer; black seedpods follow. Thrives in wet areas.

Lady fern (*Athyrium filix-femina*). 3' tall; foliage all season.

Bethlehem sage (*Pulmonaria saccharata* 'Mrs. Moon'). 12" tall; flowers in spring; blossoms are pink, later turning blue.

Canada hemlock (*Tsuga canadensis* 'Gentsch White'). Upright mounded shrub reaches 4' wide and 2' tall; new growth is silver-white.

Greedy Groundcovers

Some groundcovers are meant to be planted alone. When planted with other groundcovers, they swamp the competition. When looking through catalogs, notice the descriptions of these plants: "extremely vigorous;" "rapid spreader;" "perfect for that problem area." This usually indicates you're looking at a greedy groundcover that won't share space.

What groundcovers should be planted alone? Bishop's weed (*Aegopodium* spp.), crown vetch (*Coronilla varia*), English ivy, gooseneck loosestrife (*Lysimachia clethroides*), houttuynia (*Houttuynia cordata*), Japanese honeysuckle (*Lonicera japonica* 'Halliana'), and ribbon grass (*Phalaris arundinacea*) can all spell trouble for their neighbors. Ivy and honeysuckle will smother other plants. The rest will just crowd them out.

Greedy groundcovers do have their place in your yard. They may be perfect for areas where nothing else will grow. Just be sure that the area you're planting is hemmed in by barriers, like sidewalks, so the groundcovers will stay where you want them and not take more garden space than you're willing to give.

Solving Mowing Woes

Gardening is a pleasure, but some repetitive garden maintenance chores can seem like punishment. One task that can eat up time, energy, and money is taking care of the lawn. The idealized perfect green lawn doesn't just happen, it's a high-maintenance item. While most of us value some lawn for play area and as a rich green space to set off our flowering plants, many of us have far too much of it. If you're spending more time than you'd like on your lawn, consider these alternatives.

Boost your borders. One of the prettiest ways to pare down your lawn is to expand your existing perennial borders. If you have a rectangular yard with a border along the edge, try enlarging the border by creating an addition with a curved edge. Flowing edges are pleasing to look at and also easy to mow around. An agreeable proportion of lawn-to-border area is two-thirds lawn to one-third border. Enlarging your border will give you the opportunity to try new plants and to lift and divide the plants you already have.

Allow a margin of soil or mulch between your lawn and your perennials so that you don't accidentally chop into your plantings when you mow. Edging strips also help prevent mowing accidents. See page 229 for instructions on installing an edging strip.

A groundcover tapestry. Mixed groundcovers are another low-maintenance choice for covering a large area. Groundcovers are either clump formers, like blue lilyturf (*Liriope muscari*), or runners, like common bugleweed (*Ajuga reptans*). Runners can sometimes invade and overwhelm clump formers. If you'd rather not worry about having to cut the runners out of the clump formers, then pair two clump formers, like lilyturf and lamb's-ears (*Stachys byzantina*), also a good companion.

When planning a border between fence and lawn, make it wide. A wide border offers an opportunity to use tall, showy perennials and reduce the amount of lawn you have to mow.

Great Perennial Groundcovers

Common and Botanical Name	Hardiness and Exposure	Bloom Time and Color	Description
Common thrift *Armeria maritima*	Zones 3–8 Sun	Spring Pink	Rounded flowerheads and mounds of grasslike foliage, 10"–14" tall. Useful for covering small areas; prefers cool temperatures and low humidity.
Canada wild ginger *Asarum canadense*	Zones 3–8 Partial–full shade	Late spring Reddish brown	6"–12" tall satiny heart-shaped leaves hide jug-shaped flowers. Spreads by self-seeding and by creeping.
Lily-of-the-valley *Convallaria majalis*	Zones 2–8 Sun–shade	Spring Pink or white	Bell-shaped flowers followed by red berries on 8"–10" stems. Spreads rapidly in moist or dry soil.
Blue fescue *Festuca cinerea*	Zones 4–9 Sun	Early summer Tan	Clump-forming grass with green-blue foliage, 8"–10" tall. Never needs mowing; lift and divide every few years to increase plants.
Sweet woodruff *Galium odoratum*	Zones 4–8 Sun to shade	Spring White	Plants slowly form large, 8"-tall clumps. Good for small, partially shaded areas. Prefers moist soil.
Sun rose *Helianthemum nummularium*	Zones 5–10 Sun	Late spring–early summer Orange, pink, white, or yellow	Creeping plants are 8"–12" tall and 2'–3' wide. Requires well-drained, neutral to alkaline soil.
St.-John's-wort *Hypericum calycinum*	Zones 5–9 Sun–partial shade	Summer Yellow	Large flowers with showy stamens on 18" plant. Evergreen in warmer climates; good for slopes; cut back in early spring to induce new growth.
Golden creeping Jenny *Lysimachia nummularia 'Aurea'*	Zones 3–8 Sun–light shade	Summer Yellow	2"–4" tall chartreuse spring leaves darken to lime green in summer. Spreads by creeping stems; can be invasive. Dry soil will slow its spread.
Prickly pear *Opuntia humifusa*	Zones 4–9 Sun	Spring Yellow	4"–6" tall cactus with 3"–4" flowers and evergreen flat, spiny leaves. Forms wide clumps; likes sandy soil.
Thymes *Thymus* spp.	Zones 4–10 Sun	Spring Pink or white	Aromatic foliage, 3"–10" tall. Evergreen foliage spreads slowly with good drainage; good between stepping-stones and to drape walls.
Common periwinkle *Vinca minor*	Zones 4–9 Sun–shade	Early spring Blue or white	Glossy evergreen foliage, 6"–8" tall. Spreads by runner; good for slopes. Tolerates dry shade.

You can create a ground-cover tapestry with a theme of contrasting foliage and flowers, or pick several groundcovers with similar features. A handsome combination is a silver-leaved cultivar of spotted lamium (*Lamium maculatum* 'Beacon Silver') with Bethlehem sage (*Pulmonaria saccharata* 'Mrs.

Moon'). They both enjoy partial shade and can tolerate dry soils once established. They make a nice tapestry under a spring-flowering tree, such as a crabapple. For details on planting groundcovers, see "Ground-covers" on page 80.

Make a mini-meadow. If you have a large area of lawn

you'd like to reduce, you'll be creating a planting on a larger scale than a border: You'll be creating a mini-meadow.

Mini-meadows can be low-maintenance plantings if you thoroughly clear the site of weeds and grass before you plant. For instructions on preparing and planting a meadow, see page 38.

Plants for High-Traffic Spots

Plants That Take Abuse
These plants bounce back when you bump them. They also smell nice when you brush into them. Try them next to the sidewalk.

Artemisias (*Artemisia* spp.). 1'–6' tall; silvery-white, aromatic foliage. Zones 3–9.

Catmint (*Nepeta* × *faassenii*). 18"–24" tall; blue-violet flowers spring–early summer. Zones 3–8.

Common yarrow (*Achillea millefolium* 'Cerise Queen'). 18" tall; cherry-red flowers in summer. Zones 3–9.

Salt-Tolerant Plants
These plants will tolerate road salt and can be planted along driveways and roads.

Artemisia (*Artemesia absinthium*). 2'–3' tall; silver-gray, aromatic foliage. Zones 3–9.

Common rose mallow (*Hibiscus moscheutos*). 4'–8' tall; huge white, pink, or red flowers all summer. Zones 5–10.

Common thrift (*Armeria maritima*). 10"–14" tall; pink or white flowers late spring–summer. Zones 4–8.

Daylilies (*Hemerocallis* spp. and hybrids). 1'–6' tall; lilylike yellow, orange, pink, red, or maroon flowers in summer. Zones 2–9.

Lavender cotton (*Santolina* spp.). 1'–2' tall; yellow flowers in summer; green or silver-gray foliage. Zones 6–8.

Sea lavender (*Limonium latifolium*). 2'–2½' tall; clouds of tiny pink flowers in summer. Zones 3–9.

White-striped ribbon grass (*Phalaris arundinacea* var. *picta*). 2'–3' tall; showy white flowers appear in early summer; foliage tinged pink in spring; foliage turns beige in fall and remains attractive in winter. Zones 4–9.

Crushproof Plants
Try these between flagstones or next to pathways.

Ajuga (*Ajuga reptans*). 4"–8" tall; blue, pink, or white flowers and showy green and/or bronze leaves. Zones 3–9.

Chamomile (*Chamaemelum nobile*). 9" tall; small daisylike flowers spring–summer. Zones 3–8.

'Gold Edge' thyme (*Thymus* 'Gold Edge'). Bushy 6"–8" plants; rosy flowers, green leaves with gold margins. Zones 4–10.

Lilyturf (*Liriope* spp.). Graceful arching clumps of narrow 12"–18" long leaves; 4"–6" spikes of blue flowers in spring. Zones 5–9.

Sedums (*Sedum album, S. kamtschaticum, S. spurium* 'Dragon's Blood', 'Ruby Mantle', or 'Tricolor') 2"–6" creeping plants with silvery, yellow, or pinkish foliage; small starry pink, white, or yellow flowers spring–summer. Zones 3–9.

Sweet woodruff (*Galium odoratum*). 4"–10" tall; starry white flowers in spring. Zones 4–8.

Thymes (*Thymus herba-barona, T. serpyllum*). Creeping plants 2"–5" tall; tiny pink, lavender, or white flowers. Zones 4–7.

Violets (*Viola* spp.). 1"–12" tall; white, yellow, pink, purple, or blue flowers in spring. Zones 3–9.

Managing High-Traffic Areas

In most cases, traffic patterns will influence your landscaping choices. If there are walkways, frame them with groundcovers or outline them with crushproof plants such as mother-of-thyme (*Thymus praecox*). If there are steps or low decks without railings, expect that people will step off the sides, and use either tough plants that take some abuse or large plants that deter traffic. You might also leave a wide margin around all entryways and use mulch that footsteps won't hurt.

Planting near driveways or roads presents problems, too, as cars sometimes drive into the plants. In winter there may be road salt (although environmentally aware gardeners do not endorse its use). Snow plows—even our own—often scrape up soil and plants along with the snowbank and dump mountains of compacted snow, ice, and gravel on the heads of unsuspecting perennials. In many of these cases, hardscape (fences, sidewalks, or gravel) may be a better solution than landscape plantings. But if you prefer to use plants, select wisely, with a realistic view of what traffic the plant and you can tolerate.

Points where pedestrians turn a corner often turn into a shortcut through the adjoining lawn or garden. Hostas and a post hung with a basket of annual geraniums signal visitors to stay on the path.

Plant pretty but tough perennial herbs like lavender and pennyroyal (*Mentha pulegium*) along pathways. They offer the bonus of wonderful fragrance when they're crushed by passing feet.

Renovating an Overgrown Garden

Sometimes a garden gets out of control. When it does, you may wonder whether to reclaim it or to start fresh. The answer is subjective. If weeds or aggressive perennials dominate 30 percent of the bed, you may want to dig it all up and go from scratch. You may also want to start over if trees have grown up to shade a once-sunny border, leaving you with the wrong plants for the location. Poor drainage or soil can be reasons to start over. Or—since gardeners grow at least as fast as gardens—maybe you know much more now than when the bed was planted, and you would *like* to design a border from scratch. If any of these are the case, you may want to turn to Chapters 7 and 8 to refresh yourself on garden design and making a planting plan.

If you can't afford the time or money for a total overhaul, or if you like most of what you have, try a partial renovation. This means you keep some plants in place, divide and move others, improve some of the soil, and bring in some new plant choices.

Starting Over

Redoing a garden takes some planning. After you dream awhile and envision the big picture, sit down and make two lists: "Keepers" and "To Go." Under Keepers, make subcategories: "Leave in place" and "Wrong place—Move." Under To Go, put subheads like "Give away" and "Compost." Be tough, and send unwanted plants to the compost heap. If plants are diseased, dig them out and burn them or dispose of them with the trash.

From your list of keepers, identify the outstanding performers and good combinations. You can frequently transform an ordinary garden into a splendid one by selecting these winners and then applying some basic design principles.

When we renovate, we usually have large plants to divide. Use the divisions in groups to make an impressive show.

Garden Troubles and Solutions

Does your perennial bed exhibit these symptoms? It may be time for corrective action—or a good renovation plan!

Problem	Solution
Rampant spreaders taking over	Limit their turf by using underground barriers or containers, or place them with equal aggressors!
Too many weeds	Dig them out, rake their seedlings, and mulch, mulch, mulch!
Tall plants need staking	Choose sheltered spots, seek dwarf cultivars; place brush, stakes, or other supports out early.
High-maintenance plants	Place plants like roses in highly visible locations—you will tend them better. Also, consider less troublesome choices.
Disease-prone plants	Replace with disease-resistant cultivars; clean up debris diligently; try preventive organic sprays such as baking soda spray.
Hardiness error	Try to find a warm, sheltered microclimate on your site, or give up on the plant, and replant with something known for success in your area.
Bad drainage	Dig ditches, sink drainage tiles, build raised beds; use bog plants in known wet spots.
Not enough light	Move sun-loving plants to sunny sites if possible. Select shade lovers for the shady sites.
Not enough water	Plan in spring for the drought of August; prepare drip irrigation systems; mulch; choose drought-tolerant plants.

Ripping out a major landscape feature like a large dogwood hedge (*left*) is a drastic step, but it allows you to restyle your yard in dramatic fashion. After a few years, the gardener's new perennial landscape is thriving (*below*).

To make your garden even more effective, repeat groupings of plants in three places around your garden. Repetition of plants, colors, and textures ties a border or landscape together. Repetition suggests harmony and shows that the gardener had a plan.

Partial Renovation

Tackle partial renovations in spring or fall. In spring the soil must be workable, and plants should have emerged enough to identify. In fall, time the work so you finish at least a month before your projected first frost date.

Preparation involves soil building and weed removal. Protect short or fragile plants you're leaving in place by circling them with chicken wire or putting a bushel basket over them. Improve the soil in one small area at a time.

Sometimes you will find

perennial weeds such as quackgrass tangling around the "keeper" plants. If so, dig up the plants and wash all the soil off the roots. Remove all weed tops and roots and dispose of them. Replant the keeper plants in containers or a holding bed. Let them grow for a few weeks to be

sure no weeds appear, and then return them to the garden.

Finally, after you have moved your choices into position, mark, map, and record your achievement. Future owners of your gardens may thank you, and you will certainly thank yourself next spring.

Transform Weedy Corners

Sometimes even the best gardeners practice avoidance. Certain areas are just too easy to neglect or too difficult to face. Candidates for neglect are the areas near the mailbox and the garbage cans, or the abandoned spot where the sandbox used to be. The back corner of a suburban lot is also a prime suspect on the neglected list. Yet landscaping those neglected spots can be your chance to make an immediate impact with limited ef-fort. For a beginner, such places offer the opportunity to practice with some tried-and-true low-maintenance plants for quick success. For advanced gardeners, it's a chance to experiment with unusual choices and landscape techniques that might not fit in the traditional borders or foundation plantings. After all, you can only make it better!

The least-successful land-scaping in many yards occurs around garages, driveways, and steps. Swimming pools and sheds also tend to defeat landscape de-sign efforts. Perhaps the functional nature of these hardscape elements discourages us, or per-haps we just need a new outlook to see these non–garden areas as potential garden sites! Yet any of these can be improved with cre-ativity—and some fine perennials.

Before you plant, ask yourself why the spot has been neglected. Does the site have problems with high winds, road salt, or heavy traffic? What are the built-in per-manent features you are working with or around? What are the limitations of the site—the light, moisture, drainage, and soil? Take these factors into account when you make plant choices.

Design in a Small Space

Design basics are probably more important in a small area than in a large one because everything is more noticeable when the scale is small. The fol-lowing rules of thumb may help with your choices as you plan to rescue that abandoned corner.

Think odd. For a natural look in small spaces, plant odd numbers of plants rather than even-numbered groupings. Clusters of three or five plants will look less formal or geometrical than a group of two or four plants might. For example, plant 3 dwarf goat's beards (*Aruncus aethusifolius*), or 5 hostas, or 11 tulips.

Limit your plant choices. Several of one kind of plant

Creating a long season of interest can be challenging in a small garden. Daffodils began the color show, now taken over by tulips and Persian nepeta (*Nepeta mussinii* 'Blue Wonder'). Emerging Asiatic lilies will bloom in summer.

makes a better impression than many kinds. For example, try a bold planting of several ligularias (*Ligularia* spp.) or astilbes in a shady area.

Limit your colors. One or two definite colors is more impressive than a multicolored mix. Unless your intention is a confetti-like riot of color, limit your bloom colors and mass the plants to make a strong statement.

Frame the garden. Determine the frame or backdrop for your planting. Walls, trellises, fences, shrubs, or even buildings can provide structure and unity to your mini-garden.

Plan a focal point. A mini-garden will benefit from a center or focus. It can be a plant, birdbath, sundial, or piece of garden sculpture.

Above: Have fun with the small corners and odd spaces in your yard. Wooden ducks add a touch of whimsy while filling the triangular "hole" at the intersection of lawn, path, and water garden.

Left: Don't overdo variegation in small settings. A blue-leaved hosta and blue spruce offer a calming backdrop for golden variegated hakone grass (*Hakonechloa macra* 'Aureola') and the subtle white edging on the variegated hosta.

91

Chapter 3

Perennials for Special Regions

Climate and Hardiness • The Midwest • The Mountain West •

The Far North • The South • The Desert Southwest •

The Pacific Northwest

Climate and Hardiness

> Oh, what a blamed
> uncertain thing
> This pesky weather is;
> It blew and snew and
> then it thew, and now,
> by jing, it's friz.
>
> —Philander Chase
> Johnson

Most people think of "climate" in terms of temperature—hot or cold. But to a perennial gardener, temperature is to climate what carrots are to vegetable stew—an important ingredient, but only one of many. It's the entire soup of your region's weather—rain, snow, heat, drought, humidity, frost, wind—that determines which perennials you can and cannot grow.

If you live where snow blankets the ground all winter, for instance, you can raise perennials that might not survive warmer winters farther south. Why? Because snow acts as a protective blanket, keeping the soil frozen and insulating underground plant parts from frigid air.

It's important to take into account *all* the factors that make up your climate. What are the average first and last frost dates in your area? Is the air consistently humid or dry? Are there predictable periods of drought, heat, or heavy rain? You can learn about these factors from your local extension office, other gardeners, and local nursery owners.

Know your zone. To help gardeners choose plants suited to their regions, the USDA has established a Plant Hardiness Zone Map, shown on page 282. Zone 1 is the coldest, Zone 10 the warmest. If a plant is hardy in Zones 5–8, it should survive cold temperatures as far north as Zone 5 and heat as far south as Zone 8.

If you live in Zone 4, you'll need to choose a more cold-hardy variety. Gardeners in Zone 9 should seek a more heat-tolerant type.

Know your landscape. The climate conditions that exist *in your own yard* can vary from spot to spot. An open area on the east side of your house may be especially hot and dry. A wooded patch behind the garage might be shady with moist, still air. The west border of your property may get lots of sun, but may also be exposed to strong winds. All are good places for perennials, but vastly different types of perennials. Study your landscape, get to know its *microclimates*, or varying climatic conditions, and then choose plants that are appropriate for each site.

You can use microclimates to "stretch your zone" and grow perennials that "you just can't grow here." The tips that follow will help you take advantage of microclimates in various regions.

The Midwest

Hardiness Zones: 5–6

Growing Season: Typically May–October, or about 130–160 days

Advantages:
- Wide selection of well-adapted native perennials
- Rich soils in many areas

Challenges:
- Greatly differing conditions from year to year
- Dramatic daily or weekly temperature swings
- Cycles of heavy rain and drought
- Late spring frosts

Uncertainty is the only thing certain about Midwest weather. In order to cope, gardeners soon learn to hope for the best—and prepare for the worst.

Choose planting sites carefully. Careful plant selection and siting are especially important. Put each plant in its proper place, according to its tolerance for extremes of heat and cold, wet and drought. If your site is open and windy, use short, compact perennials such as cushion spurge (*Euphorbia epithymoides*) or snow-in-summer (*Cerastium tomentosum*), which is a low, mounded plant that forms a woolly blanket of dense white flower clusters. Place tender or semihardy perennials on the sides of buildings and fences that are protected from prevailing winds.

Ornamental grasses such as fountain grass (*Pennisetum alopecuroides* 'Hameln') and tough perennials like 'Autumn Joy' sedum can withstand the sometimes harsh conditions found in Midwest gardens.

Avoid planting precocious spring perennials on warm, south-facing sites, where they might emerge too soon only to be killed by a subsequent frost. For the same reason, leave the withered stems and tops on plants in fall to shade and cool the soil, then prune them back in spring, after all danger of frost has passed.

Bring Back the Prairie

Native prairie plants are well adapted to Midwestern soils and climates. Mix them with more traditional landscape perennials to add variety and interest, or create your own "mini-prairie." Start with a combination of native flowers and low-growing grasses, then add taller grasses two or three years later after the smaller plants have become well established. All of the prairie perennials listed here are hardy to at least Zone 5. Name is followed by bloom colors. For grasses, name is followed by height and bloom time.

Spring-Blooming Flowers

Birdfoot violet (*Viola pedata*); blue, purple, white, pink.

Pasque flower (*Pulsatilla patens*, also known as *Anemone patens*); white, pink, violet, blue.

Prairie buttercup (*Ranunculus rhomboideus*); yellow.

Prairie smoke (*Geum triflorum*); purple.

Shooting-star (*Dodecatheon meadia*); white, pink, lavender.

Summer-Blooming Flowers

Butterfly weed (*Asclepias tuberosa*); orange, yellow, red.

Gayfeathers (*Liatris* spp.); pink, purple, white.

Joe-Pye weeds (*Eupatorium purpureum, E. maculatum*); rose, purple.

Large-flowered beardtongue (*Penstemon grandiflorus*); lavender.

Missouri primrose (*Oenothera missouriensis*); yellow.

Prairie coneflowers (*Ratibida* spp.); yellow.

Prairie dock (*Silphium terebinthinaceum*); yellow.

Stiff coreopsis (*Coreopsis palmata*); yellow.

Virginia spiderwort (*Tradescantia virginiana*); blue, purple.

Wild petunia (*Ruellia humilis*); lavender, blue.

Fall-Blooming Flowers

Azure aster (*Aster azureus*); blue.

New England aster (*Aster novae-angliae*); purple.

Showy goldenrod (*Solidago speciosa*); yellow.

Smooth aster (*Aster laevis*); blue, purple.

Stiff goldenrod (*Solidago rigida*); yellow.

Grasses

Big bluestem (*Andropogon gerardii*); 4'–8'; fall.

Indian grass (*Sorghastrum nutans*); 4'–6'; fall.

Japanese silver grass (*Miscanthus sinensis* cultivars); 6'–8'; fall.

Little bluestem (*Schizachyrium scoparium*); 3'; fall.

Prairie dropseed (*Sporobolus heterolepis*); 18"; summer.

Side oats gramma-grass (*Bouteloua curtipendula*); 18"–32"; summer.

Switch grass (*Panicum virgatum*); 3'; fall.

Mulch well. Mulch plants with several inches of leaves in fall, after the ground has frozen, to moderate soil temperatures and minimize frost heaving. Remove the mulch, however, if an extended midwinter thaw creates soggy conditions. Extreme winter cold can burn evergreen groundcovers. Cover them with pine boughs to reduce the damage.

The Midwest's unpredictable cycles of rain and no rain can play havoc with plants. To make your soil less susceptible to drought conditions, work in compost and other organic matter around your plants once or twice a year. Baptisias (*Baptisia* spp.), coneflowers (*Rudbeckia* spp.), plumbago (*Ceratostigma plumbaginoides*), and 'Moonbeam' coreopsis (*Coreopsis verticillata* 'Moonbeam') are some tough perennials that can handle the fickle climate of the Midwest.

The Mountain West

Hardiness Zones: 3–5
Growing Season: Varies depending on elevation and latitude; typically 60–90 days

Advantages:
- Well-drained soils
- Strong, bright sunlight
- Low humidity

Challenges:
- Winter is dominant season (snow is possible ten months of the year in higher elevations)
- Unpredictable frosts
- Strong winds
- Hot, dry summers

The Mountain West is no place for tender plants accustomed to the comforts of an English cottage garden. Rugged conditions call for rugged plants, such as lupines (*Lupinus* spp.) and salvias (*Salvia* spp.). Perennials need irrigation to survive dry Rocky Mountain summers. For winter protection in areas without reliable snow cover, apply an 8- to 12-inch layer of evergreen boughs, hay, or straw after the ground has frozen.

Rock gardens. The conditions that make traditional perennial gardening a challenge in the Mountain West are ideal for rock gardening. The best site for a rock garden is a gentle slope that is sheltered from wind and gets full sun or dappled afternoon shade. Rock garden plants grow best in light, extremely well-drained soil. If a site has heavier or poorly drained soil, excavate the site and backfill it with rubble (small rocks, crushed brick, and similar materials) and gravel. Mixing the excavated soil with coarse sand, compost, and pea gravel also helps improve drainage. Position rocks of various sizes on the rubble, and use the excavated soil to "sculpt" the garden around the rocks.

Low-growing flowering perennials such as bellflowers (*Campanula* spp.) and candytuft (*Iberis sempervirens*) look beautiful in a rock garden. Succulents such as hens-and-chickens (*Sempervivum tectorum*) and lewisias (*Lewisia* spp.) add textural interest and fill small crevices and corners. Alpine pinks (*Dianthus alpinus*), penstemon (*Penstemon* spp.), and Rocky Mountain columbine (*Aquilegia caerulea*) can provide clusters of color.

For detailed information on planning and planting a classic rock garden, check for books on the topic in "Suggested Reading" on page 289.

Provide a fence or hedge to protect tall delphiniums and foxgloves (*Digitalis* spp.) from mountain winds. Low-growing pinks (*Dianthus* spp.) and yellow evening primroses (*Oenothera* spp.) also thrive in the Mountain West.

The Far North

Hardiness Zones: 3–4
Growing Season: Mid-May to September

Advantages:
- Consistent snow cover
- Adequate rainfall
- Cool summer nights

Challenges:
- Seven months of winter
- Unpredictable frosts
- Humid midsummer days

The harsh winds and frigid temperatures of the Far North are often harder on humans than on perennial plants. Most perennial plants, in fact, are better acclimated to frigid temperatures and a short growing season than to extended or intense heat. Woodland wildflowers such as columbines (*Aquilegia* spp.), for example, require cool temperatures and long periods of dormancy. Of course, there are some perennials that cannot survive the North's harsh winters, so Northern gardeners should be especially careful to check hardiness of plants before they buy.

Let it snow. The Northern winter supplies an insulating blanket of snow that lasts until spring and keeps perennial plants safely underground in cold storage. To take additional advantage of natural snow protection, place tender or shallow-rooted perennials in locations where snow naturally accumulates in drifts. When snow is light or blows away from beds, pile on several inches from driveways or sidewalks.

Use winter mulch. Winter mulch also prevents frost heaving. Apply the mulch *after* the ground has frozen, usually in late fall. A 6- to 10-inch layer of coarse material such as hay is best. Remove the mulch in early spring.

Other Far North tips. Well-drained soil is especially important to prevent diseases and to keep ice pockets from forming around roots. Work compost or other organic material into poorly drained beds.

Humid conditions in midsummer can lead to diseases such as powdery mildew. To prevent the problem, allow plenty of space between plants and, when necessary, prune surrounding trees or bushes to promote good air flow.

To prevent frost damage, select late cultivars of spring wildflowers and early types of fall-flowering perennials such as chrysanthemums.

Manage the microclimates in your landscape. Avoid putting spring-blooming perennials on sunny south-facing sites, where they can blossom prematurely only to be killed by a late frost. Keep tender perennials away from cold, windy sites on the north or northwest sides of buildings.

Purple coneflower (*Echinacea purpurea*), white flowering spurge (*Euphorbia corollata*), marsh mallow (*Hibiscus moscheutos* subsp. *palustris*), and bee balm (*Monarda didyma*) create a pink-themed summer garden that is hardy to Zone 4.

Perennials for Northern Gardens

Common and Botanical Name	Hardiness and Exposure	Bloom Time and Color	Description
Maidenhair fern *Adiantum pedatum*	Zones 3–8 Partial–full shade	Spring–fall Bright green foliage	Delicate lime green fronds with slender black stems. Among the loveliest of foliage plants. Purchase only nursery-propagated stock.
Columbines *Aquilegia* spp.	Zones 3–9 Sun–partial shade	Spring–summer Many colors and bicolors	Stunning five-petaled, five-sepaled blossom appears to be a flower within a flower. Some hybrids are short-lived. A favorite hummingbird flower.
Astilbes *Astilbe* spp.	Zones 3–9 Sun–shade	Late spring–summer White, pink, purple, or red	Stately plants produce plumes of feathery flower clusters. Moist soil required.
Hay-scented fern *Dennstaedtia punctilobula*	Zones 2–8 Partial–full shade	Spring–fall Light green foliage	Arching fronds form masses of feathery green. Spreads rapidly. Purchase only nursery-propagated stock.
Daisy fleabane *Erigeron speciosus*	Zones 2–9 Sun–light shade	Summer Purple, pink, blue, or white	Small asterlike flowers bloom all summer.
Cranesbills *Geranium* spp.	Zones 3–8 Sun–partial shade	Spring–summer Pink, purple, blue, white, or red	Mounding or sprawling plants yield profusion of 1" blossoms. Do not confuse with annual bedding "geraniums" (genus *Pelargonium*).
Siberian iris *Iris sibirica*	Zones 2–9 Sun–light shade	Summer Blue, purple, yellow, white, pink, or bicolors	Graceful, beardless 2"–3" flowers are borne above attractive clusters of swordlike foliage.
Virginia bluebells *Mertensia virginica*	Zones 3–9 Sun–full shade	Spring Pink turning pale blue	Delicate, nodding flowers bloom in early spring, then plant goes dormant for remainder of growing season.
Common beardtongue *Penstemon barbatus*	Zones 3–8 Sun–light shade	Spring–summer Pink or red	Produces 1' spikes of trumpet-shaped flowers. Prune spent flower stems to encourage new blooms.
Creeping polemonium *Polemonium reptans*	Zones 2–8 Sun–partial shade	Spring–summer Blue	Sprawling mounds of fernlike leaves serve as groundcover. An attractive plant under shrubs or trees.
Lungworts *Pulmonaria* spp.	Zones 2–8 Partial–full shade	Spring Blue, pink, red, or white	Flowers emerge in early spring, are followed by lush, bushy foliage (some species spotted with silver).
False lupines *Thermopsis* spp.	Zones 3–9 Sun–partial shade	Spring Yellow	Flower spikes rise among tall, gray-green pealike leaves. An excellent back-of-the-border plant.

The South

Hardiness Zones: 7–9
Growing Season: Varies; mid-March to October in northern Zone 7; nearly year-round in lower Zone 8 and south
Advantages:
- Abundant rainfall
- Mild winters
- Long growing season

Challenges:
- Extreme summer heat and humidity
- Extended periods of heavy rain or drought
- Heavy clay soils

Summertime, and the livin' *isn't* always easy for perennials (and perennial growers) in the South. Long, hot, humid days foster a multitude of plant pests and diseases and make garden chores less than pleasant work.

On the other hand, the South's mild winters offer opportunities to grow a wide variety of perennials and to have almost year-round bloom.

Look for heat tolerance and disease resistance when choosing perennials for the southern garden. Choose planting sites that provide high afternoon shade, free air movement, and well-worked, well-drained soil.

High shade. The tall, open pine trees that grace much of the South provide ideal conditions for perennials. The trees' high branches partially shade plants from the scorching afternoon sun but allow morning sun to burn off the heavy dew that fosters diseases. Slatted fences and tall, open shrubbery may have similar virtues.

Free air flow. Ensuring free air movement also helps prevent disease problems. Avoid sites that are boxed in by buildings, fences, or dense plantings. Allow plenty of space between plants. Place tall cultivars well away from shorter types.

Well-drained soil. Good soil drainage counteracts the South's heavy rains and helps prevent winter frost heaving. To improve drainage and aeration, add plenty of organic matter, such as compost and shredded leaves, to planting beds. Where possible, double-dig or create raised beds. If the soil is very heavy clay, consider excavating the top 2 feet and replacing it with a mixture of equal parts of soil, sand, and organic matter.

Southern growers can successfully raise most of the perennials offered by Northern nurseries, but only if they make allowances for their actual growing conditions. Plants recommended for full sun in the North, for instance, may well need light or partial shade in the South. Likewise, plants described as "shade-tolerant" almost certainly require shade. Not all plants listed as hardy in Zones 8 and 9 will tolerate the heat and humidity of the Deep South. When in doubt, ask local growers and nurseries to recommend cultivars.

Cannas (*Canna* hybrids) tower over red *Crocosmia* hybrids, pink globe amaranth (*Gomphrena globosa*) blossoms, and purple perilla (*Perilla fructescens*) foliage in a Southern border.

Perennials for the Hot, Humid South

Common and Botanical Name	Hardiness and Exposure	Bloom Time and Color	Description
Spiny bear's-breech *Acanthus spinosus*	Zones 7–10 Sun–partial shade	Spring–summer Purple and white	Striking fernlike evergreen foliage.
Butterfly weed *Asclepias tuberosa*	Zones 3–9 Sun	Summer Yellow, orange, or red	Attracts butterflies throughout its bloom period. Tolerates poor, dry soil. Do not move established plants.
Hardy begonia *Begonia grandis*	Zones 6–10 Partial–full shade	Summer–fall Pink	Lovely pink flowers and large pointed green leaves. Plants spread freely in humus-rich soil. Avoid hot afternoon sun.
Boltonia *Boltonia asteroides*	Zones 3–9 Sun–light shade	Summer–fall White or pink	Bushy, 4'–6' plant produces a profusion of daisylike flowers starting in late summer.
Shasta daisy *Chrysanthemum X superbum*	Zones 4–8 Full sun–partial shade	Summer White and yellow	2"–4" blooms held on sturdy stalks above deep green foliage. Choose individual cultivars suited to your hardiness zone.
Milk-and-wine lily *Crinum latifolium* var. *zeylanicum*	Zones 8–10 Sun–light shade	Summer White and purple	Handsome Deep South lily sends up spectacular funnel-shaped flowers. Forms dense clumps of straplike leaves.
Montbretias *Crocosmia* spp.	Zones 5–9 Sun–partial shade	Summer–fall Orange, red, or yellow	Intensely colored members of the lily family. Spectacular funnel-shaped blossoms rise above fans of green, swordlike foliage. Plants grow from corms and spread to form clumps.
White gaura *Gaura lindheimeri*	Zones 5–9 Sun	Spring–summer White turning pink	Native to the Deep South. 4' plant produces long-lasting blooms along slender stems.
Common rose mallow *Hibiscus moscheutos*	Zones 5–10 Sun–light shade	Summer Pink, red, or white	Traditional cottage-garden perennial produces round flowers 6"–8" in diameter. Some hybrids have blossoms up to 10".
Red spider lily *Lycoris radiata*	Zones 7–10 Sun–partial shade	Summer–fall Red	Spectacular flowers with long, arching stamens borne on 18" stems. Leaves emerge in fall, die back in early summer.
Salvias *Salvia* spp.	Zones 3–10 Sun–light shade	Summer–fall Blue, purple, or pink	Bushy plants produce clusters of flower spikes; many varieties have aromatic foliage. Avoid rich or overly moist soils.
Verbenas *Verbena* spp.	Zones 3–10 Sun–light shade	Summer Red, pink, purple, or blue	Tough plants range from trailing groundcover types such as moss verbena (*V. tenuisecta*) to upright types such as rigid verbena (*V. rigida*).

The Desert Southwest

Hardiness Zones: 8–10
Growing season: Nearly
  year-round at lower elevations
Advantages:
  • Mild winters
  • Long growing season
  • Wide selection of attractive
    desert-adapted plants
Challenges:
  • Very little rainfall
  • Long periods of extreme
    summer heat
  • Alkaline soils
  • Hot, drying winds

Traditional perennials have a difficult and often brief life in the Desert Southwest: the arid low-country regions of Arizona, Nevada, New Mexico, and much of Texas. They require lavish care and irrigation and look out of tune with the desert landscape.

A better approach is to work with the desert environment. The Southwest has a native repertoire of perennials, trees, shrubs, and groundcovers naturally suited to an arid climate. Some imports from similar climates, such as southern Australia, also do well in the Southwest.

Irrigation is a must in the Southwest. Drip irrigation systems and bubbler systems that periodically flood planting beds are good choices. All systems should include a programmable timer to control how much and how often plants are watered.

Always consult local gardeners and your community's county extension office for specific plant and soil-amendment recommendations. Soil conditions vary greatly throughout the Southwest, and, as a result, so do the plants and gardening practices appropriate for a given area.

Waterwise Landscaping

Irrigating lawns and flowers accounts for more than half of all the water used in Desert Southwest communities. To save this resource (and money as well), apply the principles of *xeriscaping,* or waterwise landscaping.

Plan around water use. Group plants with similar water needs, creating zones of high, medium, and low use so you can custom-irrigate each zone.

Limit the lawn. According to xeriscape designers, just 600 square feet of lawn provides plenty of room for play and recreation. Keep your lawn small and site it near the house to create a cooling effect. An adjacent patio provides extra "elbow room." Consider replacing some turf with pebble mulch or low-water groundcovers.

Drought-tolerant plantings, such as green and gray mounds of lavender cottons (*Santolina* spp.) and lavender-flowered *Salvia clevelandii* 'Allen Chickering', often have a silver-gray theme that blends well with Southwestern architecture.

Houseplants elsewhere, red-flowering aloes (*Aloe* sp.) and silver jade plant (*Crassula arborescens*) can grow freely in outdoor gardens in warm desert areas.

Make your soil a sponge. Work organic matter into the top foot of soil before installing plants with moderate or high water needs. (Drought-tolerant plants generally prefer unimproved soil.)

Irrigate efficiently. Use a well-tuned irrigation system with separate control valves for lawn areas and for high-, moderate-, and low-water-use plants.

Colorful Desert Perennials

These perennials are suited to many of the low desert regions of the Southwest. Plant name is followed by bloom season and color.

- **California fuchsia** (*Zauschneria californica*); spring and fall; orange.
- **Cassias** (*Cassia* spp.); spring; yellow.
- **Desert marigold** (*Baileya multiradiata*); spring–fall; yellow.
- **Golden columbine** (*Aquilegia chrysantha*); spring–fall; yellow.
- **Melampodium** (*Melampodium leucanthum*); spring–fall; white.
- **Penstemons** (*Penstemon* spp.); spring; pink, red.
- **Rush milkweed** (*Asclepias subulata*); spring–fall; white.
- **Texas betony** (*Stachys coccinea*); spring and summer; pink.
- **Trailing lantana** (*Lantana montevidensis*); spring–fall; purple, pink.
- **Tufted evening primrose** (*Oenothera caespitosa*); spring–fall; white.
- **Verbenas** (*Verbena* spp.); spring–fall; purple, pink.

Mulch unplanted areas. Mulch cools the soil, discourages weed growth, and adds color and texture to the landscape. Organic mulches, such as bark chips, are best for planting beds and other small areas. Granite pebble mulch is best for borders and other large areas. Choose a neutral or desert tone; white and dark-colored stone can reflect or absorb too much heat.

Choose low-water-use plants. Plants naturally adapted to desert conditions require far less water and care. Most Southwest nurseries offer a variety of desert natives. Use them for most of your plantings. An occasional grouping of moderate or high-water-use plants adds a touch of green.

The Pacific Northwest

Hardiness Zones: 7–9
Growing Season: Mid-February to November
Advantages:
- Long spring and autumn seasons
- Well-drained soils
- Moderate average annual temperatures
- Low humidity

Challenges:
- Dry, hot summers
- Occasional freezes
- Rainy winter season

Just as the Midwest is unquestionably the "corn belt" of North America, the Pacific Northwest (the area extending from coastal northern California to southern British Columbia, west of the Cascades) deserves to be called the "perennial belt." Nearly all woodland and traditional cottage-garden perennials flourish in the region's mild winters and long, cool spring and fall seasons. Plants grow larger. Flower colors seem brighter and more vivid. Blossoms last longer. Commercial perennial production is one of the region's leading agricultural industries.

Summer heat. In most areas, however, summers—though brief—are very hot and dry. Temperatures can reach up to 100°F, and rainfall is scant. Irrigate flowerbeds regularly. When choosing plants, look for heat- and drought-resistant cultivars. Provide dappled or afternoon shade for sun-sensitive types.

Griffith's spurge (*Euphorbia griffithii*) thrives in the Pacific Northwest. Many euphorbias are evergreen in this region and and have a much showier spring bloom than they do in other parts of the United States.

Fall and winter. Good air circulation is important in flowerbeds to prevent mildew during the long, cool autumns and

Stars of the Pacific Northwest

Some perennials that are just ho-hum in other regions of the country really shine in the Pacific Northwest. Here are some star performers.

Alumroots (*Heuchera* spp.). Attractive evergreen foliage plants; many types send up slender stems filled with bell-shaped flowers. Zones 4–8.

Anemones (*Anemone* spp.). Most species blossom in spring; Japanese anemone (*A. X hybrida*) cultivars bear flowers in late summer and fall. Zones 3–9.

Bellflowers (*Campanula* spp.). Species range from low-growing rock garden types to tall, upright specimens; provide afternoon shade from summer sun. Zones 3–8.

Columbines (*Aquilegia* spp.). Live longer in the Northwest than in most parts of the country; foliage remains green and lush long after blooms fade. Zones 3–9.

Cranesbills (*Geranium* spp.). Exceptionally long-blooming in the Northwest. Zones 3–8.

Hardy cyclamen (*Cyclamen* spp.). Showy alpine plants grow from tubers; bear lovely nodding flowers above mottled, heart-shaped leaves; *C. hederifolium* blooms late summer and autumn, *C. repandum* in spring, *C. coum* during mild winters and in spring. Zones 6–9.

Hostas (*Hosta* spp.). Many excellent new cultivars developed in the Pacific Northwest; wide selection, including the sun-tolerant 'So Sweet'. Zones 3–8.

Lungworts (*Pulmonaria* spp.). Choose mildew-resistant cultivars. Zones 2–8.

wet winters. Avoid spacing plants too closely. Prune back overhanging boughs or other dense vegetation. Don't plant in areas surrounded by hedges or walls.

Winter rains can be heavy and persistent, so be sure your soil is well-drained. Add coarse organic matter to improve drainage. If the soil is very heavy, create raised beds for your perennials.

Winter temperatures occasionally dip into the low 20s, and every few years may reach 0°F. Without a protective covering of snow or ground sufficiently frozen to allow winter mulching, plants suffer. Site tender perennials away from frost pockets at the bases of slopes and in cold, still areas.

Northwest gardeners in Zone 9 can try growing tender perennials like hybrid *Fuschias* directly in garden beds. The plants may die if winter temperatures dip too low.

2

Classic Perennials and Perennial Combinations

by Nancy J. Ondra and Jean M. A. Nick

With hundreds of perennials to choose from, the most difficult decision you face may be how to get started. To help you make choices, we've selected 75 of the most reliable, easiest to grow perennials and put together a practical portrait for each. We've included our best ideas for using these perennials in your landscape, along with tips for propagation and best performance. For each perennial, you'll also find a photograph showing you a great combination with another perennial, annuals, grasses, and even shrubs.

Chapter 4

75 Classic Landscape Perennials

Plant Combinations • Landscape Uses • Growing Tips •

75 Perennials at a Glance

We've arranged this guide alphabetically by botanical name (which is how most mail-order firms prepare their catalogs). For each genus (plant group name), there's a summary of "vital statistics," including hardiness, size, shape, bloom color, bloom time, light requirements, and soil requirements.

Some plant groups have only one species, while others have many species with widely different habits. The hardiness zone, height, color, and bloom-time ranges given reflect the extremes for all commonly grown species in a genus. Each individual species may have a narrower range within the ones given.

If you'd like an overview of all 75 perennials, or if you're looking for flowers of a certain color or that bloom in a particular season, turn to "75 Classic Perennials at a Glance" on page 144. This summary chart will help you make choices efficiently as you develop plant lists for specific beds and borders.

Achillea
(uh-KILL-ee-uh)

Yarrow

Zones: 3–9
Height: 1 to 4 feet
Shape: Spreading clumps of stiff, upright flowerstalks
Color: White, pink, red, or yellow
Bloom time: Late spring, summer
Exposure: Sun to partial shade
Soil: Average to poor

• Plant yarrow along walkways, where you will be sure to brush it and re-

'Johnson's Blue' geranium is a perfect cool companion behind lemon yellow 'Moonshine' yarrow and the bright pink blossoms of red valerian (*Centranthus ruber*).

lease its aromatic fragrance.

• Combine yellow yarrows with the blue flowers of catmints (*Nepeta* spp.) and salvias (*Salvia* spp.).

• Dry yarrow flowerheads for winter arrangements. Cut blooms before the color starts to fade and hang bunches upside down in a dark, airy room.

• Dig and divide overgrown clumps in early spring or fall; discard the woody center.

Ajuga

(uh-JOO-guh)

Ajuga, Bugleweed

Zones: 3–9
Height: 4 to 12 inches
Shape: Creeping groundcover
Color: Leaves green, purple, and/or white; flowers blue, pink, or white
Bloom time: Late spring, early summer
Exposure: Sun to full shade
Soil: Average, well-drained

• Common bugleweed (*A. reptans*) is a great choice if you need a fast-spreading groundcover for large areas. It can be a maintenance headache in small spots unless you contain it with a plastic or metal barrier.

• Geneva bugleweed (*A. genevensis*) and upright bugleweed (*A. pyramidalis*) spread moderately but are seldom invasive; try them in rock gardens and mixed shade plantings.

• Once you plant ajuga, you can have a lifetime supply of new plants; dig up and divide plants in spring or fall.

Liven up a large planting of bugleweed by mixing cultivars with different flower or foliage colors.

Alchemilla

(al-keh-MILL-uh)

Lady's-mantle

Zones: 3–8
Height: 6 to 12 inches
Shape: Soft mounds
Color: Yellow-green
Bloom time: Spring, early summer
Exposure: Sun to partial shade
Soil: Rich, moist

• When you shop for lady's-mantle, you'll most often find the species *A. mollis*, with mounds of flannel-soft, ruffled leaves and clouds of chartreuse flowers.

• Lady's-mantle makes a great groundcover, but by midsummer the leaves can

The striking contrast of chartreuse lady's-mantle blossoms and purple flowers of spotted lamium (*Lamium maculatum*) shows beautifully along a pathway.

look rather tired. Shear the whole planting to the ground to prompt a fresh batch of foliage.

• Grow lady's-mantle as an edging plant or mix it with spiky perennials such as irises.

• In hot summer areas, site these plants in partial shade for best growth and flowering.

• Lady's-mantle may self-sow where it is happy. Dig and spread the new seedlings to extend an edging of lady's-mantle all along a bed. Or, to prevent reseeding, cut off spent flowers.

Allium

(AL-ee-um)

Allium, Ornamental onion

Zones: 3–9
Height: 6 inches to 5 feet
Shape: Low tufts of leaves with upright flowerstalks
Color: Pink, purple, white, blue, or yellow
Bloom time: Spring, summer, fall
Exposure: Sun
Soil: Average to rich, well-drained to dry

• For an early summer border accent, try giant onion (*A. giganteum*); its purple-pink flower clusters bloom atop 5-foot stems. Mix them with bushy annuals and perennials to hide the foliage as it turns yellow.

• The fragrant white flowers of garlic chives (*A. tuberosum*) brighten the late-summer garden, and the edible green leaves are tasty any time!

• Snip off spent flower stems to prevent self-sown seedlings, or let the showy seedheads form, then weed out or move the resulting seedlings.

Yellow 'Moonbeam' coreopsis stands out in front of the pink flower globes of *Allium* senescens and behind fuzzy annual ageratum.

Anemone

(uh-NEM-oh-nee)

Anemone, Windflower

Zones: 3–9
Height: 4 inches to 5 feet
Shape: Varies among species
Color: White, pink, red, purple, or blue
Bloom time: Spring, summer, fall
Exposure: Sun to shade
Soil: Varies widely among species

• If you have room for only one anemone, make it a Japanese anemone (*A.* ✕ *hybrida*). This fall-blooming beauty has single or double flowers on 3- to 5-foot

White Japanese anemone ('Alba') and the yellow foliage of possum haw (*Ilex decidua* 'Warren's Red') make a great fall pair.

stems. Combine Japanese anemones with bleeding hearts (*Dicentra spectabilis*) and other early bloomers; the anemone foliage will fill the space when the other plants go dormant.

• Vigorous snowdrop anemone (*A. sylvestris*) blooms in spring. Try planting it with ferns and other shade lovers.

• To increase your anemone collection, divide spring-blooming types after flowering; summer- and fall-bloomers in spring.

Aquilegia

(ack-wih-LEE-gee-uh)
Columbine

Zones: 3–9
Height: 6 inches to 4 feet
Shape: Open clumps
Color: Wide variety
Bloom time: Spring, early summer
Exposure: Sun to partial shade
Soil: Average to rich, moist but well-drained

- Columbines' spurred flowers have a quaint and old-fashioned look that adds charm to borders, woodlands, and rock gardens.
- These delicate-looking perennials bridge the spring and summer bloom seasons. Combine

Wild columbine (*A. canadensis*) makes red exclamation points against a background of basket-of-gold (*Aurinia saxatilis*).

them with late-blooming tulips to finish the spring show, and irises and peonies to start your summer display.

- For something really different, try double-flowered 'Nora Barlow'—it has pink, green, and white petals all in the same bloom!
- Squiggly lines in your columbine leaves mean leafminers are at work; pinch off and destroy damaged leaves.
- In mid- to late summer, the urn-shaped seedpods will drop lots of seed. Pinch off spent flowers to prevent self-sowing, or transplant the seedlings.

Artemisia

(ar-teh-MEEZ-ee-uh)
Artemisia,
Wormwood

Zones: 3–9
Height: 10 inches to 6 feet
Shape: Varies among species
Color: Leaves green to silver; flowers yellowish or grayish
Bloom time: Summer, fall
Exposure: Sun
Soil: Average, well-drained

- Artemisias are indispensable for adding season-long foliage interest to sunny beds and borders.
- The gray-green or silver leaves of artemisia look stunning with red and other hot colors.

For a soothing effect, pair artemisia with flowers that sport cool hues of pink and blue.

'Silver King' artemisia wraps a stunning mantle around 'Autumn Joy' sedum in fall.

- The cultivar 'Powis Castle' forms shrubby clumps of aromatic, silvery white leaves. Try combining it with perennials with spiky foliage and flowers.
- For a soft edging, try silvermound artemisia (*A. schmidtiana*). If the mounds flop open in summer, shear them back by half to produce more compact growth.
- 'Silver King' artemisia (*A. ludoviciana* 'Silver King') forms upright, spreading clumps of silvery leaves and stems. Divide plants every 2 or 3 years in spring or fall to keep them under control.

Asclepias

(as-KLEE-pea-us)
Milkweed

Zones: 3–9
Height: 1 to 5 feet
Shape: Clumps of upright stalks
Color: Yellow, orange, red, pink, white or green
Bloom time: Summer
Exposure: Sun to light shade
Soil: Average, moist to dry

• No butterfly garden is complete without milkweeds. The leaves are the sole food source of monarch butterfly caterpillars; the flowers provide a

The complementary colors of orange butterfly weed and blue spike speedwell (*Veronica spicata*) make a vibrant fellowship.

rich nectar supply for many beautiful species of butterflies.

• These tough, adaptable plants look equally at home in borders and wildflower gardens. The blooms make excellent cut flowers.

• For hot summer color, combine butterfly weed (*A. tuberosa*) with red and yellow flowers. It needs loose, well-drained soil, while pink- to white-flowered swamp milkweed (*A. incarnata*) prefers moist conditions.

• To increase your milkweed plantings, take tip cuttings in early summer or sow fresh seed outdoors in fall.

Pink asters backed by Russian sage (*Perovskia atriplicifolia*) and yellow coneflowers (*Rudbeckia* sp.) create layers of texture and color.

Aster

(AS-ter)
Aster

Zones: 2–8
Height: 6 inches to 8 feet
Shape: Varies among species
Color: Blue, purple, red, pink, or white
Bloom time: Summer, fall
Exposure: Sun to partial shade
Soil: Varies widely among species

• Bushy and beautiful, asters offer masses of showy, daisylike blooms that are ideal for beds, borders, containers, and meadow gardens.

• Frikart's aster (*A.* ✕ *frikartii*) produces yellow-centered, lavender-blue flowers from midsummer to fall. The 2- to 3-foot plants are ideal for the middle of a border.

• For late summer and fall color, try New England asters (*A. novae-angliae*). 'Purple Dome' is a compact, 2-foot mound smothered in purple flowers; 'Alma Potschke' has vivid pink flowers on 3-foot stems. 'Autumn Snow' bears masses of white flowers.

• Stake tall asters or cut them back by half in midsummer to promote sturdier stems and more branching.

• Divide plants every year or two in spring to control their spread, rejuvenate overgrown clumps, or increase your plantings.

Astilbe

(uh-STILL-bee)
Astilbe, False spirea

Zones: 3–9
Height: 8 inches to 5 feet
Shape: Clumps with upright flowerstalks
Color: Leaves green or reddish; flowers red, pink, or white
Bloom time: Late spring, summer
Exposure: Sun to shade
Soil: Average, moist but well-drained

• Astilbes are long-lived, easy-care additions to moist-soil borders. Ferns, irises, and other moisture-loving plants are perfect companions.

• Try a mass of astilbes around a water garden; the water will reflect the colorful flower plumes.

• Snip a few of the flower plumes for indoor arrangements; leave the rest to mature on the plants for winter interest.

• Dwarf Chinese astilbe (*A. chinensis* 'Pumila') makes a great groundcover. The low, creeping plants form carpets of ferny foliage with perky pink flower clusters in late summer.

• Hybrid astilbes (*A. × arendsii*) come in a range of colors, heights, and bloom times; try a mixed planting for all-summer color.

Red, white, and pink astilbes are a simple and satisfying combination for a shady spot.

• To keep your astilbes vigorous, divide overgrown clumps every 3 to 4 years.

Basket-of-gold flourishes on rocky sites. Purple rock cress (*Aubrieta deltoidea*) makes a bold companion.

Aurinia

(aw-RIN-ee-uh)
Basket-of-gold

Zones: 3–7
Height: 10 to 12 inches
Shape: Low mounds
Color: Yellow
Bloom time: Spring
Exposure: Sun
Soil: Average, well-drained

• The glowing yellow flowers of basket-of-gold are a real standout in the spring garden. Plant them alone or combine them with other early perennials and bulbs.

• Try planting drifts of basket-of-gold in a rock garden, on a slope, or at the top of a retaining wall. These sites provide the excellent drainage this perennial needs.

• If the golden color of the species is a little too bright for your taste, try the softer yellow 'Citrinum' or peachy yellow 'Sunny Border Apricot'.

• These plants can look messy once the flowers have faded. Cut them back by about half to remove the seedheads and promote bushy new growth.

• Divide clumps in fall to expand your plantings.

Baptisia

(bap-TEEZ-ee-uh)

Baptisia, False indigo

Zones: 3–9
Height: 1 to 5 feet
Shape: Clumps of upright flower-
stalks
Color: Blue, yellow, or white
Bloom time: Late spring, early
summer
Exposure: Sun to light shade
Soil: Rich, moist but well-drained

• Plant them and forget them—that's the key to growing baptisias. These durable plants can live in the same spot for years without division, slowly forming shrub-size clumps.

• Admire the spiky flower clusters of blue false indigo (*B. australis*) in your early summer border, then enjoy the gray-green leaves for the rest of the season.

• If white flower spikes would fit better into your design, try white wild indigo (*B. alba*).

• Baptisias also produce showy gray or brown seedpods; cut them for arrangements or leave them for later interest.

• In some spots, baptisias may need staking; place rounded peony hoops over emerging clumps for support.

• To get more baptisias, divide clumps in fall, using shears or a sharp knife to cut through the tough crowns; leave at least one bud per division.

Dark pine boughs are a handsome backdrop for blue false indigo. Lady's mantle (*Alchemilla mollis*) in front completes the picture.

Delicate blossoms and foliage of *Chrysanthemum zawadskii* var. *latilobum* 'Clara Curtis' peek over the smooth, stately leaves of *Bergenia* 'Silberlicht'.

Bergenia

(ber-GEEN-ee-uh)

Bergenia

Zones: 3–9
Height: 1 to 2 feet
Shape: Mounds of leaves with
taller flowerstalks
Color: Leaves green or reddish;
flowers red, pink, or white
Bloom time: Early spring
Exposure: Sun to partial shade
Soil: Rich, moist

• Bergenia offers year-round interest—colorful flowers in spring and glossy green leaves that stay attractive through the season and turn reddish over winter.

• Grow bergenias along the front of a border, under shrubs and trees, or as accents in container plantings.

• Bergenia's bold foliage is a perfect complement to fine-textured leaves and flowers. Try pairing bergenia with ferns, bleeding hearts (*Dicentra* spp.), and hardy geraniums (*Geranium* spp.).

• Flowerbuds may be damaged by very cold temperatures. Protect them over winter by covering them with straw or coarse leaves, or grow the plants purely for foliage interest.

• Divide clumps in spring for propagation or to thin out crowded plantings.

Boltonia

(bowl-TOE-nee-uh)
Boltonia

Zones: 3–9
Height: 4 to 6 feet
Shape: Tall, rounded
Color: White or pink
Bloom time: Late summer, fall
Exposure: Sun to light shade
Soil: Rich, moist to dry

- The blue-green leaves and snowy white flowers of boltonia add a cool touch to late summer and early fall borders and wild-flower gardens.

- For an elegant all-white combination, try 'Snowbank' boltonia with a white-variegated ornamental grass and a white-

Bright clusters of pink turtlehead (*Chelone lyonii*) at center and spikes of *Celosia spicata* 'Flamingo Feather' at lower right look lovely among daisylike 'Pink Beauty' boltonia.

flowered Japanese anemone (such as *Anemone* × *hybrida* 'Honorine Jobert').

- Cut plants back by half in early to midsummer to promote bushier growth and more flowers.

- Boltonias are easy to divide in spring. Remove the dead centers and replant the vigorous outer portions.

Campanula

(kam-PAN-yew-luh)
Bellflower, Harebell

Zones: 2–8
Height: 4 inches to 5 feet
Shape: Varies among species
Color: Purple, blue, white, or pink
Bloom time: Spring, summer
Exposure: Sun to partial shade
Soil: Average to rich, well-drained

- Bellflowers are invaluable for adding bright blues and purples to the summer garden.

- Low-growing species, such as Carpathian harebell (*C. carpatica*) and Dalmatian bell-

For a clean, bright combination, plant clustered bellflower with a white daisy such as Shasta daisy (*Chrysanthemum* × *superbum*).

flower (*C. portenschlagiana*), are ideal for rock gardens and for the front of borders.

- Clustered bellflower (*C. glomerata*) and peachleaf bellflower (*C. persicifolia*) are midsize to tall perennials that look great in the middle or back of the border.

- Create stunning color combinations by grouping blue-purple bellflowers with bright yellow yarrow, pure white peonies, or pink astilbes.

- Divide bellflowers in early spring or fall to control their spread or rejuvenate crowded clumps.

Oxeye daisies (C. *leucanthemum*) and spiky foxgloves (*Digitalis* sp.) are cheerful companions in a summer border.

Chrysanthemum

(kris-AN-thuh-mum)
Chrysanthemum

Zones: 3–11
Height: 1 to 5 feet
Shape: Varies
Color: White, yellow, orange, red, pink, or purple
Bloom time: Summer, fall
Exposure: Sun
Soil: Average to rich, well-drained

- Mix several species into your sunny borders and beds to have chrysanthemums in bloom from early summer to frost.

- Shasta daisies (C. × *superbum*) are classics for the early summer garden. A drift of these white daisies paired with Siberian irises (*Iris sibirica*) is an unforgettable sight.

- What would fall be without bright garden mums (C. × *morifolium*)? Tuck them into bare spots left by worn-out annuals and perennials, or group them for colorful container plantings.

- Unlike other mums, gold-and-silver chrysanthemum (C. *pacificum*) is grown mostly for its scalloped, gray-green, silver-edged leaves; try it in containers or as a groundcover.

- Divide chrysanthemums every other year in spring to keep them healthy and vigorous.

Cimicifuga

(sim-ih-siff-YOU-guh)
Bugbane, Black cohosh, Snakeroot

Zones: 3–8
Height: 2 to 7 feet
Shape: Mounds of leaves with taller flowerstalks
Color: White
Bloom time: Summer, fall
Exposure: Sun to partial shade
Soil: Rich, moist

- Throughout the season, the ferny green leaves of bugbane make a beautiful backdrop for colorful perennials such as daylilies and garden phlox (*Phlox paniculata*).

- Black snakeroot (C. *racemosa*) produces showy flower spikes up to 6 feet tall in early to midsummer.

- 'White Pearl', a culitvar of Kamchatka bugbane (C. *simplex*), is more compact—to about 4 feet—with arching clusters of lightly fragrant white flowers. Try it in masses in a woodland garden or under trees.

- Steady soil moisture is critical for good growth; dry soil leads to stunted growth and browned leaves.

- You can divide established plants in fall, although they'll grow better if left undisturbed.

The white flowers of bugbane show their full drama against a dark background like purple-flowering Durand clematis (*Clematis* × *durandii*).

114

Coreopsis

(core-ee-OP-sis)
Coreopsis, Tickseed

Zones: 3–9
Height: 1 to 9 feet
Shape: Varies with species
Color: Yellow, pink
Bloom time: Late spring, summer
Exposure: Sun
Soil: Average to rich, moist to dry

• Cheerful yellow coreopsis flowers are a welcome sight in summer beds and borders. Removing the spent flowers can keep plants blooming for months!

• 'Moonbeam' is an outstanding selection of threadleaf coreopsis (*C. verticillata*). Its light yellow flowers look beautiful with other soft colors, including pink, blue, and lavender.

• Pink tickseed (*C. rosea*) looks very much like a pink version of threadleaf coreopsis. Unlike similar species of coreopsis, however, pink tickseed prefers soil moisture that stays relatively stable. Try it with irises.

• The puffy, golden yellow flowers of *C. grandiflora* 'Early Sunrise' make ideal companions for purple coneflower (*Echinacea purpurea*), daylilies, and ornamental grasses.

• Divide plants in spring or fall to rejuvenate old clumps or to increase your plantings.

For a foliage feature, group yellow-flowered 'Moonbeam' coreopsis, grassy yellow sedge (*Carex elata* 'Bowles Golden'), and bluish green rue (*Ruta graveolens*).

Delphinium

(dell-FIN-ee-um)
Delphinium, Larkspur

Zones: 3–8
Height: 1 to 6 feet
Shape: Varies among species
Color: Blue, purple, pink, or white
Bloom time: Late spring, summer; fall rebloom
Exposure: Sun
Soil: Rich, moist

• The towering flower spikes of delphiniums are traditional favorites to plant for early summer color in beds, borders, and cottage gardens.

Pink astilbes and white baby's-breath light up the scene around blue Chinese delphinium (*D. grandiflorum* 'Blue Dwarf').

• Create eye-catching contrasts by pairing upright delphiniums with bushy, mounded perennials such as peonies and baby's-breath.

• Encourage plants to rebloom by cutting off the spent flowers just above the top leaves. When the leafy stems begin to die back, cut them down to the new growth emerging at the base.

• Delphiniums tend to be short-lived, fading out after 2 or 3 years. Propagate new plants by taking cuttings from the new spring growth or by sowing fresh seed indoors or outdoors.

The light, airy flowers of garden forget-me-not (*Myosotis sylvatica*) seem to float like mist around a group of cheerful pinks.

Dianthus

(dye-AN-thus)
Pinks, Carnation

Zones: 3–9
Height: 3 inches to 2 feet
Shape: Mounds or mats
Color: White, pink, red, or lilac
Bloom time: Spring, summer
Exposure: Sun to light shade
Soil: Average, moist to dry

• Pinks are lovely, fragrant, old-fashioned perennials that are perfect for rock gardens or border edgings. The slender blue-green leaves hold their color year-round.

• Many pinks have delightfully fragrant flowers. Plant them in raised beds or along the top of a retaining wall so you won't have to kneel down to enjoy the scent.

• Silvery-leaved plants, such as lamb's-ears (*Stachys byzantina*) and artemisias, make striking companions for pinks' bright blooms.

• Shear off the spent flowers after the first flush of bloom; this can encourage plants to flower again later in the season.

• To keep the plants vigorous, divide them every 2 or 3 years in spring or fall.

Dicentra

(dye-SEN-truh)
Bleeding heart

Zones: 2–9
Height: 8 inches to 2½ feet
Shape: Soft mounds
Color: Pink or white
Bloom time: Spring, summer
Exposure: Sun to full shade
Soil: Rich, moist

• Common bleeding heart (*D. spectabilis*) is a classic favorite for spring borders. Combine its shrubby clumps with daffodils, primroses, and columbines (*Aquilegia* spp.) for a cheerful swirl of color.

• Common bleeding heart often goes dormant by midsummer. Grow it with bushy plants, such as asters and baby's-

Fernlike fringed bleeding heart and elegant hostas make a stunning statement. Both will thrive in shade and woodland gardens.

breath, that can fill the space.

• For a steady display of flowers from spring until frost, try fringed bleeding heart (*D. eximia*), which is much smaller than

its spring-blooming cousin.

• Divide overgrown clumps in fall or as they go dormant. Plants often self-sow; you can transplant the seedlings.

Digitalis

(dij-uh-TAL-lis)
Foxglove

Zones: 3–8
Height: 2 to 5 feet
Shape: Erect flower spikes
Color: Pink, white, yellow, or brown
Bloom time: Summer
Exposure: Sun to partial shade
Soil: Rich, moist

• The striking spikes of foxgloves perfectly punctuate the summer border. Their upright form is a welcome contrast to mounded plants such as peonies and roses.

• Foxgloves also look super with ferns and hostas in shade

Yellow foxglove mixes well with the yellow-green flowers of lady's mantle (*Alchemilla mollis*) and feathery boughs of Canada hemlock (*Tsuga canadensis*).

gardens and woodland plantings.

• Common foxglove (*D. purpurea*) reaches to 5 feet when in bloom, with dramatic flower spikes in white, pinks, and cream. Although it is biennial, common foxglove seems perennial because it produces lots of self-sown seedlings.

• For compact, easy-care color, try perennial yellow foxglove (*D. grandiflora*). The 2- to 3-foot spikes of soft yellow flowers combine beautifully with blues, pinks, and white.

• To increase your foxglove plantings, dig up the self-sown seedlings and move them to new areas of the garden.

Echinacea

(eck-in-AY-see-uh)
Purple coneflower

Zones: 2–8
Height: 1 to 6 feet
Shape: Loose clumps of erect stalks
Color: Purple, pink, or white
Bloom time: Summer
Exposure: Sun
Soil: Average, moist to dry

• Few plants provide so much show for so little work! The large, long-lasting, rosy pink blooms of purple coneflowers appear throughout the summer, while the cone-shaped seedheads stay attractive well into winter.

• These easy-care plants are a natural choice for meadow gardens, along with ornamental grasses, goldenrods (*Solidago* spp.), and yarrow.

• In beds and borders, try pairing the bright blooms with artemisias, daylilies, coreopsis, and lamb's-ears (*Stachys byzantina*).

• Purple coneflower seldom needs to be divided. If you want to expand your plantings, start new plants from seed, or transplant self-sown seedlings.

For a colorful late-summer display, pair 'Bright Star' purple coneflower and 'Goldsturm' black-eyed Susan.

Epimedium

(ep-ih-MEE-dee-um)

Epimedium,
Barrenwort

Zones: 3–8
Height: 6 to 15 inches
Shape: Spreading mats
Color: Leaves green, yellow, or reddish; flowers white, yellow, pink, or red
Bloom time: Spring
Exposure: Partial to full shade
Soil: Average to rich, moist to dry

• Epimediums are grown mainly as groundcovers, but they have a lot to offer beds and borders, too! The heart-shaped leaves complement bright summer companion flowers.

• These delicate-looking plants are actually quite tough. Try them in dry shade.

• Although often touted as evergreen, epimedium leaves tend to look tattered by midwinter. Cut them to the ground in early spring: The plants will look neater and the dainty flowers will be more visible.

• Some species, including red epimedium (*E.* × *rubrum*), have a reddish tint to the young leaves.

• Epimediums form spreading clumps that seldom need division. But if you want to propagate them, divide them in late summer or early fall.

Red epimedium leaves flow like a stream beside steps. Yuccas shoot up like fountains from their midst.

Eryngium

(er-IN-gee-um)

Sea holly, Eryngo

Zones: 2–9
Height: 1 to 6 feet
Shape: Open clumps of stiff, erect stalks
Color: Silver-gray, blue, or purple
Bloom time: Summer, fall
Exposure: Sun
Soil: Average, well-drained

• In mid- to late summer, the unique silvery flowers and foliage of sea hollies are an unforgettable addition to any sunny border.

• Plant sea hollies against a green backdrop, such as shrubs or tall grasses, or mix them with

Smooth yellow lily blossoms invite you to sniff their fragrance, but the spines of giant sea holly (E. giganteum) advise you to admire from a distance.

yellows, pinks, and other colors.

• The taproots that give sea hollies drought resistance also make the plants difficult to move. Let established plants expand to form dramatic clumps.

• The metallic-looking blooms are striking in fresh arrangements; some also keep their color when dried.

• Sea hollies often self-sow. If you want more sea hollies, move the seedlings to other parts of the garden.

Eupatorium

(you-puh-TOUR-ee-um)

Boneset, Joe-Pye weed

Zones: 2–10
Height: 2 to 14 feet
Shape: Multistemmed clumps
Color: Blue, purple, pink, or white
Bloom time: Summer, fall
Exposure: Sun
Soil: Average to rich, moist

• If you're searching for a big back-of-the-border plant, look no farther than Joe-Pye weeds (*E. fistulosum* and *E. purpureum*). Far from being weedy, these dramatic perennials have wonderful upright form, clean green leaves, and late-season rosy pink flowers.

White *Phlox paniculata* 'David' and towering spotted Joe-Pye weed (*E. maculatum* 'Atropurpureum') create a wild retreat that's perfect for nesting birds.

• Joe-Pye weeds can tower up to 14 feet, although 6 feet is more common. Too big for your border? Try using them like shrubs for a seasonal hedge or screen.

• If you like the fuzzy lavender-blue blooms of annual ageratum, try hardy ageratum (*E. coelestinum*). It blooms from midsummer to fall on 2-foot stems and doesn't need annual replanting. Give it a spot where it can spread.

• Divide plants in early spring to rejuvenate old clumps or to expand your plantings.

Euphorbia

(you-FOR-bee-uh)

Spurge, Euphorbia

Zones: 3–9
Height: 6 inches to 4 feet
Shape: Spreading clumps
Color: Leaves green or blue-green; flowers yellow, surrounded by green, yellow, white, or reddish bracts
Bloom time: Spring, summer
Exposure: Sun to partial shade
Soil: Average to rich, well-drained to dry

• Of the many kinds of euphorbias, cushion spurge (*E. epithymoides*) is one of the most popular for garden use. Combine its green leaves and glowing yellow petal-like bracts

Lemony cushion spurge backed by pale wild columbine (*Aquilegia canadensis*) makes a wonderful spring duo for a yellow theme garden.

with brightly colored tulips for a spectacular spring display.

• Griffith's spurge (*E. griffithii*) forms 3-foot shrubby clumps topped with fiery reddish orange bracts. Unlike other euphorbias, this species thrives in continually moist soil; try it with irises and astilbes.

• Divide plants in spring to rejuvenate old clumps or for propagation. All euphorbias release an irritating milky sap from broken leaves and stems, so wear gloves while working around the plants.

Filipendula

(fill-uh-PEN-djew-luh)
Meadowsweet,
Queen-of-the-prairie

Zones: 3–9
Height: 2 to 6 feet
Shape: Loose shrubby mounds
Color: White or pink
Bloom time: Late spring, summer
Exposure: Sun to partial shade
Soil: Rich, moist

Repeat flower and leaf form by pairing 'Venusta' queen-of-the-prairie and white-flowered bottlebrush buckeye (Aesculus parviflora), a shrub native to the southeast.

- The frothy flower clusters of meadowsweets float above bushy mounds of deep green, divided leaves. They look marvelous in meadow gardens, borders, and pondside plantings.

- Queen-of-the-prairie (*F. rubra*) adds a striking accent to the back of the border. Siberian meadowsweet (*F. palmata*) is a more compact midborder plant.

- In a cottage garden, group meadowswects with roses, irises, purple coneflowers (*Echinacea purpurea*), and ornamental grasses.

- Dropwort (*F. vulgaris*) has clusters of creamy white flowers and looks lovely with artemisias and catmints (*Nepeta* spp.).

- Divide clumps as needed in fall to control their spread or for propagation.

Gaillardia

(gah-LARD-ee-uh)
Blanket flower

Zones: 2–10
Height: 2 to 3 feet
Shape: Clumps with taller flowerstalks
Color: Mixtures of orange, red, yellow, and brown
Bloom time: Summer
Exposure: Sun
Soil: Average, well-drained to dry

Yellow-flowered evening primroses such as Oenothera caespitosa bring out the yellow highlights in red blanket flower blossoms.

- Nothing says summer like the bright red-and-yellow blooms of blanket flower. These tough plants can take heat, drought, neglect—even tough seaside conditions!

- A mass of blanket flowers makes an eye-catching landscape accent from early summer to fall.

- In beds and borders, pair blanket flowers with butterfly weed (*Asclepias tuberosa*) and other orange and red flowers.

- Pinch off spent flowers at the base of the stem to keep plants looking tidy and prolong the bloom season.

- Blanket flowers tend to be short-lived, so divide them every 2 or 3 years in spring.

Geranium

(jer-ANE-ee-um)
Cranesbill, Hardy
geranium

Zones: 3–8
Height: 4 inches to 4 feet
Shape: Soft mounds
Color: White, blue, purple, or pink
Bloom time: Spring, early summer
Exposure: Sun to partial shade
Soil: Rich, moist but well-drained

- Cranesbills come in an array of heights and colors that can fit into any planting scheme.
- For a striking border accent, try Armenian cranesbill (*G. psilostemon*), with black-centered, magenta flowers on 4-foot stems.
- Mounding blood-red cranesbill (*G. sanguineum*) is an

Grasses and perennials create great garden surprises, like a duo of 'Russell Pritchard' geraniums and golden variegated hakone grass (*Hakonechloa macra* 'Aureola').

indispensable front-of-the-border perennial. The species has reddish purple flowers; the variety *striatum* (also known as var. *lancastriense*) blooms in soft pink.

- While most cranesbills need moist soil, drought-tolerant bigroot cranesbill (*G. macrorrhizum*) and Endres cranesbill (*G. endressii*) grow well in either moist or dry spots.
- The hybrid cranesbill 'Johnson's Blue' is a popular companion for soft yellows, such as 'Moonbeam' coreopsis; it also looks lovely with artemisias and other silver-leaved plants.
- It's nearly impossible to have too many of these versatile, easy-to-grow perennials. Divide existing plants in fall or early spring.

Gypsophila

(jipp-SOFF-ill-uh)
Baby's-breath

Zones: 3–9
Height: 4 inches to 4 feet
Shape: Airy mounds
Color: White or pink
Bloom time: Summer
Exposure: Sun to light shade
Soil: Rich, moist but well-drained

- The airy bloom clusters of baby's-breath look as beautiful in the perennial garden as they do in flower arrangements.
- The most commonly

Low growers like yellow-flowered sedums and silvery lamb's ears are natural for edgings, but tall, misty baby's-breath also cascades beautifully over a stone wall.

available species is *G. paniculata*. Its dainty white flower clusters practically smother the shrub-size masses of blue-green leaves in summer. For a similar effect in small spaces, try creeping baby's-breath (*G. repens*).

- These fine-textured plants are natural companions for plants with spiky leaves, such as iris, and big, bold flowers, such as lilies.
- Cutting off spent flowerstalks just after the flowers fade can promote rebloom.
- Try spring or summer cuttings for propagation, or buy additional plants.

Helenium

(hel-EE-nee-um)

Sneezeweed

Zones: 3–9
Height: 2 to 5 feet
Shape: Clumps of erect stalks
Color: Yellow or orange
Bloom time: Late summer, fall
Exposure: Sun
Soil: Rich, moist

• This bold, late-blooming perennial adds bright color to the back of the fall border or the meadow garden.

• Combine sneezeweeds with other hot colors for an end-of-the-season splash. For dramatic contrasts, pair it with blues and purples, such as spiky blue salvias (*Salvia* spp.).

• To minimize the need for staking on tall sneezeweeds, pinch the stem tips once or twice in spring. Or, try 'Brilliant', a compact cultivar of *H. autumnale* that doesn't require support.

• Divide clumps every 3 to 4 years to keep them vigorous. If you want even more sneezeweeds, take stem cuttings in early summer.

Drifts of orange sneezeweed (*H. hoopesii*) and white oxeye daisy (*Chrysanthemum leucanthemum*) fill a sunny meadow with color in late summer.

Heliopsis

(hee-lee-OP-sis)

Heliopsis, Oxeye

Zones: 3–9
Height: 3 to 6 feet
Shape: Clumps of erect stalks
Color: Yellow
Bloom time: Summer
Exposure: Sun to partial shade
Soil: Average to rich, moist to dry

• The bright yellow daisies of heliopsis add welcome mid-summer color. Heliopsis has a wild, free-flowing look that blends beautifully into meadow gardens; try it with spiky gayfeathers (*Liatris* spp.), colorful asters, and bright orange butterfly weed (*Asclepias tuberosa*).

• Go for easy-care color with drifts of heliopsis, daylilies, and ornamental grasses.

• 'Golden Plume' has fluffy, double flowers; 'Summer Sun' is compact (to 3 feet) with golden yellow, semidouble flowers.

• Divide clumps in spring or fall for propagation or to control their spread.

A backdrop of yellow heliopsis to the right and black-eyed Susans to the left mix joyfully with purple coneflowers and lavender Frikart's aster (*Aster × frikartii* 'Monch').

Helleborus

(hell-uh-BORE-us)
Hellebore, Christmas
rose, Lenten rose

Zones: 3–9
Height: 10 inches to 2 feet
Shape: Clumps of flower-
stalks
Color: Maroon, purple, pink,
white, or green
Bloom time: Winter, spring
Exposure: Partial shade
Soil: Rich, moist but well-
drained

• Unless you live
where the snow cover is
deep and persistent, you
can enjoy the evergreen
leaves of hellebores
through most of the year.

Hellebores are lovely in shade
gardens and under shrubs.

• Christmas rose (*H. niger*)
seldom blooms in December, but
it can pop its flowers through
light snow in January or

Mix Lenten roses of different shades for an elegant start to the garden season.

February. The white flowers
blush with pink as they age.

• Lenten rose (*H. orientalis*)
blooms slightly later—usually
February to March—with elegant, nodding flowers in a range
of pinks, deep purples,
cream, and white.

• Lenten roses can
make great groundcovers
under trees and shrubs.
Combine them with prim-
roses and small, early-
blooming bulbs like crocus.

• Hellebores tend to
self-sow where they are
happy; transplant the
young seedlings to other
parts of the garden.

Hemerocallis

(hem-er-oh-CAL-is)
Daylily

Zones: 2–9
Height: 1 to 6 feet
Shape: Mounds of arching leaves
with taller flowerstalks
Color: Cream, yellow, orange, red,
maroon, or pink
Bloom time: Spring, summer
Exposure: Sun to partial shade
Soil: Average to rich, well-drained
to dry

• Daylilies make great companions for spring bulbs like daffodils. The bulbs bloom as the
daylily leaves emerge; then the
daylily foliage fills in as the bulb
leaves turn yellow in summer.

Use annuals like blue mealy-cup sage (*Salvia farinacea*) and low-growing snapdragons to dress up the base of daylilies.

• You'll enjoy seeing daylilies
along a winding garden path.

• Daylilies look serene and
beautiful in a reflection from a
water garden.

• There's an incredible
range of daylilies offered for sale,
so check catalog photographs or
buy plants in bloom to get just
the colors you want.

• Each daylily flower lasts
one day, but the plants produce
so many buds that they can stay
in bloom for weeks.

• Daylilies generally form
long-lasting clumps; divide them
in late summer to fall if needed.

Heuchera

(HUE-ker-uh)
Alumroot, Coral bells

Zones: 3–9
Height: 1 to 3 feet
Shape: Mounds of leaves with taller flower spikes
Color: Leaves green to dark red; flowers white, pink, or red
Bloom time: Spring, summer
Exposure: Sun to partial shade
Soil: Rich, moist but well-drained

- The flower clusters of coral bells (*H. sanguinea* and *H.* × *brizoides*) add an airy look to summer beds and borders. The mounds of evergreen foliage make an excellent edging.
- Some alumroots have showy flowers, others have colorful leaves—a few have both!

Make the most of the mixed tones of 'Palace Purple' heuchera leaves by pairing them with pure colors like bright red pansies and fresh green daylily foliage.

For exceptional season-long interest, try 'Palace Purple' with purple-brown leaves and tiny, greenish white flowers, or 'Snowstorm' with white-spotted green leaves and red flowers.

- Removing the spent flowerstalks at the base can prolong the bloom period.
- As alumroots mature, they produce woody crowns. Divide them in spring or fall.

Try pairing pink marsh mallow (*H. moscheutos* subsp. *palustris*) and feathery Culver's root (*Veronicastrum virginicum*) to make a smashing back-of-the-border combination.

Hibiscus

(hy-BISS-kus)
Hibiscus, Rose mallow

Zones: 4–10
Height: 4 to 8 feet
Shape: Shrublike clusters of sturdy, erect stalks
Color: White, pink, or red
Bloom time: Summer
Exposure: Sun to light shade
Soil: Rich, moist

- "Bold and beautiful" sums up the attractions of common rose mallow (*H. moscheutos*). Its broad leaves and large, showy flowers make this a striking accent plant in any perennial garden. Try a row of common rose mallow as a colorful summer hedge or screen.
- Mix mallows with Joe-Pye weeds (*Eupatorium* spp.), ironweeds (*Vernonia* spp.), and other moisture-loving perennials in meadow gardens.
- Mallows prefer steady soil moisture, but they'll adapt to drier conditions by producing more compact growth.
- Established plants may self-sow freely. Propagate cultivars that won't come true from seed by taking tip cuttings in midsummer (remove the flowerbuds).

Hosta

(HOSS-tuh)
Hosta, Plantain lily

Zones: 3–8
Height: 6 inches to 3 feet
Shape: Wide mounds of leaves with taller flower spikes
Color: Leaves green, yellow, blue-green, and/or cream; flowers lilac or white
Bloom time: Summer to fall
Exposure: Light to full shade
Soil: Average to rich, moist

• Hostas are the workhorse of shady gardens. Try a circle of them under a tree or plant a bed of hostas along a shaded wall of your house.

• Hostas boring? Never! Plant assorted cultivars and enjoy the wide range of solid and var-

Greenish gold *H. fortunei* 'Gold Standard' glows next to the dark green leaves of blue hosta (*H. ventricosa*) and complements the intricately variegated foliage of *H. sieboldiana* 'Frances Williams'.

iegated green, blue-green, yellow, and almost white leaves.

• Interplant them with ferns and wild ginger for a beautiful shady groundcover.

• Plant hostas with early-spring bulbs and wildflowers. The hostas will unfurl their leaves just when the bulb foliage starts to look moth-eaten.

• While hostas are not usually grown for their flowers, *H. plantaginea* bears spikes of 5-inch-long, fragrant white trumpets in summer over glossy, heart-shaped leaves.

• Hostas expand slowly to form broad, showy clumps. You can divide them in spring if desired for propagation.

Iberis

(eye-BEER-iss)
Candytuft

Zones: 2–9
Height: 3 to 12 inches
Shape: Low creeping mats
Color: White
Bloom time: Early spring
Exposure: Sun to light shade
Soil: Average, well-drained

• You can't beat perennial candytuft as an edging for beds, borders, and walkways. It also grows well in rock gardens.

• Shrubby perennial candytuft (*I. sempervirens*) offers tidy mounds of evergreen leaves that

are smothered in white flowers in early spring. 'Autumn Snow' reblooms in fall.

• Try candytuft in raised beds or atop retaining walls, where it can cascade over the side.

• Shear plants back by about one-third after bloom to remove the spent flowers and promote compact growth.

• Combine candytuft with other early bloomers, such as spring bulbs and bleeding hearts (*Dicentra* spp.).

• For propagation, dig up and transplant rooted stems, or take tip cuttings in early summer.

White perennial candytuft and purple rock cress (*Aubrieta deltoidea*) paired with tulips will give your garden abundant color from early through late spring.

Yellow flag iris, ferns, and white columbine (*Aquilegia* sp.) are a graceful trio for a lightly shaded spot with moist, well-drained soil.

Iris

(EYE-ris)

Iris

Zones: 2–10
Height: 4 inches to 4 feet
Shape: Upright spiky clumps
Color: White, yellow, orange, brown, pink, purple, and blue
Bloom time: Spring, summer
Exposure: Sun to light shade
Soil: Varies widely among species

- It's hard to imagine a perennial garden without irises. After their short but glorious bloom season, you can enjoy the spiky foliage all season long.
- Siberian iris (*I. sibirica*) is a classic choice for an early-summer perennial border comprised of peonies, hostas, cranesbills (*Geranium* spp.), and columbines (*Aquilegia* spp.).
- Bearded irises (*Iris* bearded hybrids) bloom in nearly every color. Their sword-shaped leaves make a dramatic contrast to mounded companions.
- Yellow flag (*I. pseudacorus*) is ideal for wet spots and water gardens.
- Crested iris (*I. cristata*) is a charmer for the woodland garden. The short-stemmed flowers bloom amid spreading clumps of arching, blue-green leaves.
- Divide bearded irises in mid- to late summer; other species in early fall.

Kniphofia

(nee-FOFE-ee-uh)
Torch lily, Red-hot poker

Zones: 5–9
Height: 3 to 5 feet
Shape: Arching clumps of narrow leaves with tall flower-stalks
Color: Red, orange, and/or yellow
Bloom time: Late spring, summer
Exposure: Sun
Soil: Rich, well-drained

- Spiky torch lilies are unforgettable border accents. For a cool white-and-yellow combination, try 'Primrose Beauty' with shasta daisies (*Chrysanthemum* × *superbum*).
- Many torch lilies have two-toned flowerheads of orange or red and yellow. They look great with other hot-colored perennials, such as yellow yarrow and red or orange daylilies.
- For dramatic color contrast, try torch lilies with blue balloon flower (*Platycodon grandiflorus*) or catmint (*Nepeta* spp.).
- Cut spent flower stems off at the base to make plants look neat and encourage rebloom.
- Torch lilies prefer to be left undisturbed, but you can remove a few of the outer crowns in fall if needed for propagation.

For a knockout hot-color garden, mix the orange flower torches of 'Royal Standard' torch lily with sunflowers (*Helianthus* sp.) and violet sage (*Salvia* × *superba*).

Lamium

(LAY-mee-um)
Lamium, Dead nettle

Zones: 3–8
Height: 6 to 12 inches
Shape: Creeping, open ground-cover
Color: Leaves silver-green, variegated; flowers white or pink
Bloom time: Spring, summer
Exposure: Partial to full shade
Soil: Rich, moist but well-drained

• Lamiums are lovely groundcovers for shady gardens. Their silvery leaves brighten up dark areas and combine beautifully with all shades of green.

• These tough plants can even tolerate dry shade. Try them with hostas, ferns, and spring bulbs.

• 'White Nancy' is a popular cultivar with snowy white flowers from spring into summer. 'Pink Pewter' and 'Shell Pink' look similar but have pink flowers; 'Beacon Silver' is more purplish pink.

• Shear plants lightly after bloom to keep plants compact.

• Lamiums can spread fairly quickly in favorable conditions but generally aren't rampant enough to be invasive. Simply pull out unwanted plants or divide them in fall or spring.

'White Nancy' lamium, glossy violet leaves, and golden barberry (*Berberis thunbergii* 'Aurea') paint a rich foliage portrait.

Lavandula

(lav-AN-djew-luh)
Lavender

Zones: 5–9
Height: 2 to 3 feet
Shape: Shrubby mounds with long flowerstalks
Color: Foliage gray; flowers purple, blue, pink, or white
Bloom time: Summer
Exposure: Sun to light shade
Soil: Average to rich, well-drained to dry

• Lavender isn't just for the herb garden—it's great with traditional perennials, too! Use it to edge a border or in masses as an accent.

• Create a fragrant garden by grouping lavender with roses, pinks (*Dianthus* spp.), oriental lilies, yarrow, and artemisia.

• For an icy-cool color combination, try a planting of lavender, lamb's-ears (*Stachys byzantina*), and sea hollies (*Eryngium* spp.) or globe thistle (*Echinops ritro*).

• The "evergray" foliage may look a little tired in winter. However, you may not want to cut it back because it will still release its unforgettable summer scent when you brush against or rub the leaves.

• It's hard to have too much lavender. To make more plants, take stem cuttings from side shoots in summer.

Lavender flowers, silvery artemisia leaves, and bluish green rue (*Ruta graveolens*) are perfect fragrant companions for edging a walkway.

Liatris

(lee-AH-tris)
Gayfeather, Blazing-
star

Zones: 3–9
Height: 6 inches to 3 feet
Shape: Clumps of upright flower-stalks
Color: Purple, pink, or white
Bloom time: Summer
Exposure: Sun
Soil: Average to rich, well-drained

• There's nothing like gayfeathers for adding zip to summer beds and borders. Their upright, fuzzy flower spikes are unmistakable.

• Gayfeathers are a natural choice for meadow gardens and prairie plantings; they're favorites with butterflies, too!

• Pick up the pinkish purple color with purple cone-flowers (*Echinacea purpurea*), then tone it down with silvery lamb's-ears (*Stachys byzantina*) and artemisias, or jazz it up with yellow yarrow and coreopsis.

• Don't forget to include a few plants in the cutting garden; they're great for arrangements.

• Leave gayfeathers alone to form large clumps, or divide them in fall for propagation.

Pair pink spike gayfeather (*L. spicata*) with yellow coneflower (*Rudbeckia* sp.) for a floral version of exploding fireworks.

Ligularia

(lig-you-LAIR-ee-uh)
Ligularia, Golden-
ray, Groundsel

Zones: 3–10
Height: 18 inches to 6 feet
Shape: Mounds of bold leaves with tall flower spikes
Color: Yellow, orange
Bloom time: Summer
Exposure: Partial shade
Soil: Rich, continuously moist

• There's nothing delicate about ligularias. Give them moist soil and room to spread, and they'll form big, bold clumps of broad leaves and bright flowers.

• Grow ligularias in bor-

The spectacular flower spikes of 'The Rocket' ligularia echo the form of the green fronds of lady fern (*Athyrium filix-femina*).

ders, in bog gardens, or along streams with other moisture lovers such as meadowsweets (*Filipendula* spp.), astilbes, large-leaved hostas, and irises. Tall ferns, such as ostrich fern (*Matteuccia struthiopteris*) and royal fern (*Osmunda regalis*), are also excellent companions.

• 'Desdemona', a cultivar of *L. dentata,* produces rounded leaves that are reddish purple when young; the leaves age to deep green with deep purple undersides and stems. Glowing orange-yellow daisies bloom in late summer.

• For propagation, divide plants in spring or fall.

Lilium

(LILL-*ee*-um)

Lily

Zones: 2–9
Height: 1 to 7 feet
Shape: Tall, slender stalks topped with a cluster of flowers
Color: White, yellow, orange, red, or pink
Bloom time: Spring, summer
Exposure: Sun to partial shade
Soil: Average, well-drained

'Enchantment' hybrid lily at left and tawny daylily (*Hemerocallis fulva*) at right make a great orange pair.

- For late-summer flowers and fragrance, try pink-and-white Japanese lilies (*L. speciosum* var. *rubrum*) or oriental hybrids, such as pure white 'Casa Blanca' or white-and-yellow 'Platyphyllum'.
- Midsummer regal lilies (*L. regale*) are also scented and sensational. Try them with pink flowers or purplish leaves (such as *Heuchera* 'Palace Purple') to complement the purple-blushed buds; yellow-flowered companions can accent the flower's yellow throat.
- Plant lilies with baby's-breath, hostas, asters, and other bushy perennials that will hide the base of the lily stems.
- Many lilies produce small, dark "minibulbs" along their stem. Remove these and plant them; they'll bloom in a few years.

Linum

(LIE-num)

Flax

Zones: 3–9
Height: 1 to 2 feet
Shape: Open clumps of wiry stems tipped with flowers
Color: Blue, yellow
Bloom time: Summer
Exposure: Sun to light shade
Soil: Average, well-drained to dry

- Blue flax (*L. perenne*) has delicate-looking leaves and flowers, adding a casual, airy touch to border plantings from late spring to midsummer.

For a meadow garden look on a hot, dry site, interplant blue flax and blanket flowers (*Gaillardia* sp.).

- Contrast fine-textured flax with bold leaves and flowers, such as lilies, daylilies, bearded irises, and yuccas (*Yucca* spp.).
- The soft blue flowers look lovely against silvery foliage, such as lamb's-ears (*Stachys byzantina*) and artemisia.
- Flax forms hazy mounds that are great for softening hard edges along paths, driveways, walls, and steps.
- For propagation, take stem cuttings in early summer, divide plants in spring or fall, or transplant self-sown seedlings.

Liriope

(lih-RYE-oh-pea)
Lilyturf

Zones: 5–9
Height: 12 to 18 inches
Shape: Tufted mounds with short flowerspikes
Color: Purple, blue, or white
Bloom time: Spring
Exposure: Sun to shade
Soil: Average to rich, well-drained to dry

• Lilyturf adds a neat grasslike texture to perennial plantings in sun or shade.

• Use blue lilyturf (*L. muscari*) to edge beds and borders or as a groundcover. The cream-edged leaves of 'Variegata' add extra excitement.

Smooth and shiny leaves of European wild ginger (*Asarum europaeum*) snuggled against the spiky foliage of variegated blue lilyturf are a compatible shade-loving couple.

• Creeping lilyturf (*L. spicata*) can quickly crowd out less agressive plants. Save it for a tough spot where other plants don't thrive, such as dry shade under trees.

• If lilyturf foliage looks tattered after a tough winter, mow the leaves to just above the soil; new foliage will form in spring.

• Divide clumps in spring or fall to control their spread or to get more plants.

For a rainforest feeling, group red cardinal flower, great blue lobelia, and annual common perilla (*Perilla frutescens*) foliage.

Lobelia

(low-BEE-lee-uh)
Lobelia

Zones: 2–9
Height: 2 to 4 feet
Shape: Erect spikes
Color: Red, purple, blue, white, or pink
Bloom time: Summer, fall
Exposure: Sun to partial shade
Soil: Rich, constantly moist

• Perennial lobelias produce tall, spiky flowers that look much different from their mounding annual cousins.

• The dazzling red bloom spikes of cardinal flower (*L. cardinalis*) add can't-miss color to moist-soil borders, meadows, and streamside plantings. Plus, hummingbirds like them!

• Great blue lobelia (*L. syphilitica*) has a more subtle sky-blue color that is easy to mix into beds and borders. Try it with daylilies, sneezeweeds (*Helenium* spp.), goldenrods (*Solidago* spp.), and ornamental grasses.

• Perennial lobelias tend to be short-lived, but they can produce many seedlings. (Remove the flower spikes after blooming if you want to prevent self-sowing.) Dividing clumps in early fall can help existing plants perform well for several seasons.

Lupinus

(lew-PIE-nus)

Lupine

Zones: 2–7
Height: 18 inches to 5 feet
Shape: Mounds of leaves with taller flower spikes
Color: White, pink, purple, blue, or red
Bloom time: Spring, summer
Exposure: Sun to light shade
Soil: Rich, moist but well-drained

• Lupines are a favorite for early-summer cottage gardens and perennial borders. They thrive in areas with cool summers and suffer in hot temperatures.

• Classic companions for lupines include bearded irises, peonies, and oriental poppies (*Papaver orientale*).

• Seed-grown lupines usually come in mixed colors. For single colors, look for cultivars such as pink-and-white 'The Chatelaine' and deep reddish 'My Castle'.

• Cut off spent flower spikes to promote possible rebloom, or let the seeds mature so plants can self-sow.

• For propagation, separate sideshoots from the clumps in fall. Or, if you don't mind mixed colors, sow seed in pots outdoors in late summer or indoors in winter. (Soaking the seed in warm water overnight can speed germination.)

Don't let groundcovers be boring. A stately purple lupine adds a wonderful accent in a planting of common periwinkle (*Vinca minor* 'Bowles Variety').

Lychnis

(LICK-nis)

Campion, Catchfly

Zones: 3–9
Height: 10 inches to 3 feet
Shape: Loose clumps
Color: Orange, red, pink, or white
Bloom time: Spring, summer
Exposure: Sun to partial shade
Soil: Average, well-drained to dry

• Love it or hate it—the magenta color of rose campion (*L. coronaria*) is definitely eye-catching. Its shocking blooms and subtle silver leaves and stems look great against green leaves. Or try them with silvery blue

The lavender blossoms of spiderwort (*Tradescantia* sp.) are a soothing foil for rose campion's eye-popping flowers.

globe thistles (*Echinops* spp.) or sea hollies (*Eryngium* spp.)

• If the bright flowers of the species aren't to your liking, choose the white-flowered cultivar 'Alba'.

• Maltese cross (*L. chalcedonica*) produces vivid scarlet flowers that are great for the back of the border. Yellow or white blooms can make cheerful companions.

• Both rose campion and Maltese cross self-sow freely. Cut off spent flowerheads, or allow the seeds to form if you want seedlings for transplanting.

Monarda

(mow-NAR-duh)

Bee balm, Bergamot

Zones: 3–9
Height: 1 to 4 feet
Shape: Spreading patches of upright stems
Color: Red, pink, white, purple, or yellow-green
Bloom time: Summer
Exposure: Sun to partial shade
Soil: Rich, moist

• Bee balm (*M. didyma*) isn't just for bees—it's popular with butterflies and hummingbirds, too. Try it in beds, borders, and meadow gardens.

Team up 'Gardenview Scarlet' bee balm and *Achillea ptarmica* 'The Pearl' to attract hummingbirds and butterflies.

• Wild bee balm usually blooms in bright red, but you can get other colors too. Look for white 'Snow Queen', light pink 'Beauty of Cobham', and purplish 'Violet Queen', among others.

• Many bee balms are prone to powdery mildew, a fungal disease that produces a dusty white coating on leaves and stems. Prevent powdery mildew problems by planting resistant cultivars, such as bright pink 'Marshall's Delight'.

• Divide clumps every 2 or 3 years in spring or fall to control their spread or for propagation.

Nepeta

(NEP-uh-tuh)

Catmint

Zones: 3–8
Height: 1 to 2 feet
Shape: Soft, sprawling mounds
Color: Blue, purple
Bloom time: Spring, early summer
Exposure: Sun to light shade
Soil: Average, well-drained

• Misty mounds of catmint make a marvelous edging for beds, borders, and paths.

• The silver-gray leaves and lavender-blue flowers look great with pale yellow 'Moonbeam' coreopsis (*Coreopsis verticillata* 'Moonbeam') and 'Moonshine'

For a free-spirited look, pair annual orange California poppies (*Eschscholzia californica*) with a sweep of Persian catmint (*N. mussinii*).

yarrow. Or go for the gold with bright yellow evening primroses (*Oenothera* spp.) and daylilies.

• 'Six Hills Giant' is a tall catmint (to 3 feet) that's ideal for the middle of the border.

• After the first flush of bloom, shear off the spent flowerheads to promote rebloom.

• For propagation, dig up and transplant rooted stems, or take stem cuttings in summer.

Oenothera

(ee-no-THEE-ruh)

Evening primrose, Sundrops

Zones: 3–8
Height: 4 inches to 3 feet
Shape: Varies among species
Color: Yellow, white, or pink
Bloom time: Spring, summer
Exposure: Sun
Soil: Average to rich, well-drained to dry

- Dependable, easy-care evening primroses add bold sweeps of sunny blooms to summer beds and borders.
- Yellow-flowered sundrops (*O. fruticosa* and *O. tetragona*) are terrific companions for yarrow, butterfly weed (*Asclepias tuberosa*), and globe thistle (*Echinops ritro*).
- With its soft pink flowers, showy evening primrose (*O. speciosa*) may look delicate, but it's not! It can spread rampantly. Give it a hot, dry site where it can spread to its heart's content, or be prepared to divide or thin plants each year to keep them in bounds.
- Lift clumps and separate the leafy rosettes in spring or fall to control their spread or expand your plantings.

Turn a hot, dry site into a breathtaking garden by planting glowing yellow sundrops next to Persian catmint (*Nepeta mussinii* 'Blue Wonder').

Hosta foliage and pink peonies make a pretty combination that's practical, too: The hostas serve as natural supports for the floppy peonies.

Paeonia

(pay-OHN-nee-uh)

Peony

Zones: 2–8
Height: 1 to 5 feet
Shape: Loose, flower-topped mounds
Color: White, pink, red, or yellow
Bloom time: Spring, early summer
Exposure: Sun to light shade
Soil: Rich, moist

- Peony flowers are so exquisite that you can forgive them for the briefness of their bloom. The rest of the season, their shrubby clumps of green foliage make a great background for other colorful perennials.
- The heavy blooms of double-flowered peonies tend to fall over, especially after rain. Support the stems with hoop stakes or stakes and string. Single-flowered types don't need staking.
- A row of peonies can make a glorious early-summer hedge. Mix several cultivars to extend the bloom season.
- Classic companions to peonies include irises, foxgloves (*Digitalis* spp.), and columbines (*Aquilegia* spp.).
- Peonies often grow happily for many years without division. But if blooms become sparse, divide the clumps in late summer or early fall. Be sure to leave several buds on each piece.

Papaver

(pa-PAH-ver)
Poppy

Zones: 2–7
Height: 1 to 3 feet
Shape: Loose clumps
Color: Orange, red, pink, white, or yellow
Bloom time: Spring, early summer
Exposure: Sun
Soil: Rich, well-drained

Delicate pink Oriental poppies go dormant quickly after flowering. Fill the gaps by interplanting long-blooming cranesbills (*Geranium* spp.) and perennial salvia (*Salvia* spp.).

- There's nothing subtle about the orange-scarlet, black-centered flowers of Oriental poppy (*P. orientale*). They're sure to catch your eye in any early summer planting.

- If you're looking for a softer, less strident color, choose a cultivar such as salmon-pink 'Helen Elizabeth' or silky pink 'Cedar Hill'.

- Bushy perennials that bloom after early summer, such as Russian sage (*Perovskia atriplicifolia*) and boltonia (*Boltonia asteroides*), make good companions for Oriental poppies.

- To propagate poppies or to rejuvenate crowded clumps, divide plants just as the new leaves emerge in late summer.

Perovskia

(per-OFF-skee-uh)
Russian sage

Zones: 4–9
Height: 3 to 5 feet
Shape: Airy, shrublike mound
Color: Blue
Bloom time: Summer
Exposure: Sun
Soil: Average, well-drained to dry

The breathtaking hazy flower spikes of Russian sage add life and movement spilling out over 'Carefree Wonder' shrub roses.

- Russian sage (*P. atriplicifolia*) adds a cool touch to the late-summer garden. This tough, trouble-free perennial laughs at heat, drought, and pests. Try it in masses for a low-maintenance landscape feature, or as an accent in borders and cottage gardens.

- Cut the woody stems of Russian sage down to about 1 foot in late fall or early spring to promote fresh new growth.

- Compatible companions include ornamental grasses, goldenrods (*Solidago* spp.), daylilies, and showy stonecrop (*Sedum spectabile*).

- Propagate Russian sage by taking stem cuttings in early summer.

Phlox

(FLOCKS)
Phlox

Zones: 2–9
Height: 4 inches to 4 feet
Shape: Varies among species
Color: White, pink, red, orange, purple, or blue
Bloom time: Spring, summer
Exposure: Sun to full shade
Soil: Varies among species

Garden phlox can be a centerpiece for a color-theme garden. Joe-Pye weed (*Eupatorium* sp.) rises behind the phlox, while pink astilbe waves soft plumes beside it. Annual impatiens adds a touch of hot pink in front.

• Garden phlox (*P. paniculata*) is a traditional favorite for borders. Its mounded flower clusters come in many colors and combine well with other summer bloomers.

• Wild blue phlox (*P. divaricata*) forms clumps of light blue spring flowers on 1-foot stems. Creeping phlox (*P. stolonifera*) is another spring bloomer and has pink, blue, or white flowers. Both have evergreen leaves and thrive in shade.

• For propagation, divide spring-flowering phlox after bloom; others in fall or spring.

The pink flower spikes in 'Vivid' obedient plant call out the pink highlights in the open blossoms of grape leaf anemone (*Anemone tomentosa* 'Robustissima').

Physostegia

(fie-so-STEE-gee-uh)
Obedient plant

Zones: 3–9
Height: 3 to 4 feet
Shape: Spreading clumps of upright flowerstalks
Color: Pink, purple, or white
Bloom time: Late summer
Exposure: Sun to partial shade
Soil: Average, moist

• The species *P. virginiana* is commonly known as obedient plant, even though it's anything but obedient! This vigorous, easy-care perennial spreads to form broad sweeps of spiky, rosy pink flowers in late summer.

• The spiky flowers of obedient plant look fabulous with ornamental grasses, asters, goldenrods (*Solidago* spp.), and Joe-Pye weeds (*Eupatorium* spp.).

• You can find several cultivars of obedient plant in catalogs. 'Vivid' is a popular cultivar with deep pink flowers on 2-foot stems. 'Summer Snow' has white flowers. 'Variegata' has cream-edged leaves and pink flowers.

• If you grow obedient plant in borders, divide it every 2 or 3 years in fall or spring to keep it in bounds. You can also propagate it by stem cuttings in early summer.

Platycodon

(plah-tee-KOE-don)
Balloon flower

Zones: 3–8
Height: 1 to 3 feet
Shape: Loose clumps
Color: Blue, pink, or white
Bloom time: Summer
Exposure: Sun to light shade
Soil: Average to rich, well-drained

• The unique, puffed-up buds of balloon flowers burst open to produce cupped, star-shaped blooms that combine well with many perennials. They look lovely with bright

Blue balloon flowers look soft and mysterious next to spiny dark pine needles.

or pastel flowers and green or silvery foliage plants.

• Balloon flower shoots appear late in spring. Be sure to mark their location to remind yourself not to dig there.

• Pinching off spent flowers can prolong the bloom season.

• Balloon flowers form long-lived clumps and prefer to be left undisturbed. If you want to propagate them, lift and divide the clumps in spring or early fall, digging deeply to get the roots. Or grow new plants by sowing seed outdoors in late summer or fall.

Polygonatum

(poe-lig-oh-NAY-tum)
Solomon's seal

Zones: 3–9
Height: 1 to 3 feet
Shape: Arching stems with dangling flowers
Color: Leaves green or varigated; flowers white
Bloom time: Spring
Exposure: Partial to full shade
Soil: Rich, moist

• Solomon's seals add a graceful, arching accent to shady gardens. Bell-shaped flowers dangle from the

stems in spring, followed by dark blue-black berries in summer. The foliage turns a showy yellow-brown in fall.

The arching branches of Solomon's seal behind the delicate curves of maidenhair fern (*Adiantum pedatum*) create a serene shade garden, while hostas round out the scene.

• Hostas, ferns, wild gingers (*Asarum* spp.), lamiums (*Lamium* spp.), and other shade lovers are ideal companions.

• Brighten up a dreary corner with variegated fragrant Solomon's seal (*P. odoratum* 'Variegatum').

• In evenly moist soil, the stems of Great Solomon's seal (*P. commutatum*) can grow up to 6 feet tall.

• To propagate, divide the branching rhizomes in spring or fall.

Primula

(PRIM-you-luh)

Primrose

Zones: 2–8
Height: 2 inches to 2 feet
Shape: Rosettes of leaves, taller flowering stems
Color: Yellow, white, pink, purple, or red
Bloom time: Spring, early summer
Exposure: Sun to partial shade
Soil: Rich, moist

• Perky primroses are among the first flowers to bloom in spring. They are charming in beds, borders, woodlands, and wet areas.

• Japanese primroses

Blue forget-me-not flowers repeat the starry shape of the yellow centers of polyanthus primroses.

(*P. japonica*) just love a spot with dependably damp soil. They'll re-

seed to produce sweeps of leafy rosettes topped with rose, pink, or white flowers.

• Polyanthus primroses (*P. × polyantha*) bloom in lots of colors. Many have more than one color in each flower. Try them with tulips for a bright spring show.

• Fragrant cowslip primrose (*P. veris*) produces dainty yellow, orange, or reddish blooms. It looks great with daffodils, hellebores (*Helleborus* spp.), and lungworts (*Pulmonaria* spp.).

• Divide clumps after flowering to relieve overcrowding or to expand your plantings.

Pulmonaria

(puhl-muhn-AIR-ee-uh)

Lungwort, Bethlehem sage

Zones: 2–8
Height: 9 inches to 2 feet
Shape: Loose clumps
Color: Leaves green or variegated; flowers pink, blue, red, or white
Bloom time: Spring
Exposure: Partial to full shade
Soil: Rich, moist

• The showy, silver-spotted leaves are reason enough to love lung-

worts. But lungworts also produce pretty spring flowers.

• 'Mrs. Moon' is an excellent broad-leaved cultivar of

Spotted Bethlehem sage and glossy European wild ginger (*Asarum europaeum*) make a rich foliage combination for moist shade.

Bethlehem sage (*P. saccharata*). Its flowers open pink and turn blue as they age. 'Sissinghurst White' has white flowers.

• Planted singly as accents or in groups, lungworts brighten up shady spots under trees and shrubs.

• Combine lungworts with colorful spring-flowering bulbs, bleeding hearts (*Dicentra* spp.), hellebores (*Helleborus* spp.), and hostas.

• Divide plants in fall to rejuvenate crowded clumps or for propagation.

137

Rudbeckia

(ruhd-BECK-ee-uh)
Coneflower, Black-
eyed Susan

Zones: 3–9
Height: 18 inches to 6 feet
Shape: Broad clumps of stiff, branched stalks
Color: Orange, yellow
Bloom time: Summer
Exposure: Sun to light shade
Soil: Average to rich, moist but well-drained

• Nothing says summer like the bright blooms of coneflowers. These tough plants are invaluable for beds, borders, and meadow gardens and perfect combined with grasses, gayfeathers (*Liatris* spp.), and purple coneflowers (*Echinacea purpurea*).

• 'Goldsturm', a cultivar of *R. fulgida*, is a widely planted selection. Its orange-yellow, dark-centered daisies bloom on 2-foot stems.

• For a different look, try 'Herbstsonne', a cultivar of shining coneflower (*R. nitida*). It has bright yellow, green-centered daisies on 6-foot stems and makes an ideal back-of-the-border plant.

• Pinch off spent flowers to promote rebloom, or let the seed-

'Goldsturm' black-eyed Susan looks stunning next to ornamental grasses like blue oat grass (*Helictotrichon sempervirens*).

heads form for winter interest.

• Divide clumps in spring for propagation, or dig up self-sown seedlings.

Salvia

(SAL-vee-uh)
Salvia, Sage

Zones: 3–10
Height: 1 to 4 feet
Shape: Mounded to shrubby
Color: Blue, purple, red, or pink
Bloom time: Summer, fall
Exposure: Sun to light shade
Soil: Average, well-drained to dry

• Spiky salvias are super mid-border or edging plants for sunny plantings. Their upright habit contrasts beautifully with mounded plants, such as cranesbills (*Geranium* spp.) and threadleaf coreopsis (*Coreopsis verticillata*).

• Violet sage (*S.* × *superba*)

Create contrasts of color and form by showcasing 'East Friesland' violet sage between pale 'Moonshine' and bright 'Coronation Gold' yarrows.

has several popular cultivars. 'Blue Queen' offers violet flowers on 2-foot stems. 'Rose Queen' has rosy pink flowers.

• 'Purple Rain', a cultivar of *S. verticillata*, has long spikes of reddish purple blooms over compact mounds of silvery green leaves through most of the summer.

• Cutting the spent flower stems off your salvias can promote a second flush of bloom in late summer.

• Divide overgrown clumps in fall or early spring. Division is also an effective method for propagation, as is taking stem cuttings in early summer.

Scabiosa

(scab-ee-OH-suh)
Scabious,
Pincushion flower

Zones: 3–7
Height: 18 inches to 2 feet
Shape: Clumps with long flower stems
Color: Blue, pink, white
Bloom time: Summer
Exposure: Sun to light shade
Soil: Rich, well-drained to dry

• Pincushion flower (*S. caucasica*) has a quaint, old-fashioned look that is charming in cottage gardens and informal borders. The blooms are also excellent for cutting.

Blue pincushion flowers and yellow heliopsis make a great pair, both in the garden and as cut flowers for indoor arrangements.

lilac-blue flowers on 1-foot stems. 'Pink Mist' has a similar habit with rose-pink blooms. Both are great at the front of the border and in containers.

• Daylilies, yarrows, and coreopsis (*Coreopsis* spp.) all make wonderful summer companions for pincushion flower.

• Removing the spent flowers at the base of the stem will keep the plants looking neat and encourage repeat bloom.

• 'Butterfly Blue' is a long-blooming selection with lacy,

• Divide crowded clumps as needed in spring.

Sedum

(SEE-dum)
Sedum, Stonecrop

Zones: 3–9
Height: 2 inches to 2 feet
Shape: Spreading mats to upright clumps
Color: Leaves green, red, yellow, or silver; flowers yellow, pink, or white
Bloom time: Spring, summer
Exposure: Sun to partial shade
Soil: Average, well-drained to dry

• Sedums come in many shapes and sizes, providing interesting foliage and showy flowers with little or no fuss.

• 'Autumn Joy' is a popular hybrid that looks great in several seasons. Its neat mounds of succulent stems and leaves are

'Ruby Glow' sedum and the wispy leaves of cottage pinks (*Dianthus plumarius*) are a study in color harmony and contrasting shape.

topped in late summer with green buds that open to reddish pink flowers. The flowerheads hold their shape well into winter.

• 'Vera Jameson' is a cultivar with blue or purplish leaves that add interest to a garden in spring.

• 'Dragon's Blood', a cultivar of *S. spurium*, forms mats of red-tinted leaves topped with flat clusters of rose-red flowers in summer.

• Sedums are easy to propagate. Divide them in spring or fall, or take cuttings in summer.

Solidago

(sole-ih-DAY-go)
Goldenrod

Zones: 3–9
Height: 1 to 5 feet
Shape: Clumps of upright stalks
Color: Yellow
Bloom time: Summer, fall
Exposure: Sun
Soil: Average, moist but well-drained

'Crown of Rays' goldenrod and daisylike *Aster* × *frikartii* 'Monch' offer joyful colors in a sunny fall garden.

- Goldenrods are easy-care perennials that look as good in beds and borders as they do in meadows and wild areas.
- 'Golden Fleece' dwarf goldenrod is a compact, free-blooming selection of *S. sphacelata* that makes a great ground-cover or edging.
- Group goldenrods with asters, coneflowers (*Echinacea* and *Rudbeckia* spp.), Joe-Pye weeds (*Eupatorium* spp.), and grasses.
- Don't hold goldenrods responsible for your fall hay fever; they are mistakenly blamed for the irritating pollen that's produced by ragweed.
- For propagation, divide plants in spring.

Stachys

(STAY-kiss)
Lamb's-ears, Betony

Zones: 2–8
Height: 6 inches to 2 feet
Shape: Spreading mats with upright flower stems
Color: Leaves green, silver; flowers purple, pink, white
Bloom time: Spring, summer
Exposure: Sun to light shade
Soil: Varies among species

- The soft, fuzzy leaves of lamb's-ears just beg to be touched. Try them along a path where you'll brush by them frequently.
- Lamb's-ears are ideal for the front of the border or herb garden. The silver-gray foliage and flower spikes are a perfect complement to green leaves and both bright- and soft-colored flowers.

'Autumn Joy' sedum between *Phlox paniculata* 'Bright Eyes' and silver-gray lamb's-ears create an effective combination.

- In hot, humid conditions, the leaves may die back due to rot. If this happens, cut the leaves and stems to the ground; new foliage should sprout when things cool off. The cultivar 'Helen von Stein' is less prone to rot.
- Cut the flower stems to the ground after bloom to keep plants looking neat.
- Lamb's-ears will spread quickly in ideal conditions. Divide clumps in fall to control their spread or for propagation.

Tiarella

(tee-uh-REL-uh)
Foamflower

Zones: 3–8
Height: 6 to 10 inches
Shape: Spreading mat with taller flower clusters
Color: White, pink
Bloom time: Spring
Exposure: Partial to full shade
Soil: Rich, moist

• Foamflowers are favorites for shady borders and woodland gardens, and make great groundcovers under trees and shrubs.

• Two similar selections are

White Allegheny foamflower between 'Francee' hosta and woolly blue violet (*Viola sororia*) forms a lovely trio for a woodland garden.

Allegheny foamflower (*T. cordifolia*) and Wherry's foamflower (*T. wherryi*). Both have fuzzy, heart-shaped leaves and brushy spikes of white to pale pink flowers.

• Allegheny foamflower grows from long, leafy runners. It spreads fairly quickly but is rarely considered invasive.

• Group foamflowers with shade lovers such as hostas, epimediums (*Epimedium* spp.), Solomon's seals (*Polygonatum* spp.), and lamium (*Lamium maculatum*).

• For propagation, dig up rooted runners or divide plants in fall or spring.

Tradescantia

(trad-es-KANT-ee-uh)
Spiderwort

Zones: 3–9
Height: 1 to 3 feet
Shape: Clumps of arching, grasslike leaves
Color: Purple, pink, white, or blue
Bloom time: Late spring, early summer
Exposure: Sun to partial shade
Soil: Average to rich, moist but well-drained

• Spiderworts are interesting accents for the late spring garden. Each spiderwort bloom lasts one day (or less in hot weather), but the plants produce many buds and can bloom for as long as several weeks.

• After flowering, spiderworts can look fairly shabby. Cut them to the ground for a fresh batch of foliage.

• Common spiderwort (*T.* × *andersoniana*) is the kind most commonly grown in gardens. Several cultivars of common spiderwort are available, including white 'Snowcap', reddish pink 'Red Cloud', and pale blue 'James C. Weguelin'.

• Spiderwort blossoms look best in informal areas, paired with hostas, columbines (*Aquilegia* spp.), drumstick primroses (*Primula denticulata*), and other perennials.

• For propagation, divide plants in spring.

'Red Cloud' spiderwort and ferns mingle happily in moist, shady conditions.

141

Silky lamb's-ears repeat the color and texture of towering mullein flower spikes.

Verbascum

(ver-BASS-kum)
Mullein

Zones: 4–8
Height: 2 to 5 feet
Shape: Rosette of leaves with tall flower spikes
Color: Yellow or white
Bloom time: Summer
Exposure: Sun
Soil: Average, well-drained to dry

• Majestic mulleins make a dramatic statement in the summer perennial garden.

• Nettle-leaved mullein (*V. chaixii*) has broad green leaves and 3-foot spikes of purple-centered, yellow flowers. 'Album' is similar but has white petals.

• Olympic mullein (*V. olympicum*) forms gorgeous rosettes of fuzzy silver leaves. Their branched spikes rise up to 6 feet tall, with yellow flowers.

• Cut off the first flower spike of the season when it's done blooming to promote flowering sideshoots. Let the sideshoots mature to set seed.

• Mulleins look great with ornamental grasses and many perennials, including daylilies, yarrows, and cranesbills (*Geranium* spp.).

• Mulleins tend to be short-lived perennials. For propagation, dig up and transplant the self-sown seedlings.

Verbena

(ver-BEAN-uh)
Verbena, Vervain

Zones: 4–10
Height: 4 inches to 5 feet
Shape: Varies among species
Color: Pink, purple, white, or blue
Bloom time: Summer
Exposure: Sun to light shade
Soil: Average, well-drained to dry

• Bright-flowered verbenas are invaluable for summer beds and borders. Use tall types as accents and short types as edgings.

• These tough plants take heat and drought in their stride, and they bloom dependably through the summer. Good companions include artemisias, ornamental grasses, mulleins (*Verbascum* spp.), and coreopsis (*Coreopsis* spp.).

• Brazilian vervain (*V. bonariensis*) produces 3- to 4-foot slender stems topped with small clusters of purplish pink flowers. It usually only overwinters in Zones 7–10, but it will reseed itself in cooler areas.

• Rose verbena (*V. canadensis*) is hardier (usually Zones 5–10) and shorter (12 to 18 inches), with pink flowers. Shearing off the spent flowerheads in mid- to late summer can extend the bloom season.

• Verbenas are easy to propagate by stem cuttings in summer.

Rose verbena looks cheery peeking out from under the drooping seedheads of fountain grass (*Pennisetum alopecuroides*).

Veronica

(ver-ON-ih-kuh)
Speedwell

Zones: 3–8
Height: 4 inches to 6 feet
Shape: Varies among species
Color: White, pink, purple or blue
Bloom time: Spring, summer
Exposure: Sun to light shade
Soil: Average to rich, moist but well-drained

• Compact and practically care-free, speedwells are dependable, long-blooming perennials that are perfect for beds, borders, and rock gardens.

• Spike speedwell (*V. spicata*) forms spreading, 1- to 3-foot

Spiky *Veronica grandis* 'Blue Charm' and purple coneflowers are a super duo for a sunny garden.

clumps that make great edging or accent plants. The species has thin, blue flower spikes. 'Minuet' offers soft pink blooms; 'Red Fox' is a bright reddish pink.

• 'Sunny Border Blue' is a popular hybrid that produces deep violet-blue flower spikes from summer to frost.

• Almost any plant looks good with speedwells. They combine well with virtually every flower form and color.

• Pinch off spent flower spikes to keep plants blooming.

• For propagation, divide plants in spring or fall or take stem cuttings in summer.

Yucca

(YUK-uh)
Yucca, Adam's-
needle

Zones: 3–10
Height: 4 to 15 feet
Shape: Spiky mounds with tall flowerstalks
Color: White
Bloom time: Summer
Exposure: Sun to light shade
Soil: Average, well-drained to dry

• The fabulous form of yuccas makes an unforgettable accent in the perennial garden. The large rosettes of sword-shaped evergreen leaves are dramatic, even without the

Emphasize the swordlike quality of Adam's-needle (*Y. filamentosa*) by surrounding it with delicate plants such as white rock cress (*Arabis* sp.) and moss pinks (*Phlox subulata*).

addition of the tall, showy spikes of white blooms in summer.

• Yuccas are ideal companions for big, bright flowers, including yarrows, daylilies, and

coneflowers (*Echinacea* and *Rudbeckia* spp.).

• Most yucca leaves are silvery green. For extra excitement, try cream- or yellow-striped 'Color Guard' or 'Gold Sword' cultivars.

• Contrast the bold foliage with lacy-leaved perennials, such as rose verbena (*Verbena canadensis*), cranesbills (*Geranium* spp.), and threadleaf coreopsis (*Coreopsis verticillata*).

• For propagation, separate rooted offsets from the main clumps in spring or fall.

75 Classic Perennials at a Glance

Plant name	Flower Color	Height	Bloom Time	Exposure	Soil	Zones
Achillea		1'–4'	Late spring, summer	Sun to partial shade	Average to poor	3–9
Ajuga		4"–12"	Late spring, early summer	Sun to full shade	Average, well-drained	3–9
Alchemilla		6"–12"	Spring, early summer	Sun to partial shade	Rich, moist	3–8
Allium		6"–5'	Spring, summer, fall	Sun	Average to rich, well-drained to dry	3–9
Anemone		4"–5'	Spring, summer, fall	Sun to shade	Varies widely among species	3–9
Aquilegia		6"–4'	Spring, early summer	Sun to partial shade	Average to rich, moist but well-drained	3–9
Artemisia		10"–6'	Summer, fall	Sun	Average, well-drained	3–9
Asclepias		1'–5'	Summer	Sun to light shade	Average, moist to dry	3–9
Aster		6"–8'	Summer, fall	Sun to partial shade	Varies widely among species	2–8
Astilbe		8"–5'	Late spring, summer	Sun to shade	Average, moist but well-drained	3–9
Aurinia		10"–12"	Spring	Sun	Average, well-drained	3–7
Baptisia		1'–5'	Late spring, early summer	Sun to light shade	Rich, moist but well-drained	3–9
Bergenia		1'–2'	Early spring	Sun to partial shade	Rich, moist	3–9
Boltonia		4'–6'	Late summer, fall	Sun to light shade	Rich, moist to dry	3–9
Campanula		4"–5'	Spring, summer	Sun to partial shade	Average to rich, well-drained	2–8
Chrysanthemum		1'–5'	Summer, fall	Sun	Average to rich, well-drained	3–11
Cimicifuga		2'–7'	Summer, fall	Sun to partial shade	Rich, moist	3–8
Coreopsis		1'–9'	Late spring, summer	Sun	Average to rich, moist to dry	3–9

Plant name	Flower Color	Height	Bloom Time	Exposure	Soil	Zones
Delphinium		1'–6'	Late spring, summer; fall re-bloom	Sun	Rich, moist	3–8
Dianthus		3"–2'	Spring, summer	Sun to light shade	Average, moist to dry	3–9
Dicentra		8"–2½'	Spring, summer	Sun to full shade	Rich, moist	2–9
Digitalis		2'–5'	Summer	Sun to partial shade	Rich, moist	3–8
Echinacea		1'–6'	Summer	Sun	Average, moist to dry	2–8
Epimedium		6"–15"	Spring	Partial to full shade	Average to rich, moist to dry	3–8
Eryngium		1'–6'	Summer, fall	Sun	Average, well-drained	2–9
Eupatorium		2'–14'	Summer, fall	Sun	Average to rich, moist	2–10
Euphorbia		6"–4'	Spring, summer	Sun to partial shade	Average to rich, well-drained to dry	3–9
Filipendula		2'–6'	Late spring, summer	Sun to partial shade	Rich, moist	3–9
Gaillardia		2'–3'	Summer	Sun	Average, well-drained to dry	2–10
Geranium		4"–4'	Spring, early summer	Sun to partial shade	Rich, moist but well-drained	3–8
Gypsophila		4"–4'	Summer	Sun to light shade	Rich, moist but well-drained	3–9
Helenium		2'–5'	Late summer, fall	Sun	Rich, moist	3–9
Heliopsis		3'–6'	Summer	Sun to partial shade	Average to rich, moist to dry	3–9
Helleborus		10"–2'	Winter, spring	Partial shade	Rich, moist but well-drained	3–9
Hemerocallis		1'–6'	Spring, summer	Sun to partial shade	Average to rich, well-drained to dry	2–9
Heuchera		1'–3'	Spring, summer	Sun to partial shade	Rich, moist but well-drained	3–9
Hibiscus		4'–8'	Summer	Sun to light shade	Rich, moist	4–10

(continued)

75 Classic Perennials at a Glance—Continued

Plant name	Flower Color	Height	Bloom Time	Exposure	Soil	Zones
Hosta		6"–3'	Summer to fall	Light to full shade	Average to rich, moist	3–8
Iberis		3"–12"	Early spring	Sun to light shade	Average, well-drained	2–9
Iris		4"–4'	Spring, Summer	Sun to light shade	Varies widely among species	2–10
Kniphofia		3'–5'	Late spring, summer	Sun	Rich, well-drained	5–9
Lamium		6"–12"	Spring, summer	Partial to full shade	Rich, moist but well-drained	3–8
Lavandula		2'–3'	Summer	Sun to light shade	Average to rich, well-drained to dry	5–9
Liatris		6"–3'	Summer	Sun	Average to rich, well-drained	3–9
Ligularia		18"–6'	Summer	Partial shade	Rich, continuously moist	3–10
Lilium		1'–7'	Spring, summer	Sun to partial shade	Average, well-drained	2–9
Linum		1'–2'	Summer	Sun to light shade	Average, well-drained to dry	3–9
Liriope		12"–18"	Spring	Sun to shade	Average to rich, well-drained to dry	5–9
Lobelia		2'–4'	Summer, fall	Sun to partial shade	Rich, consistently moist	2–9
Lupinus		18"–5'	Spring, summer	Sun to light shade	Rich, moist but well-drained	2–7
Lychnis		10"–3'	Spring, summer	Sun to partial shade	Average, well-drained to dry	3–9
Monarda		1'–4'	Summer	Sun to partial shade	Rich, moist	3–9
Nepeta		1'–2'	Spring, early summer	Sun to light shade	Average, well-drained	3–8
Oenothera		4"–3'	Spring, summer	Sun	Average to rich, well-drained to dry	3–8
Paeonia		1'–5'	Spring, early summer	Sun to light shade	Rich, moist	2–8
Papaver		1'–3'	Spring, early summer	Sun	Rich, well-drained	2–7

Plant name	Flower Color	Height	Bloom Time	Exposure	Soil	Zones
Perovskia		3'–5'	Summer	Sun	Average, well-drained to dry	4–9
Phlox		4"–4'	Spring, summer	Sun to full shade	Varies among species	2–9
Physostegia		3'–4'	Late summer	Sun to partial shade	Average, moist	3–9
Platycodon		1'-3'	Summer	Sun to light shade	Average to rich, well-drained	3–8
Polygonatum		1'–3'	Spring	Partial to full shade	Rich, moist	3–9
Primula		2"–2'	Spring, early summer	Sun to partial shade	Rich, moist	2–8
Pulmonaria		9"–2'	Spring	Partial to full shade	Rich, moist	2–8
Rudbeckia		18"–6'	Summer	Sun to light shade	Average to rich, moist but well-drained	3–9
Salvia		1'–4'	Summer, fall	Sun to light shade	Average, well-drained to dry	3–10
Scabiosa		18"–2'	Summer	Sun to light shade	Rich, well-drained to dry	3–7
Sedum		2"–2'	Spring, summer	Sun to partial shade	Average, well-drained to dry	3–9
Solidago		1'–5'	Summer, fall	Sun	Average, moist but well-drained	3–9
Stachys		6"–2'	Spring, summer	Sun to light shade	Varies among species	2–8
Tiarella		6"–10"	Spring	Partial to full shade	Rich, moist	3–8
Tradescantia		1'–3'	Late spring, early summer	Sun to partial shade	Average to rich, moist but well-drained	3–9
Verbascum		2'-5'	Summer	Sun	Average, well-drained to dry	4–8
Verbena		4"–5'	Summer	Sun to light shade	Average, well-drained to dry	4–10
Veronica		4"-6'	Spring, summer	Sun to light shade	Average to rich, moist but well-drained	3–8
Yucca		4'-15'	Summer	Sun to light shade	Average, well-drained to dry	3–10

3 Creating Garden and Landscape Designs

by Barbara W. Ellis

What's the difference between gardening with perennials and landscaping with perennials? If you're an experienced gardener, you've probably planted perennials in several areas of your yard and have many ideas for planting still more perennials. Designing a perennial *landscape* may be as simple as taking inventory of your ideas, finding creative ways to combine them, and drawing a plan. In this section, you'll learn how to make an overall landscape plan for your yard, or just a part of your yard. You'll also learn how to design gardens from scratch using your own ideas and combinations. There's no formal training required! Just follow the simple steps through the process of getting to know your landscape, mapping out a plan, and designing fabulous perennial gardens.

Chapter 5

Dreaming and Discovering

Becoming Your Own Designer • Sizing Up Views • Evaluating

Your Yard • What's Your Style? • Putting Your Ideas Together

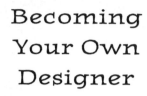

Becoming Your Own Designer

Is your yard exactly the way you'd like it to be? Few of us can answer that question with an unqualified "Yes!" Perhaps you live in a new development where the yards are 95 percent lawn. Or, if you live in an established neighborhood with plenty of gardens and shade trees, you probably have some landscape problems—especially in those shady spots.

If you'd like to improve your yard's appearance, you may want to try designing your own landscape plan. You may feel intimidated by the thought of creating your own design. It seems like a huge undertaking that requires special skills and training. But the truth is, you can easily improve your yard using some basic ideas and techniques that are also used by professional designers. Choose a project you can feel confident trying. You can give your whole yard a

face-lift, redesign the backyard only, or just redo the area around your patio.

Be creative. Whatever the scale of your project, you'll find that landscaping, especially with perennial flowers, is a great chance to be creative and have fun. Perennials can express your personality—your likes, dislikes, and style. For example, if you're a collector at heart, you'll aim to grow as many different plants as you can, not worrying about the fine points of design. Or, you may find that perennials bring out the artist in you. You'll thrive on plotting borders and rearranging plants to present an exquisitely planned garden picture every season of the year.

As with any creative process, there's more than one way to tackle designing a landscape project. If you're a natural organizer, you'll enjoy mapping your project and developing plant lists. If you're a spur-of-the-moment sort, you may never get the details on paper. But whatever your style, take some time

to read or browse through the process of developing a landscape plan presented here. You're sure to find tips and examples that will help you shape your ideas. Then take a walk and look at gardens. You'll find ideas for garden styles as well as plants that are well-adapted to your local climate. Take snapshots of appealing plantings—they'll be reminders when you're drawing up designs.

Trust yourself. As you develop ideas, remember that there are no wrong answers when it comes to landscaping with perennials, just different ones. Experiment! Grow plants that appeal to you. Don't worry too much about following rules. Talk to other gardeners and look at their gardens. Try to learn from their successes and failures. But above all, have fun.

Landscaping with perennials is guaranteed to add life and excitement to your yard. An average lawn can become a sweeping, flower-lined path that draws visitors to the house. ➤

Using Design Terms

A perennial garden isn't just one kind of garden. That's one of the things that makes them so fun and exciting to plant. But the terms used to describe the different categories of perennial gardens can be confusing. Understanding the terms is useful in developing landscape ideas, though, so it's worth your while to sort them out.

Mass plantings. Mass plantings are group plantings of a single kind of plant. Easy-care, low-maintenance plants are the

Perennial gardens don't have to be complicated to be attractive. In the right site, a mass planting of daylilies can be just as beautiful as a border filled with a vast array of plants.

Plant perennials in foundation beds close to the house, where you can enjoy them daily. If your foundation area is filled with shrubs, try creating a colorful flowerbed between the lawn and front walk.

Fill your perennial borders with masses of color if they'll be viewed from a distance. Daylilies, lamb's-ears (*Stachys* sp.), and lilies make a pleasing border combination.

best choice for mass plantings. For a low-maintenance garden on a sunny, dry site, masses of 'Autumn Joy' sedum, black-eyed Susans (*Rudbeckia* spp.), daylilies, or ornamental grasses would be spectacular.

Mixed plantings. Mixed plantings are a variety of plants growing together in one garden. They combine herbaceous perennials with trees, shrubs, vines, annuals, and other plants. They're a perfect choice for a site that needs year-round interest—they don't leave a bare expanse of ground in winter.

Perennial beds. A garden along a

An island bed of perennials planted under pines creates a charming figure eight of foliage and flowers. On the practical side, it eliminates the need for fussy mowing and trimming around the tree trunks.

patio or foundation or at the edge of the lawn is usually called a bed. Island beds are plantings—perennials alone, or a mixed planting—surrounded by a sea of lawn. Beds are designed to be seen from more than one side. Because beds are for viewing close up, plant them with perennials that have long flowering periods and attractive foliage.

Perennial borders. Borders are longer than beds and generally are planted along a fence or at the boundary of a yard. Borders can also edge one or both sides of a walk or driveway. They're usually designed to be seen from one side only. A garage, fence, or hedge behind a border provides an excellent backdrop. Masses of asters, 'Autumn Joy' sedum, chrysanthemums, daylilies, peonies, Siberian iris (*Iris sibirica*), and ornamental grasses all make fine plants for a sunny border.

The Possibilities of Perennials

Perennials make any yard a special place to be. Whether they're arranged in practical, low-maintenance plantings or jumbled together in cheerful confusion, perennials add color, fragrance, texture, and movement to the landscape. As shown in the sample landscape on this page, perennials are multipurpose plants that can reduce maintenance, create mystery, welcome visitors, attract wildlife, and much more. Keep the possibilities of perennials in mind as you launch your own plan for redesigning some or all of your property.

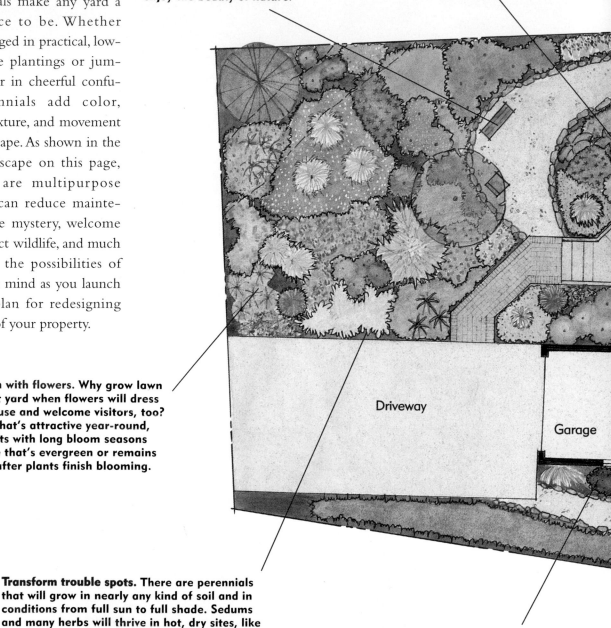

Create an outdoor retreat. A garden bench surrounded by perennials is a wonderful spot to relax, relieve stress, and enjoy the beauty of nature.

Add eye appeal. One of the best reasons to plant perennials is simply that they're beautiful. They'll add appeal to your yard whether they're planted in the lawn, around a patio, along a walkway, at the edge of your yard, or in front of a fence.

Driveway

Garage

Greet them with flowers. Why grow lawn in the front yard when flowers will dress up your house and welcome visitors, too? For a bed that's attractive year-round, mix in plants with long bloom seasons and foliage that's evergreen or remains attractive after plants finish blooming.

Transform trouble spots. There are perennials that will grow in nearly any kind of soil and in conditions from full sun to full shade. Sedums and many herbs will thrive in hot, dry sites, like the area along this paved driveway. Moisture-loving perennials like hostas, astilbes, and ferns will transform a wet site from an ugly quagmire into a garden.

Dress up ho-hum features. Surround an otherwise plain garage or edge dull-looking steps with cheerful perennials to dress up your landscape in one easy step.

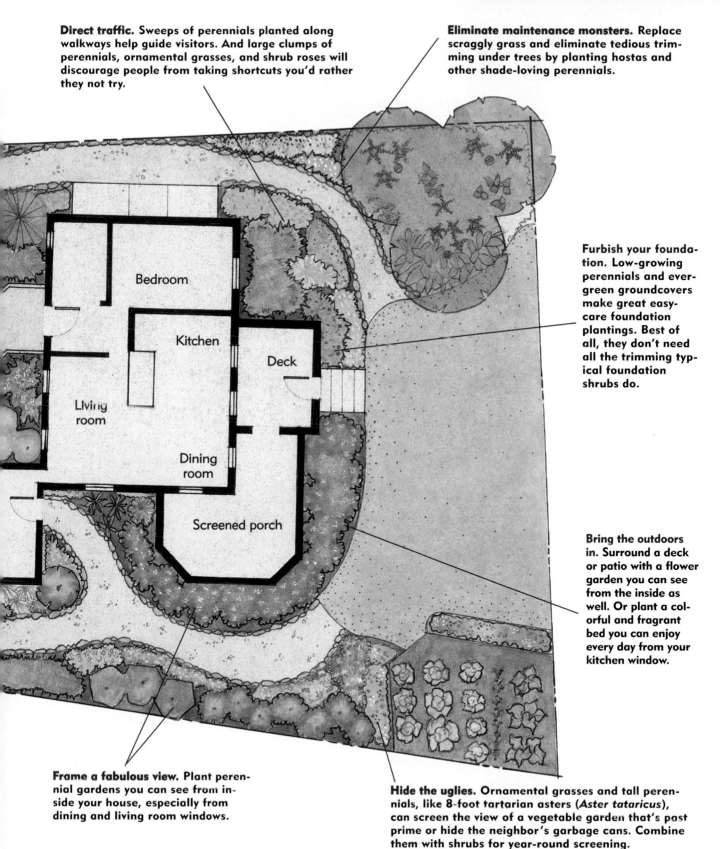

Direct traffic. Sweeps of perennials planted along walkways help guide visitors. And large clumps of perennials, ornamental grasses, and shrub roses will discourage people from taking shortcuts you'd rather they not try.

Eliminate maintenance monsters. Replace scraggly grass and eliminate tedious trimming under trees by planting hostas and other shade-loving perennials.

Furbish your foundation. Low-growing perennials and evergreen groundcovers make great easy-care foundation plantings. Best of all, they don't need all the trimming typical foundation shrubs do.

Bring the outdoors in. Surround a deck or patio with a flower garden you can see from the inside as well. Or plant a colorful and fragrant bed you can enjoy every day from your kitchen window.

Frame a fabulous view. Plant perennial gardens you can see from inside your house, especially from dining and living room windows.

Hide the uglies. Ornamental grasses and tall perennials, like 8-foot tartarian asters (*Aster tataricus*), can screen the view of a vegetable garden that's past prime or hide the neighbor's garbage cans. Combine them with shrubs for year-round screening.

Bedroom

Kitchen

Deck

Living room

Dining room

Screened porch

Design gardens that offer great window views in all four seasons. A perennial garden with a geometric layout will make a pleasing scene in fall and winter, too.

Sizing Up the Views

Imagine living in the middle of a garden. Flowers and foliage surround you. Patterns of sunlight and shadow play upon the ground, and pleasant fragrances waft by on the breezes. A flower-lined path leads off in one direction, beckoning you to follow it into a shady clump of trees. A glance in another direction reveals a bench surrounded by herbs and sun-loving perennials. Why not put your *house* in the middle of that garden?

All too often, we think of gardens as out in the yard somewhere—completely separate from the house. But the most satisfying home landscapes surround the house with the garden.

Think for a minute. How often do you look out your kitchen window? If it's 10 times a day, that's 3,600 times each year. What could be nicer than to see beautiful flowers outside every window? That's what putting your house in a garden means.

This isn't as difficult to accomplish as it might seem. Fortunately, you don't have to plant flowers on every square inch of your yard. You *will* need to spend some time thinking about the placement of your perennial plantings in relation to your house.

It's all too easy to make spur-of-the-moment choices and end up with flowerbeds scattered randomly around your yard. But for gardens that give maximum pleasure, begin by discovering what parts of your yard are visible when you're inside, looking outside. Once you know that, you can plant perennials to fill the spaces framed by your windows and create views that will put a smile on your face every time you see them.

Start Indoors

Gather up a pencil and a sketchbook or notebook, and spend a few minutes looking out each window of your home. Linger longer in front of windows that are most important to you—the kitchen or living room windows, perhaps.

Draw an outline of each room and indicate where the

Plan for "Face" Value

To give your house an appealing public face, take a look at it from the street, too. An effective design will add a neat, welcoming look to a house. It creates attractive views for your neighbors, and will delight you every time you return home. Here's an added bonus: Studies show that when you sell your home, you'll realize a return on investment of 100 to 200 percent on money spent on landscaping.

windows are. Make notes or pictures of what you see—flowerbeds, trees, the patio, the garbage cans, the neighbor's pool, a park across the street, mountains in the distance.

Next, write down your ideas for improving the view, or any other ideas that pop into your head. Would a cluster of shrubs make the patio seem cozier and more appealing? How about adding flowerbeds along a walkway? What about planting herbs and flowers under the window in the breakfast nook?

If trees and shrubs have obliterated the view from a window, try to look past them and think what you *might* see. If the window overlooks the neighbor's house or a busy street, you may want to leave things as they are. But if a shrub or tree branch blocks an otherwise beautiful view of your garden, consider doing some selective pruning to improve the view.

Check the Big Picture

After you've checked all your window views, go outside and look from your garden back to your house. Walk around the edges of your yard and follow paths you normally travel. Then, get off the beaten track so you have a fresh view of your house and the surrounding yard.

Again, jot down your ideas as you walk. Look at the "fit" between the house and the landscape. Is it a rambling, comfortable-looking house that seems surrounded by stiff, uncomfortable-looking plantings? Does the house look "plopped down" on the lot—a huge structure surrounded by scattered gardens that seem too small?

Don't worry about solving these problems now. We'll get to that in the coming chapters. For now, just record your impressions so you can refer to them later.

When you plan your landscape, create attractive views for your neighborhood, too. Purple coneflower (*Echinacea purpurea*) and lavender flower spikes of Russian sage (*Perovskia atriplicifolia*) highlight a pleasant scene for the neighbors to enjoy.

Evaluating Your Yard

What details of your yard can you picture in your mind's eye? Does it have walkways, raised beds, steps, or terraced slopes? How big are they and what do they look like? What are the problem spots that need improvement? These details are the foundation of your landscape. As you create your new landscape, you'll use perennials to improve these features and also to add new features.

If you're someone who thinks on paper, it's best to make a written site assessment of your yard's features. (Visual thinkers may do this more informally, with just a few jotted notes.) Taking snapshots is also a great way to record the features of your yard.

Take a tour of your front, back, and side yards. As you go, sketch your yard and make notes about what you have to work with. Your goal is to collect as much information as you can, and also to begin cooking up landscape ideas that might appeal to you. Use the list below to help you decide what to record.

Your house. Describe the exterior of your house from all angles. Include distinctive details, the style and mood of the architecture, and the materials the house is made of.

Perennials play a major role in taming trouble spots. Transform a rough, hard-to-mow slope by adding an attractive set of steps bordered by 'Goldsturm' black-eyed Susan, variegated sedge (*Carex* sp.), a creeping form of sedum, and annual sweet alyssum.

Solid features. These include walks, walls, fences, terraces, lampposts, decks, and outbuildings (such as sheds). Note the materials they're made of and the style or mood they suggest. Also make notes about whether their style seems compatible with your house.

Plants and gardens. Note the locations of individual large trees and shrubs, shrub borders, wooded areas, or foundation plantings. Also include the outlines of flower and vegetable gardens.

Utilities. Your design will need to accommodate underground cables, septic fields, and other utilities, so don't forget to record their approximate locations.

Water. Mark streams and ponds if you have them, as well as water spigots, rain barrels, or other water sources.

Traffic patterns. Formal walkways aren't the only traffic routes in your yard. Record unofficial paths as well—your route to the garage or compost pile, and the cut-through to the neighbor's yard. Make a note if paths need to accommodate a garden cart or wheelbarrow, and record areas where cars are occasionally parked or driven.

Shade and sun. Observe your yard at several times of day to see which parts are shady or sunny, and which receive sun or shade for only part of the day. (See "Success with Shady Sites" on page 58 for more information about sun and shade.)

Problem spots. Challenging sites like slopes, wet spots, rock outcrops, and areas with compacted soil will figure prominently in your design, so mark them down. For more on such sites, see "Get Personal with Problem Sites" on page 172.

But Do You Like It?

It's all too easy to get caught up in visual details—like walkways and lampposts—at this stage. After you've dealt with what you see, try to write down your *feelings* about your yard. What areas appeal to you? What are the eyesores you'd like to hide or redo?

You'll probably end up with a jumble of sketches and notes. Later on you'll sort them and figure out what you *really* have time and room to do. For now, dream happily, get to know your yard, and reach for as many ideas as you can imagine.

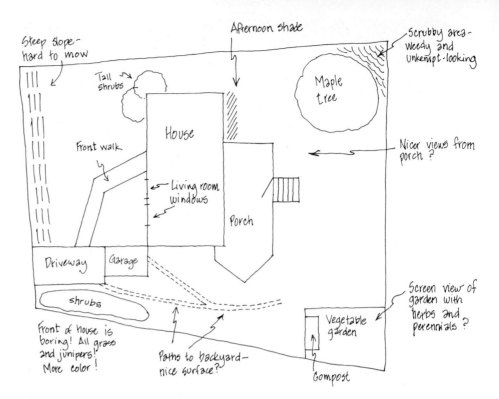

A rough sketch is a starting point in your journey from idle dreams to a detailed landscape plan. Be loose—don't worry about drawing to scale—and include questions and ideas as they come to mind.

Look for small, subtle opportunities to add beauty around your yard. Dalmatian bellflower (*Campanula portenschlagiana*) looks lovely entwined with yellow pansies and annual sweet alyssum in the crannies of stone steps.

If big, bold, and bright is your style, go ahead and express it in your garden. Try a riotous planting of hot-color perennials like scarlet poppies and bright yellow coreopsis.

What's Your Style?

Understanding your personal style—whether you are quiet and contemplative or exuberant and colorful, for example—is an enormously powerful design tool. It will help you figure out what you want and need in your garden, as well as what kinds of garden features *aren't* suited to your personality.

Think about the way you like to do everyday tasks such as setting the table or keeping house. The way you accomplish them can say a great deal about the kind of garden you'd enjoy most. For example, when you set a table, do you prefer the cheerful confusion of mismatched tableware, or the quiet simplicity of matched pieces? Your answer says something about whether you would feel more comfortable in a riotous cottage garden where flowers tumble over one another, or in an elegant formal garden with orderly beds of flowers.

Is your house comfortably "lived-in," or is it neat and or-derly, with everything in its place? The answer to this question will not only help you discover the right garden style for you, it may help you avoid main-tenance nightmares. For example, if you prefer the everything-in-its-place approach, a garden with bold, clean lines and wide, easy-to-maintain paths is probably a good choice. You'll also probably be less able to tolerate the sight of faded flowers, flopping stems, and scruffy foliage than someone who loves the lived-in look. To keep maintenance manageable, choose plants that need minimal deadheading, stand tall without staking, and remain attractive through the season.

Formal or Informal?

If you like well-organized flowerbeds in regular patterns, you prefer formal gardens. If fluid, free-form beds are more your style, informal gardens will appeal to you. Nearly all gardens are either formal or informal in style, although some use elements of both styles. Here are some characteristics that distinguish the two.

Formal style. Gardens with a formal style look peaceful and balanced. They feature rectangular, oval, or round beds; sheared, geometrically shaped hedges and evergreens; and stone, brick, concrete, or gravel walkways. Materials, shapes, or plantings—such as boxwood hedges—are repeated throughout the garden. You'll often see statues, sundials, and simple water features in formal gardens.

Informal style. Informal gardens are more dynamic and exciting to look at than formal ones. Natural, organic-looking shapes predominate. Instead of brick walkways, you'll see mulched paths and rustic features like split rail fences. And instead of matching beds of perennials,

In an informal garden (*right*), flowerbeds flow along the contours of the land or look like water pooling on the landscape. Formal gardens (*below*) have clear symmetry. Mirror-image plantings border a central walkway.

an informal garden might feature two free-flowing beds with unmatched mixtures of flowering shrubs and perennials.

Special Styles

The existing conditions in your yard will also influence the style of your gardens. Your yard may have a grove of mature trees that cries out to be underplanted with an informal garden of shade-loving hostas, wildflowers, and azaleas. Perhaps your yard already has some formal rectangular beds and clipped hedges. You may decide to add your personal touch by planting some of your favorite perennials in the existing gardens. Incorporating existing "hardscape," like brick pathways, is usually a good idea, too.

The style of your house can and should affect the landscape you plan. You'll be most satisfied if they harmonize with each other. For example, if you have a single-story ranch house, a large, free-spirited cottage garden filled with tall perennials could overwhelm the front yard. Or, if you have a home with period architecture—Colonial or Victorian, for example—you may want a garden that features plants from that era.

Regional style also can determine the kind of gardens you plant. Mediterranean-style gardens are classic California choices; an informal planting of

prairie plants might be a good Midwestern choice.

Here are some of the most popular special styles for American gardens.

Colonial style. This style can be quite formal, with boxwood hedges or knot gardens of clipped lavender cotton (*Santolina chamaecyparissus*). But Colonial gardens can also be informal mixed beds filled with herbs, like lavender and thyme, and old-fashioned flowers,

like cranesbills (*Geranium* spp.), peonies, pinks (*Dianthus* spp.), and violets.

Country style. Rustic and relaxed looking, country-style gardens are generally informal, although they may have formal features like square beds or weathered brick terraces. The plants are a joyful jumble: herbs, salad greens, and old-fashioned perennials like daisies, hollyhocks, irises, and peonies.

If you like sharp contrasts in your gardens, try a modern planting like blue fescue (*Festuca cinerea*) and Swiss mountain pine (*Pinus mugo*) paired with showy stonecrop (*Sedum spectabile*) and 'Ruby Glow' sedum.

Cottage style. Plants take center stage in a cottage garden. These informal, even wild-looking gardens feature old-fashioned perennials, like primroses (*Primula* spp.) and pinks (*Dianthus* spp.); fragrant roses and other flowering shrubs; herbs; and reseeding annuals like sweet alyssum. Narrow paths allow plants to be enjoyed up close.

Mediterranean style. Sunbaked terraces, fragrant herbs, and formal, rectangular pools are classic features of Mediterranean gardens. Shady sitting areas under trees, awnings, or umbrellas provide relief from the sun. Paved areas—and the containers that decorate them—often feature terra-cotta and various ceramics.

Modern style. Formal or informal in style, modern gardens feature bold, simple shapes and strong contrasts. Mass plantings create striking groups with different colors and textures, using plants such as ornamental grasses, yuccas, showy stonecrop (*Sedum spectabile*), and large-leaved hostas.

Natural landscapes. These informal gardens are inspired by nature's gardens. They feature plants that are native to the region—or at least look as if they are. Natural materials (native stone walls, for example) and areas designed to attract butterflies and other wildlife are also characteristic of natural landscapes.

Nature-loving gardeners will enjoy naturalistic plantings like a meadow garden filled with jubilant tall perennials (*above*), and a woodland garden that offers the mystery and tranquility of a forest (*below*).

163

Plant perennials to screen your vegetable garden from view. If you need to put your vegetable garden in the center of your yard to get full sun, surround it with a picket fence and fabulous perennial plantings.

Putting Your Ideas Together

You've probably discovered by now that you've gathered an exciting array of ideas for your landscape. You have views to improve, features to highlight and others to screen from sight, garden styles to try, and an impressive list of "must grow" perennials.

There are any number of ways to sort through your ideas. If you have a computer, you can type them all in and organize them with the stroke of a key— or move them around with a mouse, for that matter. If you're a

list maker, sheets of lined paper and a pencil may suffice. An easy, low-tech way to organize your ideas is to write them out on 3 × 5 cards.

Sort Your Ideas

Gather all your notes, sketches, and snapshots, and spread them out on a table. (An out-of-the-way spot where you

A single well-chosen bed of perennials can beautify your yard, attract butterflies, and screen out the street or other unwanted views.

164

A perennial border flanking a house and patio provides great views for cooks both inside and out, simplifies lawn maintenance, and adds a cheery face to the house.

can leave them for several days is ideal.) You'll also need a pack of 3 × 5 index cards and/or some lined paper, as well as a couple of sharp pencils. Depending on how fancy you want to get, colored pens, pencils, or markers may come in handy, too.

To turn the 3 × 5 cards into a handy system for sorting out all the ideas you've gathered, write each of your major ideas onto a card. Start with the ideas you came up with when checking views out windows and around your yard. If that's an overwhelming number of ideas, just make cards for the most important ones. For example, you may have imagined a mixed bed of perennials and flowering shrubs around the terrace in front of the living room window.

Next, make cards for each of the major features of your yard. You'll want ones on both good and bad features—major trees and shrubs, existing plantings, hardscape features like concrete walkways and walls, utility areas, and problem sites like slopes or wet spots.

Finally, look over your notes about the garden styles that appeal to you. Make a card for each type of individual garden and planting you'd like to have. For example, you may want an herb garden, a country garden, and a planting that attracts butterflies.

Now you have a neat stack of cards. Look through them and think about what you've missed. Ask yourself—and other family members—what you want and need your landscape to do. Nongardening family members will have definite opinions, too: You may need an area for playing ball, working on a car, or placing a swing set. Or you may want a spot for growing divisions of your great-aunt's peonies or a frog pond—make cards for them, too. (You also may want to use colored markers to color-code the different kinds of cards or to rank the importance of the ideas.)

Play the Garden Game

It's time to transform your ideas into garden projects. Have you already started to see links between your ideas? For example, would raised beds or terraces on the sunny slope turn it from a problem into the perfect spot for the herb garden you've always wanted? If so, put those cards together in a pile. Could you position the herb garden so it provides a pleasing view from

the kitchen window? If so, add that card to the pile, and so forth.

As you sort your cards, look for ways to combine different ideas into a single garden or planting. For example, many of us would love to have a perennial border, an herb garden, a rose garden, room for a peony collection, *and* a bird garden. But most of us don't have enough space or time to devote to so many different gardens. Try combining all those ideas: A perennial border

A perennial garden is a great low-maintenance alternative to struggling with scraggly lawn in a shady spot. Hostas and many other perennials thrive in shade and require little care.

easily could include herbs, low-maintenance shrub roses, the peony collection, and flowers that attract hummingbirds. Rosehips and seed from perennials and flowering shrubs would provide food for seed-eating birds; a birdbath or small rock-edged pool would provide water.

An island of perennials can create a private retreat in an otherwise open yard.

You'll have cards that don't fit easily into any of your piles. Some you'll have to discard. With others, you may just have to look for the best fit. If you want a private outdoor retreat but don't quite know where to put it, you may want to write "Outdoor retreat?" on several cards and put it into several of your piles to serve as a reminder that you want to include that feature.

When you finish, each pile represents a project to tackle. Keep the cards! When you get ready to design your bed or border, your pile of idea cards will help you decide what kinds of plants to include. Cards on views and problem spots in the same pile will remind you of important issues, such as the need to make your border visible from the living room and the path to the neighbor's yard that must be maintained.

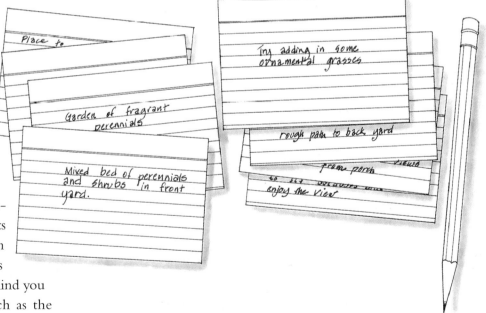

Use 3 × 5 cards as a simple but versatile tool for sorting and grouping your landscape ideas. You can arrange your cards in neat piles, toss them into heaps, or fan them out neatly so you can read each one.

167

Chapter 6

Mapping and Planning

Make a Working Map • Get Personal with Problem Sites •

Draw Your Dream Landscape • A Gallery of Landscape

Ideas • Prioritize Your Projects • Before You Plant

Make a Working Map

A working map of your yard will help you get from the *idea* stage of landscaping to the *doing* stage. You'll use your working map as the base sketch for drawing landscape plans, calculating how much space you have, determining how many plants you'll need to buy, and much more. Your map doesn't have to be an artistic accomplishment. Think of it as a picture of what you're starting with.

The first thing you need to do is gather materials: one standard and two colored pencils, a ruler, a clipboard, scrap paper, some large sheets of graph paper and tracing paper, and a compass.

If you have a survey map of your property, dig it out, too. You can draw your working map on a photocopy of the survey map, or just refer to it to draw the outline of your property. If you

don't have a survey map, you can locate your property corners as you make your map.

You'll also need something to measure with, such as a 100-foot measuring tape, along with a helper to hold one end. Or you can make a homemade measuring device fashioned from stakes, string, and tape. First, tie one end of a long (200 to 250 feet) piece of string to a stake. Then measure and mark 10- or 20-foot intervals along the string. Wrap the marked string around the stake and tie the free end to a second stake.

To use the measurer, stake it at the point you're measuring from, then stretch it to the feature you want to locate. Count up the marks along the string, multiply by your interval (10 or 20 feet), and that's the distance.

Next, make a list of features in your yard to include on your map. Include the property corners (unless you're using a

survey), existing plantings, and all other features, as shown in the illustration on the opposite page.

Step-by-Step Mapping

There's a simple mathematical technique that will help you draw an accurate map. It's called triangulation, and it's shown in the illustration on page 171. But before you start drawing, you must measure the distances to all the features on your list from a set of reference points. Here's what to do:

1. Sketch your property on a piece of scrap paper. Use this to record measurements.

2. Pick two reference points to measure from, such as the two corners on one side of your house. Measure the distance between the two reference points and write it on your sketch.

3. Circle each reference point with a different color pencil—

Pathways and doors. Draw in concrete or brick walkways and other paths that you commonly use.

Major trees and shrubs. Draw the spread of the branches of large trees. For mass plantings of shrubs, outline the entire planting and mark the main trunks.

Underground features. Record the locations of water mains, wells, gas lines, electric lines, underground tanks, and septic fields.

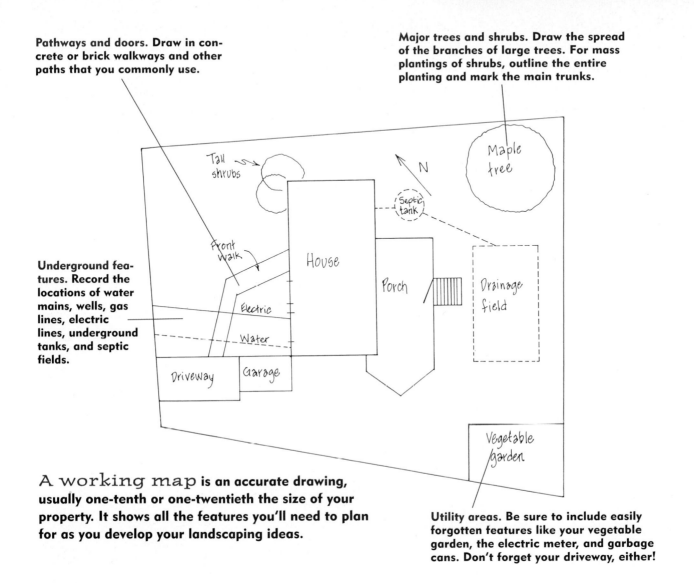

Tall shrubs

Maple tree

N

Septic tank

Front Walk

House

Porch

Drainage field

Electric

Water

Driveway

Garage

Vegetable garden

A working map **is an accurate drawing, usually one-tenth or one-twentieth the size of your property. It shows all the features you'll need to plan for as you develop your landscaping ideas.**

Utility areas. Be sure to include easily forgotten features like your vegetable garden, the electric meter, and garbage cans. Don't forget your driveway, either!

say red and blue. You'll record all the measurements made starting from the red reference point in red and from the blue reference point in blue (this will help you keep things straight later on when you're drawing your working map).

4. Measure the distance from one of your reference points to a feature on your property that you want to map, such as a tree or the corner of a peren-

nial border. (If you want to map the boundaries of your yard, the first measurements you should take are the distances from your reference points to the corners of your property.)

5. Measure the distance from the other reference point to the same feature. (Be sure you're using the right color pencil to record the distances!) Record these measurements either on your features list or on your

map, whichever is more helpful to you as you work.

6. Repeat steps 4 and 5 for all other important features in your yard.

7. Go inside and start drawing your map on graph paper. Choose your scale, and pencil in your reference points.

8. Using triangulation, mark the location of each feature you measured onto your map.

If your yard has lots of features to record, you may want to alternate measuring and mapping, plotting just three or four features at a time. Or if you're good at keeping notes and numbers organized, you may be able to do all your measuring in one outdoor session. Either way, work carefully because accuracy is the most important feature of a working map.

If you don't have a helper when you're measuring, try this variation on the technique. Pound in a stake at one reference point and attach your measuring string or tape to it. Then measure the distance between that reference point and several features, moving the free end of the tape or string from feature to feature. Then switch and measure from the other reference point to the same features.

You may need to pick new reference points when you switch from measuring your front yard to your backyard, or to map features that are unreachable from your first set of reference points.

You'll bring your personal style to the map you make. The

Measure and map major features like a wooded border *before* you set off to buy plants or bags of mulch. Otherwise, you'll play guessing games at the garden center and may run short of plants and materials.

Step 1. Select a scale. Here, 1 inch equals 20 feet.

Step 2. Set your compass. To draw a feature 50 feet away from the first reference point (Point 1), open the compass to 2½ inches. Holding the metal compass end on Point 1, draw an arc with the pencil end.

Step 3. Reset your compass to the new distance. Hold the metal compass end on the second reference point (Point 2) and draw another arc. The point where the two arcs cross locates the feature.

For large features like a perennial border or shed, you'll need to triangulate to more than one point of the feature.

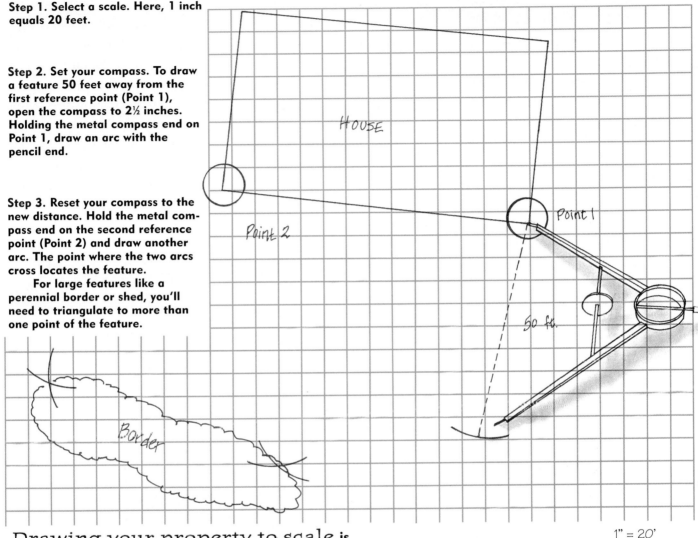

1" = 20'

Drawing your property to scale is easy when you use a simple geometric technique called **triangulation. With a compass, you'll mark the distance from two reference points to features of your landscape, resulting in an accurate map of your yard.**

detail-oriented among us probably will enjoy drawing an accurate scale map; others may find it tedious and end up with a looser rendition.

Whatever you think of the process, consider it a one-time investment in your landscape design. Once you've drawn it, you can lay sheets of tracing paper over the map to sketch endless design variations. Or, you can make a set of photocopies of the original map and sketch directly on them. Either way, you can draw to your heart's content and never have to redraw your working map.

Read on for more features that you'll want on your working map before you begin designing.

Get Personal with Problem Sites

You know where they are—those nasty sites that bog down your mower, turn into raging rivers during rainstorms, or sprout lush crops of weeds no matter what you do. An important part of planning your landscape is finding solutions for those problem sites. To design a plan that does away with problem sites forever, you need to get to know them "up close and personal." As you find the problem sites in your yard, mark them on a copy of your working map for reference.

Ramble in the Rain

There's no better way to figure out what to do about surface water drainage than to get an umbrella, put on a pair of galoshes, and go outside during a rainstorm. You'll see firsthand where water cuts runoff paths across your property, as well as where it puddles up. *Don't* plan to simply direct this water off your property and into the storm sewer as quickly as possible. Instead, look for ways to slow or redirect its flow and help it soak into the soil.

Solving runoff problems. You may be able to redirect water that flows across your yard or puddles next to your foundation by bringing in soil to build up a berm. Treat the berm like a raised bed and plant it with shrubs, ornamental grasses, and perennials.

Another option is to plant the site with perennials like daylilies that will tolerate the runoff. Or, you can double-dig the soil and/or add terraces to slow the flow of water. Double-dug soil will hold a considerable amount of water, especially if you cover it with a heavy layer of mulch.

Solving puddling problems. Sites where water tends to puddle are perfect for moisture-loving perennials like hostas, ferns, and Japanese iris (*Iris ensata*). Another option is to dig a water garden—but before you do, check whether the site collects water from neighboring yards as well as your

A small stream on your property can be a fabulous gardening opportunity when edged with moisture-loving perennials like bergenia (*Bergenia* sp.) and foxglove (*Digitalis* sp.).

Don't struggle to maintain lawn in shaded areas. Instead, create a private sitting nook surrounded by a garden of shade-tolerant annuals and perennials.

own. If any of your neighbors use garden chemicals, those chemicals may end up in your yard, possibly killing the fish or plants in your water garden.

Scrutinize Your Shade and Sun

Take time to look for sunny and shady pockets in your yard. Knowing where they are will help you pick the right plants for your landscape. To really figure out sun and shade patterns, you'll need to observe your yard several times during the course of a day. Some sites never get any direct sun—on the north side of your house next to an evergreen, for example. Others are sunny or shady only in the morning or afternoon. Note patterns on a copy of your working map, using slashing lines in one direction to indicate morning sun and another direction for afternoon sun.

Check the Traffic

Check your yard for compacted soil and scraggly grass—the signs of unofficial pathways. Accommodate these paths rather than fight them. For example, if an unofficial path to the neighbor's house runs through a site you covet for a perennial border, plan to install stepping-stones through the border.

Mull Over Your Mowing

During your next few mowing sessions, notice what your mowing problems are. Are there awkward spaces around shrubs or trees? Slopes that leave you panting? Rough areas of scraggly grass that are hard on the mower—and you? Target these areas for planting with groundcovers or mass plantings of perennials.

Search for Sad Soil

Stunted plants—or no plants at all—are one clue that your soil is less than wonderful. Problem soil areas may need cultivation or generous enrichment with organic matter. Or, you may just need to figure out what types of plants would be happy in those conditions. You'll learn more later about matching plants to soils. For now, just make note of problem areas.

As you develop your landscape ideas, include special features like steps leading to a garden seat, a group of flowering shrubs, or a water garden as focal points for your design.

Draw Your Dream Landscape

Now that you've brainstormed ideas, mapped your property, and made special note of problem sites, you're ready to create a landscape plan. Drawing a landscape plan is something like putting together a jigsaw puzzle. The objective is to blend all your ideas and the existing features of your landscape into a picture that will please you. It's a fun and creative process, as well as a challenge. But don't worry, you don't have to be an artist to create a workable design. And remember, you don't have to make a plan for your whole property. You may want to draw a plan for just your front yard, for example.

Sketch Your Ideas

To start, gather the 3 × 5 cards or other notes that summarize your ideas. (See "Putting Your Ideas Together" on page 164.) You'll also need the working map of your landscape, pencils, a ruler, sheets of tracing paper, and any ideas you've collected from books or magazines.

Put a piece of tracing paper over your working map. You'll sketch ideas on the tracing paper, which is usually called an *overlay*. (You can use photocopies of your map instead if you prefer.) You may want to pencil in some reference points (like the outline of your house) on each overlay before you start sketching. This will help you realign the overlay if it shifts position while you're sketching.

Review the pile of cards that has your most important ideas in it. For example, you may want a perennial garden in a sunny spot that you can see from both the kitchen and the living room. You may have a specific site in mind—the only spot that's in full sun and visible from both rooms, for example—or there may be more than one site that would work.

Next, start sketching ovals or rectangles on those sites to represent the garden. At this point, stick to general concepts. You'll work out detailed bed shapes and plant choices later. Landscape plans of this sort are often called "bubble diagrams," and one is shown on this page.

When you're done with the first pile of cards, move on to the next one. As you work, look for connections between spaces—you may find activities that seem to fit together. For example, if you position an herb and flower garden next to a sitting area, you'll get extra enjoyment from your garden when you sit outdoors.

Whenever you have too many ideas on an overlay, cover the overlay with a new sheet of tracing paper. Trace the parts of the design you like, and continue drawing. (Since you may want to refer back to previous overlays, don't throw any of them away until you have a finished design.)

You probably will run out of landscape space before you run out of ideas. If you do, try to incorporate leftover ideas into areas you've already assigned. In the end, you may have to discard some ideas. Just be sure they are the ones that are least important to you. If they aren't, go back and rework your design to fit them in.

Make a Practicality Check

Before you draw up a final plan like the ones shown on pages 180-181, take a minute to step back and look critically at your plan. Two important practical considerations are installation costs and required maintenance. For example, say your rough design features a brick walkway flanked by two 100-foot perennial borders. Do you have the money to buy all those plants and bricks, and the time to maintain such large plantings? Perhaps two smaller borders of mixed groundcovers and a crushed stone walk would be more practical and economical. You could design a smaller perennial garden at another site.

If you're planning on stone walls or brick walkways, make a few phone calls to find out approximate costs of materials. This safeguards you from getting stuck in an overly ambitious project.

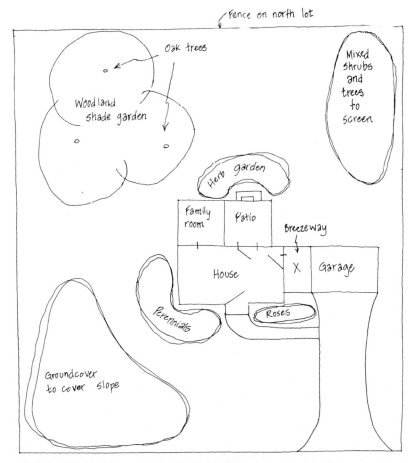

Drawing bubble diagrams lets you test your landscape ideas quickly and easily. You may create several bubble diagrams with gardens arranged in different locations before you finalize your plan.

Formalize Your Drawing

A final, detailed drawing of your plan will help you calculate your material needs for walls and walkways, tally how many plants you'll need, and figure out the best way to install your new landscape. On pages 180-181 you'll find three examples of finished landscape plans.

Start with your working map, your bubble diagram, and a new sheet of tracing paper. You may want to collect some tools that will help you draw shapes: A compass and a triangle may be helpful, especially for formal designs. For drawing informal sweeping curves, experiment with a set of French curves and/or a flexible curve (a flex-

Calm, open lawn balances lush perennial gardens. As you design your landscape, keep in mind that too many plantings with no open space can be overwhelming or claustrophobic.

ible wire coated with plastic that has one flat side you can trace against). Both of these drawing tools are available at craft and office-supply stores.

You'll use these tools to create customized shapes in place of the simple ovals or rectangles on your bubble diagram. It's easiest to start with a defining feature in your plan—perhaps a sweeping bed around a clump of trees or a long, low wall along a slope. Draw that feature in first; it will help you figure out how the rest of the elements will fit. For example, you may want to echo the shape of the bed you drew

Clear pathways help keep flowers from being trampled. A flagstone walk guides visitors and can also add complementary cool colors to a garden featuring yellow 'Moonbeam' coreopsis and hot pink petunias.

around the trees on the other side of your yard.

Another excellent option is to use a grid to structure your design. Using a grid helps ensure that your plan puts your house at the center of your garden. For more instructions on using a grid, see "Consider a Grid" on page 178.

The Finishing Touches

There's a saying that "good bones make good gardens." Although gardens don't seem the least bit bony when they're in the full flush of summer bloom, well-designed gardens do have a structure that holds them together to create a unified picture. These bones (structure) are the shapes, colors, textures, and materials repeated throughout a garden. The bones of a garden are especially important in winter: When perennials are dormant, the bones are still there to make your landscape pleasant to look at. The bones of a garden also often help guide visitors from one part to another.

Create a structure. Using a certain material throughout your garden creates its bones. Stone, brick, or flagstone in walls, terraces, and walkways become garden bones. Trees and shrubs, especially evergreens, also serve as garden bones, as do ever-

green groundcovers. Hedges and fences also can play a role in the bones of your garden.

Plan to use several materials or types of plants to create the bones of your garden. For example, you may want to use rug junipers to edge crushed stone walkways throughout your garden, and then set off your perennial plantings with a backdrop of mixed evergreens and an edging of blue fescue (*Festuca cinerea*) in front to echo the color of the evergreens. In summer, the structure of your garden could take on a whole different dimension if you use yellow- or blue-flowered perennials throughout.

A pathway to a secret garden lures visitors to explore. A brick wall certainly blocks views, but you can also use tall perennials or a vine-covered trellis to create a secluded retreat.

A graceful archway and bench offer an inviting seat in a beautiful garden. Plantings screen views of the neighbors. A central open lawn offsets abundant gardens, and brick pathways direct traffic through the flowers.

Consider a Grid

A grid is nothing more than a series of squares, drawn on a piece of tracing paper and placed over the working map of your landscape. The secret is that the size of the squares and their placement relate directly to your house, and the garden is designed around the grid squares. This helps to create a landscape plan in which the gardens and other features are proportional to your house,

Pick a prominent feature to base the grid on. In this example, each grid square is the same size as the existing patio. Major plantings generally take up one or more individual grid squares.

Don't select a grid square that's too small: It leads to a fussy, overcomplicated design. After you draw in your grid, fill in landscape features, working out from your house. This will ensure that the landscape unfolds from the house and the house is at the center of beautiful gardens.

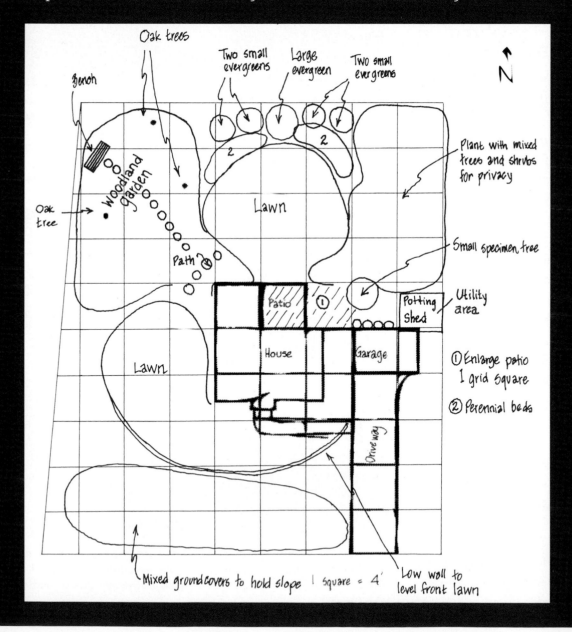

Oak trees

Two small evergreens

Large evergreen

Two small evergreens

Bench

Woodland garden

Oak tree

Lawn

Path

2

2

Plant with mixed trees and shrubs for privacy

Small specimen tree

Utility area

Patio

①

Potting Shed

House

Garage

Lawn

① Enlarge patio 1 grid square

② Perennial beds

Drive way

Mixed ground covers to hold slope

1 square = 4'

Low wall to level front lawn

Connect the spaces. As you look at your plan, imagine how visitors will walk from one area to the next. For example, if you plan a flowerbed around your patio, how will your visitors know not to tramp across your perennials in winter? You may want a low fence or hedge to separate the patio from the garden, as well as a pair of evergreens or stone pilings on either side of the designated path.

Repeat shapes. Repeated shapes create harmony. Use rectangles, ovals, or sweeping curves that echo one another—such as the edges of mixed plantings along either side of a yard.

Simple is effective. For small yards, a simple, formal garden is often most effective. Or plan on a design with strong structure—like a path that winds into the backyard between beds of mixed flowers and shrubs.

Balance garden and open space. Take an extra look at the shapes defined by areas of lawn, patios, or mass plantings of groundcovers. Designers call this the negative, or open, space in a design. Open spaces should have clean, pleasing shapes. A central oval- or hourglass-shaped lawn is much more visually pleasing than a lawn that has complicated zigzag edges. Strive to balance the negative space and positive (filled-in) space, which

To test the size and layout of a proposed flowerbed, arrange a hose or a length of plastic tape to mark the bed. Leave it in place for a few days to see if the bed is practical and comfortable to work around.

you'll plant with perennials, shrubs, trees, or mixed groundcovers.

Look for outdoor rooms. Try to enclose some areas, at least partially, with shrubs and perennials or hedges. Add easy-care shrub roses, ornamental grasses, and perennials around a patio to screen it from neighboring yards.

Include surprises. Paths that wind out of sight, steppingstones that lead visitors through a garden, or unexpected clumps of color in an otherwise green landscape create surprise and fun in your garden.

Visualize Your Design

It's tough to imagine what your rough drawing will look like as a finished landscape. For a

test, try to imagine yourself actually *doing* things in your planned yard. Are there paths to follow, sitting areas to enjoy? Does your yard have spaces for all the activities you enjoy?

To get an idea of how large you'd like your plantings to be, try piling up plastic bags filled with leaves or arranging lawn chairs on a proposed site to get an idea of the total volume of plants. If you're trying to either screen a particular view or make sure you don't cover one up, have a helper hold up a pole to estimate how tall you'll need your plantings.

Snapshots of your house are a good visualizing tool. Sketch in rough shapes of the proposed plantings on the photos (or photocopies of the photos).

A Gallery of Landscape Ideas

There's no one right way to landscape your property. What you're after is finding *your* way to landscape it. Here's an example: Three different gardeners created a landscape plan for the house and lot shown on pages 154–155. (The basic plot plan is also shown in the top illustration on this page.) As you can see, each plan reflects a different personality.

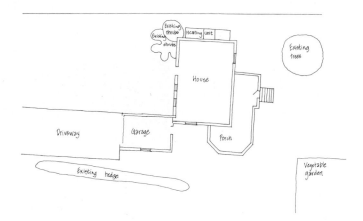

This base plan shows the house, garage, and existing trees and shrubs on a typical suburban lot. Three gardeners created three very different landscape plans for this lot, as shown on these pages.

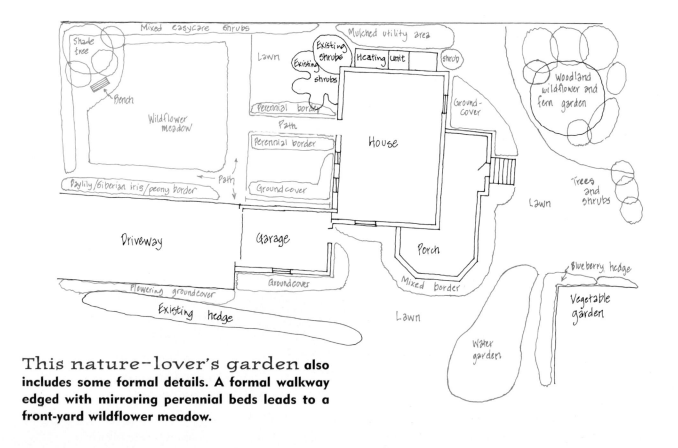

This nature-lover's garden also includes some formal details. A formal walkway edged with mirroring perennial beds leads to a front-yard wildflower meadow.

180

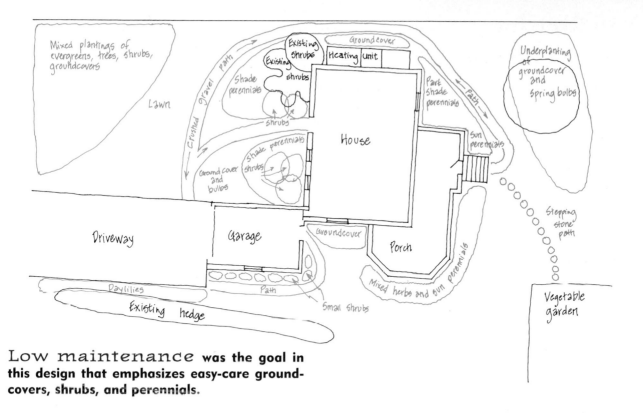

Low maintenance was the goal in this design that emphasizes easy-care groundcovers, shrubs, and perennials.

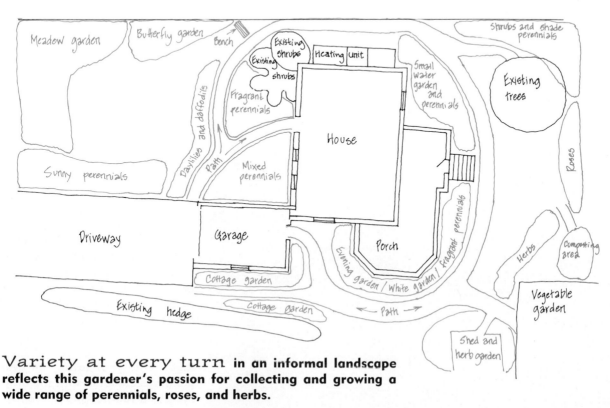

Variety at every turn in an informal landscape reflects this gardener's passion for collecting and growing a wide range of perennials, roses, and herbs.

Prioritize Your Projects

Once you've polished your plan on paper, it's time to inject a little dose of reality. Much as you'd like to plant your entire dream landscape *right now,* undoubtedly you don't have enough time, money, and muscle to do so. You need to take a hard look at your plan and pick the project or projects that you want to implement first.

One way to choose is to start with the site you see most clearly from the house. Or, you may decide to start with the project that will be the most enjoyable, such as planting the shady wildflower garden you've always wanted. Solving your worst maintenance nightmare often comes out as top priority.

When you're choosing your "do-first" projects, try to include one simple project on your list: The reward of seeing one finished, lovely spot in your unfinished yard is worth it.

Make a Practical Plan of Action

In most cases, you'll install your priority projects over time. Simple projects may take only a weekend or two. But depending on your budget, how ambitious your projects are, and the time you have to spend, others may take as long as several years to complete. That's one of the reasons having a simple project high on your list is so important. You can plant a small bed around a lamppost or on either side of a short set of steps in a single weekend, giving you pride in accomplishment and readying you to tackle more complicated projects over a longer span of time. Here are some suggestions to help you with scheduling.

Plan around hardscape. If your plan calls for adding a patio, house addition, walls, or walkways, don't plant around those sites until the building project is complete. Otherwise, you'll spend time repairing plantings after construction.

Plant woodies first. Give trees and shrubs a head start by planting them first, especially if shade is at a premium in your yard. As they're growing, you can add perennials and groundcovers as time and budget allow. If you're planning an island of trees and shrubs, mulch them well after planting to control weeds. Then gradually plant perennials among the mulch.

Mulch and grow. You can avoid digging on some sites by trying no-dig soil improvement. Scalp all weeds on the site, then

Left: Planting a perennial border in stages is one way to budget your time and money. Tall switch grass (*Panicum virgatum* 'Strictum'), golden common sneezeweed (*Helenium autumnale* 'Riverton Beauty'), and pink New England asters (*Aster novae-angliae*) stand out in the original portion of a border that is being expanded.

Right: One year later, the new plantings combine with the originals as a full-fledged border. ➤

cover it with a newspaper layer 12 to 15 sheets thick. Then spread 4 to 5 inches of straw, and top it off with 2 inches of decorative mulch. If you have it, add 1 inch of compost under the mulch. You can make planting holes right in the mulch, fill them with purchased soil, and plant them with annuals to cover the site in the summer. Keep the site mulched for a year, then plant with perennials.

Cost-Cutting Tips

There's no doubt about it, installing a landscape can be expensive. Sometimes doing it yourself is the best option; other times it's not. Here are some tips to help you keep your pocketbook under control.

Learn a skill. Check books out of your local library or attend a workshop to learn a landscape skill like bricklaying or building stone walls.

Rent, don't buy. You can rent nearly any kind of equipment or tool to make landscape installation easier. Instead of hiring someone with a tractor or buying one yourself, rent one to move soil or accomplish other tasks that your landscaping plan requires.

Use nursery services. If your plan calls for large trees and shrubs, having the nursery plant them may pay off in the long run. Many nurseries will guarantee specimens they plant, but extend a more limited warranty for specimens you plant yourself.

Opt for local materials. Consider a variety of materials for each project, then select the one that's least expensive in your area. Limestone paving slabs may be much cheaper than bluestone in some areas, for example. Also keep an eye out for used materials you can acquire—used brick, for example.

Before You Plant

So you've settled on your top-priority project and you're ready to go! But as one last step, check out the microclimate and soil on your project site. The information you gather will be invaluable in selecting the right plants for the site.

Climate on a Small Scale

The amount of shade or sun a site receives is just one factor in the microclimate of a site. If you haven't already determined how much sun and/or shade your site

receives, read "Scrutinize Your Shade and Sun" on page 173. Also evaluate the wind, exposure, and slope conditions.

Wind. Prevailing winds can wreak havoc with perennial plantings—drying plants out, ruining blossoms, and blowing them over. If your site is windy, consider making a windbreak part of the project. A fence is a quick solution, but barrier plantings will last longer and provide better protection. You'll find information on planting barriers in "Creating a Mixed Border Screen" on page 75.

Exposure. South-facing sites along a building or wall are gen-

erally warmer and more exposed in winter than north-facing ones. And the extra heat given off by the wall or fence behind a south-facing site warms these sites in spring. For this reason, they're a good place to plant spring bulbs. But broad-leaved evergreens can suffer from leaf scorch on a south-facing site both in summer and on unusually warm winter days.

Plants on a north-facing site are protected from both winter and summer sun. And west-facing sites that receive afternoon sun tend to be hotter than east-facing ones.

Slope. Perennial ground-covers are fairly easy to establish

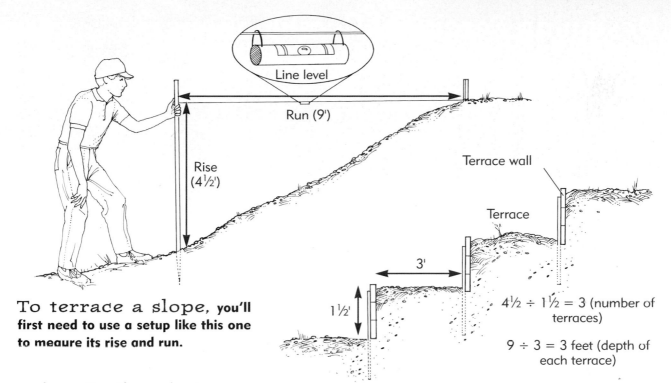

Line level

Run (9')

Rise (4½')

Terrace wall

Terrace

3'

1½'

4½ ÷ 1½ = 3 (number of terraces)

9 ÷ 3 = 3 feet (depth of each terrace)

To terrace a slope, you'll first need to use a setup like this one to meaure its rise and run.

To determine how many terraces you need, divide the rise by the planned height of each terrace. Divide the run by the number of terraces to calculate the depth of each terrace.

on slopes. But if you plan to plant a mix of perennials, you'll need to build terraces and level planting beds.

Planning terraces requires a little mathematical figuring. The first step is to measure the rise and run of the slope. From that, you can figure out how many terraces you'll need, as shown in the illustration on this page. (You'll find how-to instructions for constructing terraces in the illustration on page 232.)

◄ **Plan gardens on slopes carefully. Daffodils, azaleas, English ivy, and moss pinks (*Phlox subulata*) grow well in sun and well-drained soil. Rock and bark mulch prevent soil erosion and keep down weeds. The brick retaining wall provides a sturdy base.**

Looking at What's Down Under

Complete your site examination by taking a look at the soil. Dig a few test holes with a garden fork or spade. Poorly drained soil, compacted soil layers, and too-sandy or too-clayey soil are some of the common problems you may face. Certainly, you can work to improve your soil before you plant. But in the long run, your plants will do best if you match their needs to the soil. For example, if you have very light, sandy soil, perennials like ligularias (*Ligularia*

spp.) that need rich, moist soils just won't grow well.

If you strike rocks repeatedly while you're digging, consider building a raised bed over the area or planting shallow-rooted groundcovers around the rocks. Another option is to dig up some of the larger rocks and stack them in a low wall.

Roots are another matter. If you hit roots at every turn, you are dealing with a shallow-rooted tree. If you face this situation, refer to "Planting under Trees" on page 61 for suggestions on how and what to plant.

Chapter 7

Designing Perennial Combinations

Secrets of Successful Combinations• Contrast • Mass Plantings •

Foliage Interest • Adding Height • Matching Plants to Site • Hot and

Cool Colors • Combining Plants for Season-Long Color

Secrets of Successful Combinations

Putting perennials together in great combinations is easy and fun. What's more, creating combinations of perennials is the first, most important step in designing an entire perennial garden from scratch.

In the preceding chapters, you've worked through the process of deciding where you want to plant perennials in your yard and what styles of gardens you want. Now you're ready to try designing beautiful combinations of perennials.

In this chapter, you'll find a series of perennial combinations with explantions of how color and design principles were used to choose the plants. You'll learn how to work with attractive foliage, plant forms, and other features in perennial combinations. Once you understand how to put plants together in attractive

combinations, you'll find it a natural progression to design an entire perennial garden.

Designing with Color

Many gardeners find designing with color intimidating. They're afraid they'll make a mistake and combine flowers that don't look attractive together. Or they're simply overwhelmed by all the plants to choose from—each more beautiful than the last!

The key to comfort with combining colors is to get out there and experiment. Try out some of the combinations you see in this book, or design some of your own. Granted, you may end up with a dreadful combination or two. But that's what shovels are for—you can always move one of the offending plants somewhere else and try a new combination the next year.

Using the color wheel. In elementary school art classes, you probably learned about the pri-

mary colors—red, yellow, and blue—and how to mix them to make other colors. Those early experiences playing with paints are similar in some ways to combining colors in gardens.

The color wheel shown on the opposite page can provide the basis for choosing good perennial combinations if you know how to use it. It can also help you look at color more critically and figure out what's working in a particular combination and what isn't.

For example, *complementary* combinations—blue and orange, red and green, yellow and violet—have lots of contrast and are bright and exciting to look at. Colors that *harmonize* share the same pigments—yellow, yellow-orange, orange, and orange-red, for example. You can make stunning combinations by starting with complementary colors—violet and yellow, for example—and then adding harmonizers, such as blue-violet and red-violet, to the picture.

Flowers usually don't come in the pure colors you see in the wheel. Instead, you'll be dealing with colors like peach, lemon yellow, apricot, burgundy, deep purple, or lilac. Sometimes surrounding colors can influence our perception of color. To determine a flower's true color, try holding a solid white card behind the bloom to neutralize the influence of nearby foliage.

You'll find that light also influences color. Combinations that are so-so in the early morning can literally glitter in late afternoon sun. Ornamental grasses are particularly spectacular when backlit.

Getting Started

Besides color, when you design combinations you'll also want to consider things like plant height and form, leaf shapes, and bloom time. It can get complicated! Try not to get lost in the "rules" of garden design. If you do, you may forget what's really important—filling your yard with plants that appeal to you and grow well together. That's not to say you should throw all design principles out the window. If you look closely at great-looking combinations and gardens, you'll see that flower shapes, heights, forms, and textures all play a role in the design. And repeating certain elements—like color or

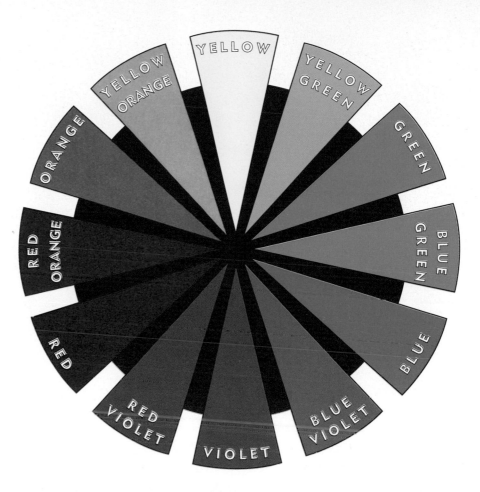

The color wheel is a tool that can help you pick pleasing combinations of colors. Colors directly across from one another on the wheel are called *complementary* colors, while colors adjacent to one another are said to *harmonize*.

texture—throughout a design helps it become a unified, visually appealing picture.

As you look at the plant combinations that follow, keep in mind that color preferences are highly subjective. You may not like all the color combinations you see here. Figuring out what you *do* like is most important. In fact, you're sure to like the combinations you design if you use

your favorite colors.

Don't get caught up in trying to apply all these principles at the same time—there's simply too much to remember. Just use them as well as you can. And remember, a shovel is your plant eraser. You can always add new plants or move some if your combinations don't turn out quite right at first. You'll find out that's half the fun!

Contrasts Create Excitement

This lush perennial garden uses contrasts between plants to form a dynamic picture. At the same time, it also uses repetition—plants that look alike in some way—to pull the garden together. The rounded mound of 'Autumn Joy' sedum, which echoes the shapes of its individual blooms, provides a solid, clean-looking anchor for the planting. It balances the exuberant and unruly explosion of New York ironweed above it. The white-striped foliage of the variegated Japanese silver grass, echoed in miniature by the creeping lilyturf in the front of the border, provides color and texture contrast to the sedum. And the ribbonlike shape of these two plants repeats in contrasting colors both in the rough-stemmed goldenrod blossoms and the ironweed leaves.

Photo Key

1 **'Autumn Joy' sedum** (*Sedum* 'Autumn Joy')

2 **Rough-stemmed goldenrod** (*Solidago rugosa* 'Fireworks')

3 **New York ironweed** (*Vernonia noveboracensis*)

4 **Variegated Japanese silver grass** (*Miscanthus sinensis* 'Variegatus')

5 **Purple coneflower** (*Echinacea purpurea*)

6 **'Moonbeam' coreopsis** (*Coreopsis verticillata* 'Moonbeam')

7 **Smoke tree** (*Cotinus coggygria*)

8 **Creeping lilyturf** (*Liriope spicata*)

Mass Plantings Make a Bold Statement

In mass plantings like this one, blocks of color and texture take precedence over the shapes of individual flowers. This planting features flowing drifts of color, which is more effective than hard-edged rectangles of plants. Note that the heights of the plants vary, so each mass of color shows to best effect.

A mass planting is especially effective from a distance, where the bold blocks of color would be most dramatic. Planting at a distance has another advantage: You can enjoy all the color without having to worry about picking off spent blooms.

Photo Key

1 **Shining coneflower (*Rudbeckia nitida* 'Herbstsonne', also called 'Autumn Sun')**

2 **Spotted Joe-Pye weed** (*Eupatorium maculatum* 'Atropurpureum')

3 **Feather reed grass** (*Calamagrostis* × *acutiflora* 'Stricta')

4 **Brazilian vervain** (*Verbena bonariensis*)

5 **Feathertop grass** (*Pennisetum villosum*)

6 **Russian sage** (*Perovskia atriplicifolia*)

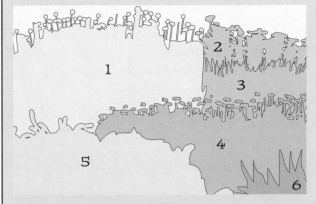

Use Foliage for 4-Season Color

Great gardens are more than just flowers! As perennials come in and out of bloom, foliage is fundamental for keeping a garden looking its best. That's why it often makes sense to mix evergreen shrubs in perennial beds and borders.

This mixed planting will have foliage interest year-round. The dwarf eastern white pine and 'Blue Star' juniper will provide winter color. In summer, the Chinese astilbe foliage will remain green and attractive all season, while the fine foliage of 'Moonbeam' coreopsis provides a colorful skirt for the garden.

Photo Key

1 **Dwarf eastern white pine** (*Pinus strobus* 'Nana')
2 **Chinese astilbe** (*Astilbe chinensis* var. *pumila*)
3 **'Blue Star' juniper** (*Juniperus squamata* 'Blue Star')
4 **'Moonbeam' coreopsis** (*Coreopsis verticillata* 'Moonbeam')

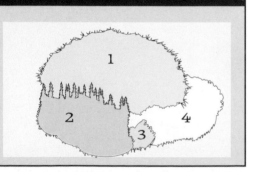

Combine Tall and Short Plants
for Heightened Interest

Vines clambering on trellises add a casual country look to a bed or border. They're a perfect solution if you need nearly instant height in a newly planted bed, or if you have space for only a narrow border. In a deep border, you can create contrasts in height by planting clumps of 5- and 6-foot-tall perennials at the back, and scale down to 1-foot mounds at the front. But in tight spaces, tuck a vine like this Jackman clematis at the back of the border to add height. (Since vines grow up, not out, they don't need the space that larger perennials require.)

Clematis like to grow with their heads in the sun and their feet in the shade, so this type of site is ideal. If you need extraquick results, try annual vines like morning glories trained in a similar manner.

Photo Key

1 **Jackman clematis** *(Clematis jackmanii)*
2 **Hybrid delphinium** *(Delphinium elatum)*
3 **Persian onion** *(Allium aflatunense)*

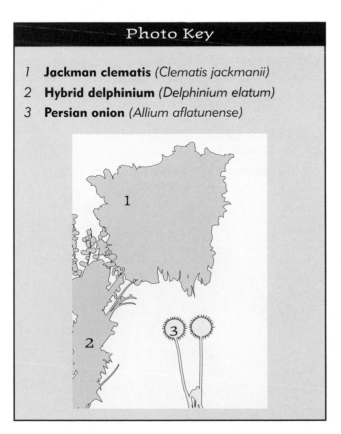

Choose Plants That Suit Your Site

Matching plants that will grow well together is the secret to planting an attractive garden that stays that way. Once you've selected several plants that you think would look nice together, check out the cultural conditions they require. You'll have the best results if you stick to plants that all need the same type of site and soil. In this garden, even though the 'Autumn Joy' sedum is much more drought-tolerant than the 'Montgomery' Colorado spruce, both will grow well in rich, well-drained soil. Note that these garden companions will also make an arresting winter picture. Both sedum and 'Goldsturm' black-eyed Susan have attractive seedheads that persist through winter, and the spruce will add a spot of silver-blue.

Photo Key

1 **'Goldsturm' black-eyed Susan** (*Rudbeckia fulgida* 'Goldsturm')

2 **'Autumn Joy' sedum** (*Sedum* 'Autumn Joy')

3 **'Montgomery' Colorado spruce** (*Picea pungens* 'Montgomery')

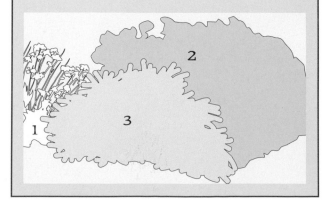

Use Dramatic Plants to Accent Your Landscape

Specimen plants like this August lily are the exclamation points of garden design. Technically, a specimen plant is one that is grown alone in the landscape so its shape and form can be appreciated from all sides. Use one to mark the entrance to a garden path or set off one part of your yard from another. But be judicious: Too many exclamation points can create confusion— and lots of obstacles to mow around.

The best specimen plants are attractive for much or all of the growing season. Shrubs or small trees are an obvious choice, but large hostas or heucheras (*Heuchera* spp.) also make great specimen plants in a shady garden. For a sunny site, you might use variegated yuccas or large ornamental grasses.

Photo Key

1. **August lily** (*Hosta plantaginea*)
2. **English ivy** (*Hedera helix*)

Match the Shape of a Garden to the Site

Shapes, texture, and movement play important roles in the design of this lush foliage garden. The fountain sets the shape of the bed and the plantings in it. Water pouring from the jug in the child's arms seems to cascade out into the garden to create ripples of plants. The net effect is a sculpture integrally linked to the setting: It's hard to imagine it without the surrounding plants.

Photo Key

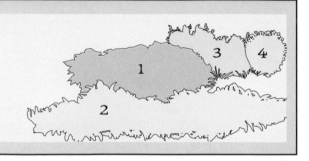

1 **'Palace Purple' heuchera** (*Heuchera micrantha* 'Palace Purple')

2 **'Silver Carpet' lamb's-ears** (*Stachys byzantina* 'Silver Carpet')

3 **Artemisia** (*Artemisia* sp.)

4 **'Goldmound' spirea** (*Spiraea* 'Goldmound')

Watch for Great Combinations
That Happen by Chance

You can blanket your yard with blocks of annuals and be be able to predict with some certainty that it will look the same in June, July, August, and September, but what fun is that? Perennials create their own combinations, and those combinations change all the time. One plant may spill over onto another, as these Japanese anemones have toppled onto asters.

Or, one year a perennial may bloom earlier or later than normal, creating a combination you hadn't planned. As the years go by, perennials also reseed and spread to make their own combinations—some good, some bad. Your job as the master color cordinator is to guide your plants with a gentle hand toward color combinations you find appealing, however long they last.

Photo Key

1 **Japanese anemone** (*Anemone* X *hybrida*)

2 **Aster** (*Aster* sp.)

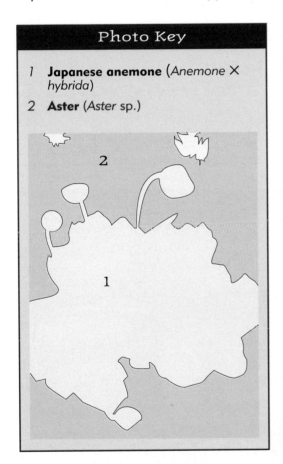

Combine Complementary Colors

One way to start a design is with complementary colors like yellow yarrows and lavender-blue cranesbills. Select the complements you want to use and then build around them by picking different flowers in similar colors.

When you try to select perennials of a particular shade, you'll find that flower color isn't always easy to define. For example, if you check descriptions in several mail-order catalogs for *Geranium* 'Johnson's Blue', you'll find it described as brilliant blue, clear blue, lavender-blue, and blue. Because flower colors are difficult to capture on film and in print, photographs of it vary as well—you'll see depictions from brilliant blue to lilac. In the end, the only true test is to grow the plant in your own garden and decide for yourself what color it is.

Photo Key

1 **'Johnson's Blue' cranesbill** (*Geranium* 'Johnson's Blue')
2 **'Moonshine yarrow'** (*Achillea* 'Moonshine')

Plant Ribbons of Hot Color
for Maximum Impact

When subtle just won't cut it, bright, cheerful hot colors may be the answer. Hot colors are the color of fire—red, orange, and yellow. They pop out in the landscape and make things look closer than they really are. Notice how the bright clumps of color at the back of this landscape seem to pop out in front of the green foliage that surrounds them.

Photo Key

1 **Bee balm** (*Monarda didyma*)
2 **Coneflower** (*Rudbeckia* sp.)
3 **Threadleaf coreopsis**
   (*Coreopsis verticillata*)

Use Cool Colors for Calming Effects

Rows of cool colors are at the forefront of this elegant spring scene. Cool colors are the color of water—blue, green, and violet, as well as silver, gray, blue-green, and gray-green. They create a garden with a serene feeling, and they also appear to make things recede. A small garden planted with blues and purples, for example, will look larger because everything seems farther away. Pale pink is also considered a cool color, while hot pink is a hot color.

Photo Key

1 **Blue atlas cedar** (*Cedrus atlantica* 'Glauca')

2 **Bearded iris** (*Iris* bearded hybrid)

3 **Juniper** (*Juniperus* sp.)

1 **Lilies** (*Lilium* spp.)
2 **'Superba' fall astilbe** (*Astilbe taquetii* 'Superba')

Startling Color Contrasts Can Make Stunning Combinations

Although pink and orange aren't high on many gardeners' lists of plants they'd like to see growing together, they work beautifully together in this garden. The pink plumes of 'Superba' fall astilbes, set off against dark green foliage, set the tone for this scene. Beyond the fence, the lilies act as an exclamation point that foreshadows more excitement in the border beyond. Yellow lilies alone would have worked, but the garden would lack that "Look at me!" excitement.

199

Use a Color Theme to Unify Your Garden

Gardens that celebrate a passion for a certain color like yellow, blue, or white have a long tradition in perennial gardening. Whether you plant just a corner of your yard with your favorite color or use it to fill an entire garden, it's great fun sleuthing out all the color possibilities. For example, there are hundreds of yellow-flowered perennials to choose from.

Yellow tulips, daffodils, irises, and primroses would extend the summer color scheme of this planting into the spring. Plants with variegated leaves, such as golden-striped ornamental grasses or *Yucca filamentosa* 'Bright Edge', or gold-colored foliage, such as golden oregano (*Origanum vulgare* 'Aureum'), are also a great option.

Photo Key

1 **'Statuesque' daylily**
(*Hemerocallis* 'Statuesque')

2 **'Coronation Gold' yarrow**
(*Achillea* 'Coronation Gold')

3 **'Moonbeam' coreopsis**
(*Coreopsis verticillata* 'Moonbeam')

Don't Forget the Power of White Flowers and Foliage

White is actually a strong color that can hold its own against more brightly hued garden residents. In this garden, white plumes of delphiniums and steely silver flowers of giant sea holly are every bit as bright as the yellow daisylike flowers of heartleaf oxeye. White is also useful for mediating disputes between clashing colors in a border. For example, a white bank of baby's-breath between clumps of orange-red lilies and pink cranesbills (*Geranium* spp.) can do wonders. Silver-leaved plants like 'Powis Castle' artemisia also make *effective* moderators. In an emergency, you can also add clumps of annual dusty miller between color combatants.

Photo Key

1 **Giant sea holly** (*Eryngium giganteum*)
2 **Delphinium** (*Delphinium* hybrid)
3 **Heartleaf oxeye** (*Telekia speciosa*, also known as *Buphthalmum speciosum*)

Design with Rivers of Color

One look along a country roadside during the height of summer will confirm that nature isn't subtle about painting colors across the landscape. You can take a cue from nature and plant your garden in meadowlike drifts of color. This technique is especially effective in large borders that you'll view from a distance. In a small garden, you can get a similar effect by planting a few clumps of each perennial. Either way, planting color drifts reduces the hodgepodge effect that can result when a garden has too many small dabs of color.

Photo Key

1 **'Goldsturm' black-eyed Susan** (*Rudbeckia fulgida* 'Goldsturm')

2 **'Autumn Joy' sedum** (*Sedum* 'Autumn Joy')

3 **Foerster's feather reed grass** (*Calamagrostis arundinacea* 'Karl Foerster')

Include the Backdrop in Your Design

This border has it all. Clumps of soft color march across the garden providing height and a sense of movement. It also has something that's easily missed: a deep green hemlock backdrop that sets off the soft colors of the perennials. The color scheme of this border would fade away against a light backdrop.

Before you plan a garden, take a minute to figure out what you'll see it against. If you are planning a perennial bed or island that you'll usually see silhouetted against the lawn, consider brighter colors that would stand out against grass green. And while perennials will show effectively against a solid board fence or dark siding, consider your colors carefully if your house is white, yellow, or pastel-colored.

Photo Key

1 **Mullein** (*Verbascum* sp.)
2 **Penstemon** (*Penstemon* sp.)
3 **'Autumn Joy' sedum** (*Sedum* 'Autumn Joy')
4 **Speedwell** (*Veronica* sp.)
5 **Clary** (*Salvia sclarea*)

Plan around Foliage Colors

Since most perennials bloom for only a few weeks in summer, foliage is often the real work-horse that keeps a garden looking great day in and day out. The spring green hosta leaves light up this shady garden as much as the fleeting pink flowers of dame's rocket. The clump of lady fern makes an especially interesting companion: Although it is the same green as the hosta, its lacy leaves stand out against the dark forest floor, creating a stunning textural contrast.

Photo Key

1 **Pagoda dogwood** (*Cornus alternifolia*)
2 **Dame's rocket** (*Hesperis matronalis*)
3 **Lady fern** (*Athyrium filix-femina*)
4 **'Piedmont Gold' hosta** (*Hosta* 'Piedmont Gold')

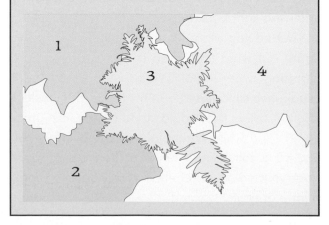

Foliage Makes the Show in Shade

Foliage can light up a shady garden all summer if you'll let it. There are plenty of perennials with variegated leaves that will add color and interest to even the darkest spot. In addition to the ones shown here, hostas, hardy cyclamen (*Cyclamen hederifolium*), and variegated Solomon's seal (*Polygonatum odoratum* 'Variegatum') will bring whites, golds, yellows, and greens to your garden. All add flowers for at least a few weeks. In this small corner of a garden, the mazus provides a carpet of white flowers and the lungwort bears rosy wine blooms to herald spring.

Photo Key

1 **'Excalibur' lungwort** (*Pulmonaria* 'Excalibur')

2 **White-flowered mazus** (*Mazus reptans* 'Albus')

3 **Persian ivy** (*Hedera colchica* 'Dentato-variegata')

Combine Plants with a Goal
of Season-Long Color

One of the challenges of working with colors in a perennial garden is that the colors of individual flowers come and go. One way to plan a summer-long display of color is to take a spring combination like this one and look for later-blooming perennials that will repeat it in other seasons.

Try peonies with Siberian iris (*Iris sibirica*) or maiden pinks (*Dianthus deltoides*) with bell-flowers (*Campanula* spp.) for early summer bloom. Follow it up with balloon flowers (*Platycodon grandiflorus*) and bee balm (*Monarda didyma*) for summer. Sum up the year with hot pink and blue asters.

Photo Key

1 **Tulip** (*Tulipa* hybrid)
2 **Forget-me-not** (*Myosotis* sp.)
3 **Lamb's-ears** (*Stachys byzantina*)

Perennials Can Provide Great Fall Color

Colors can signify the season as clearly as the weather. Fall brings silvers, bronzes, yellows, and golds to gardens as surely as it puts a nip in the air. Fall's colors are more subtle than those of the early spring and summer garden, but they are no less beautiful. This late fall garden won't be finished with the first frost of the season. And many of the plants here will continue to provide color and interest through the winter. Ornamental grasses will turn a lovely beige, adding color and texture until they're cut to the ground in early spring. Seedheads of sedums, which turn paler bronze, and coneflowers, which turn dark brown, will stand through the winter as well.

Photo Key

1 **'Sarabande' Japanese silver grass** (*Miscanthus sinensis* 'Sarabande')

2 **'Powis Castle' artemisia** (*Artemisia* 'Powis Castle')

3 **Aster** (*Aster* sp.)

4 **Cleome** (*Cleome hasslerana*)

5 **Butterfly bush** (*Buddleia* sp.)

6 **Purple smoke tree** (*Cotinus coggygria* 'Royal Purple')

7 **Purple coneflower** (*Echinacea purpurea*)

8 **Lamb's-ears** (*Stachys byzantina*)

9 **Salvia** (*Salvia* sp.)

10 **'Autumn Joy' sedum** (*Sedum* 'Autumn Joy')

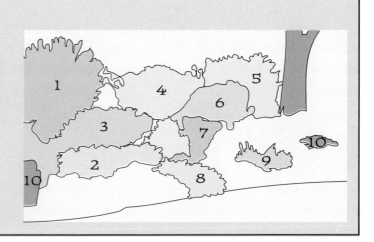

Chapter 8

Planning Your Perennial Gardens

Start with Your Plant List • Chart Your Plants • Make a Planting

Plan • Test Your Design

Start with Your Plant List

Spend ten minutes browsing at a well-stocked garden center or paging through mail-order catalogs, and you'll find there's no shortage of perennials to choose from. It's a cinch to find 50 or 60 perennials you'd love to grow. The challenge lies in winnowing down that list to select the plants that will look best and grow best in your garden.

If you're like most gardeners, you love the annual onslaught of catalogs with their tempting offerings. But it's easy to get caught in the trap of buying everything that looks and sounds appealing. Making a plant list is the best way to ensure that you buy wisely. It takes time but allows you to evaluate each plant, as well as make comparisons between plants.

You're not a list maker? Are you prone to impulse purchases? Or are you simply overwhelmed when you visit a garden center or try to wade through catalogs?

Don't despair. Try one of these suggestions for developing a list of plants.

Start with your site. Choose plants with your site conditions in mind. If you have a hot, sunny site, consider only plants that will thrive under those conditions and eliminate all the others. If you're tempted to buy whatever looks interesting or new, take a written summary of your site conditions with you to the garden center. Hold it in your hand as you compare your description to the cultural information on the plant labels. If they don't match, don't buy!

Review your style. Picking a garden style or color scheme first can help you pick plants. A cottage garden theme, for example, suggests old-fashioned reseeding perennials and biennials like peach-leaved bellflower (*Campanula persicifolia*) and foxgloves (*Digitalis* spp.).

Start your design with classic plants that epitomize your style. If you have a particular color scheme in mind—yellow and

blue, for example—that narrows your choices as well. And if you like cutting and arranging flowers, you may want to choose perennials with bloom colors that will match the colors of the furniture or wallpaper in your dining or living room.

Build on combinations. Select a perennial combination—perhaps one shown in Part 2 of this book—and check whether it will grow well on your site. If it will, use that combination as the basis for your design. This will focus your search. For an example of a combination and plants to add, see the photograph on page 206.

Keep in mind that gardens don't have to contain lots of different kinds of perennials to be beautiful and satisfying. You can also create a perfectly lovely garden simply by making mass plantings of the two or three plants in one combination.

Include some sentiment. Planning beds and borders around plants that provide special memories adds a wonderful di-

Waiting for a planting plan to come to life as a real garden is suspenseful and thrilling. To see how this pink color theme garden was planned, compare it to the plant chart and plot plan on pages 211 and 213.

mension to any garden. Perhaps there are specific plants that remind you of happy childhood experiences, dear friends or relatives, or a neighborhood where you used to live.

For example, if plants have been passed down through generations—like peonies that grew in a grandmother's garden—they can be the centerpiece of a family memory garden.

Start with a professional design. You may want to contract the task of creating a specific garden to a professional garden designer. If you do, tell the designer as much as you can about the site, and the style of garden you want. Make a list of

favorite plants that you'd like included in your garden, and discuss it with your designer. Another alternative is to adapt an existing design and plant list to suit your site. For ideas, turn to Part 1, where you'll find designs for a color theme garden, butterfly garden, perennial herb garden, and many others.

Chart Your Plants

Making an organized plant list can seem like a chore. It's easier and more fun to circle plants that catch your eye in a catalog, or to scribble down a quick list of choices. But once you discipline yourself to make a formal list, you'll never regret it. An organized list—actually a chart—is invaluable when you design a garden. If you take time to record some basic facts about each plant, you can use it to evaluate your overall list of choices at a glance.

To generate a plant chart like the one shown on the opposite page, you need graph paper and a clipboard, a pencil, a ruler, a 3 × 5 card, and a packet of colored pencils or markers. You'll also need reference materials, such as the plant descriptions in Part 2 of this book, mail-order catalogs, and possibly a perennials encyclopedia.

First, write a very brief summary of the conditions at your site on the 3 × 5 card. A few words will do, such as "Dry shade" or "Full sun, hot, well-drained soil." Clip this card on your clipboard, sticking out from behind the graph paper. Each time you see a plant that appeals to you, check whether it will grow in the conditions you've listed. If it won't, put it on a wish list of plants for another site.

Line the graph paper, as shown on the opposite page, and begin listing plants. Use colored pencils or markers to make the color bar that indicates bloom season and color. Don't worry if the bloom color isn't exact. You'll use it to make overall judgments, such as: Are there too many yellows and not enough pinks? Does anything on the list bloom in early fall?

In the "Comments" column, list the general shape of the plant first. Then note suggested combinations (many catalogs provide them), or notes about special care.

Once you've finished, evaluate your list. Start crossing plants off, eliminating ones with bloom seasons that are too short, foliage that isn't attractive for most of the season, or that aren't quite suited to the site. Also be sure you have a good assortment of heights and shapes. You may want to eliminate plants that need special care like staking or frequent division.

When planning your gardens, start with a solid perennial combination, such as daylilies, drumstick chives (*Allium sphaerocephalum*), and yarrow. Then plant annuals like salvia and snapdragons in front to provide season-long color.

KEY #	PLANT	EARLY SPRING	SPRING	EARLY SUMMER	SUMMER	EARLY FALL	FALL	LONG-LASTING FOLIAGE	WINTER INTEREST	HEIGHT UNDER 1'	2'	3'	5'	OVER 5'	COMMENTS
1	Black snakeroot Cimicifuga racemosa			■				yes						X	Vertical form; dramatic background plant
2	Mallow Malva alcea 'Fastigiata'				■						X				Upright form; prefer cool nights
3	Hollyhock Alcea rosea				■									X	Vertical form; accent plant for back of border; rust can be a problem
4	Purple coneflower Echinacea purpurea 'Bright Star'			■	■				yes seed heads			X			Erect mounds; division not recommended; plants may self-sow
5	Echinacea tennesseensis			■	■						X				Not highly vigorous
6	Hibiscus 'Red Cutleaf'				■							X			Shrublike form; bold flowers
7	Sedum 'Vera Jameson'				■			yes reddish foliage		X					Spreading form
8	Sedum 'Autumn Joy'			■	■	■		yes	yes dried flower heads			X			Mound-forming; cut back plants growing in partial shade in late June
9	Spike speedwell Veronica spicata 'Red Fox'			■	■			yes		X					Compact form; divide in spring or fall if they spread too much
10	Celosia spicata 'Flamingo Feather'			■	■	■						X			Bushy form; annual; flowers are good for drying
11	Moor grass Molinia caerulea				■	■				X					Clumping habit; old flowers and foliage break off the plants by themselves at end of season

A plant chart offers at-a-glance answers to questions such as: Does your list include enough spring-blooming perennials? Is there a good mix of colors? Do plant heights vary?

How Many Kinds of Plants?

Perennials need anywhere from 2 to 4 square feet of space per plant at maturity. So, to fill a 120-square-foot garden, you'll need between 30 and 60 plants. That doesn't mean you'll need 30 to 60 different species or cultivars; for an effective design, you'll want to plant drifts of some plants and repeating clumps of others throughout the garden to unify it. You probably actually need 15 to 30 different kinds of plants.

It's easy to let the collector's instinct take over and order one of everything. But you'll design a far better-looking garden if you steel yourself and limit your list. It's possible to have a fabulous-looking garden with only a handful of carefully chosen plants. And once you get your main perennials established, you can experiment with other plants that appeal to you.

Make a Planting Plan

Once your plant list is trimmed to size, it's time to turn it into a garden. To do that, you'll experiment with planting plans—arrangements on paper of your carefully chosen perennials.

Start by drawing your garden site to scale on a piece of graph paper. A good scale to start with is 1 inch equals 1 foot. For a large garden, you may need to try 1 inch equals 3 or 4 feet, or tape several sheets of graph paper together.

To position plants, begin drawing circles, ovals, or other shapes to represent clumps of plants. Start with one of the more important plants on your list—one that will provide color over a long season or that you want in a prominent place, for example. Then add others around it. Try to keep the shapes to scale. If you are planning a drift of a single perennial, be sure your bubble accommodates two, three, or more plants. It's easiest to number the plants on your list, and use the numbers (rather than writing out names) to identify each bubble on your diagram.

If you're designing a perennial border, draw the taller plants in the back and add layers of shorter plants in front. For an is-

In a woodland setting, tree roots and existing plants may dictate your planting plan. The results will be simple groupings, like a trio of masterwort (*Astrantia major*), purplish bigleaf ligularia (*Ligularia dentata*), and Allegheny foamflower (*Tiarella cordifolia*).

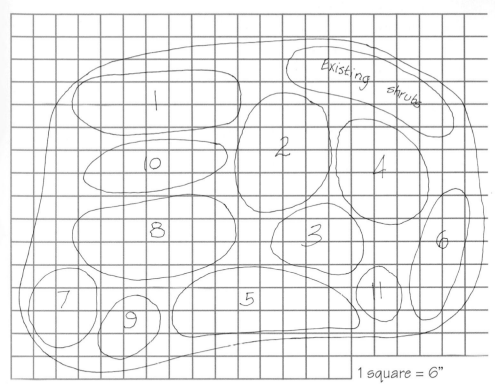

Existing shrub

1 square = 6"

A garden plot plan shows how plants in a garden will look when they've reached their mature spread. This plan shows the arrangement of the plants listed on page 211 and shown in the photo on page 209.

land bed, position the tallest plants in the center and add layers of shorter plants around them. For a formal rectangular garden, you may want to plant rows of a single plant along the edges with a contrasting plant in each corner. Here are some other tips to help you position plants and evaluate your design.

Plant in clumps. Design dramatic clumps of perennials, with three or more plants in each clump. A design filled with single plants will make an unsatisfying, spotty-looking garden with random bits of color here and there.

Repeat colors and textures. Place clumps of perennials with outstanding foliage or especially long bloom seasons throughout the garden. This helps unify the design and ensures you'll have attractive foliage and flowers to look at much of the time.

Move the color around. Arrange colors evenly throughout the site. If all your pink- or yellow-flowered plants are in one place, you'll end up with a lopsided garden.

Vary heights. Keep most of the tallest plants at the back (or in the center for an island bed),

bringing a few forward a bit to create depth and variety. Bring some medium-height plants into the front row as well. Avoid a soldierlike lineup of plants of equal height.

Think season to season. Spread the bloom for each season through the whole border. You'll find a technique for checking seasonal bloom in the illustration on page 215.

Try planting on centers. One technique that works effectively for meadow and prairielike gardens is to divide the site into 1-foot squares and plant a perennial or grass in each square. (Small plugs or 2½-inch pots are used for this technique.) Arrange the plants in drifts, with three, four, or more perennials planted in adjacent squares. Then let the plants spread and fill as they will.

Limit your plant list. If you run out of space on your plot plan before you run out of plants on your list, resist the temptation to squeeze in each and every plant. Instead, check the list of leftover plants against the plan. If some favorites are still on the list, substitute them for a plant that's on the plan. After you double-check, set the list aside. Keep those leftover plants in mind for replacement possibilities in the event that ones you've selected don't grow as well as you had hoped.

Test Your Design

You may want to test your design before you commit to it. You'll see two simple tests for visualizing designs in the illustrations on this page and the opposite page.

If your sketches reveal a bloom shortage in one season or another, readjust your plan, and then recheck it. You may want to add an extra mass of an especially long-blooming perennial to even out the bloom sequence. If you discover a "hole" in your garden, recheck your original plant list for that special perennial to fill the space.

How Many to Buy?

Let your plot plan tell you how many individual perennials you need to buy. To do so, lightly draw circles the size of mature plants over each clump of plants. Or draw a dot to indicate the center of each proposed plant in a clump, with lines radiating out to indicate spread. Then count the circles or dots.

There's also an easy way to figure out how many plants you'll need for a massed planting.

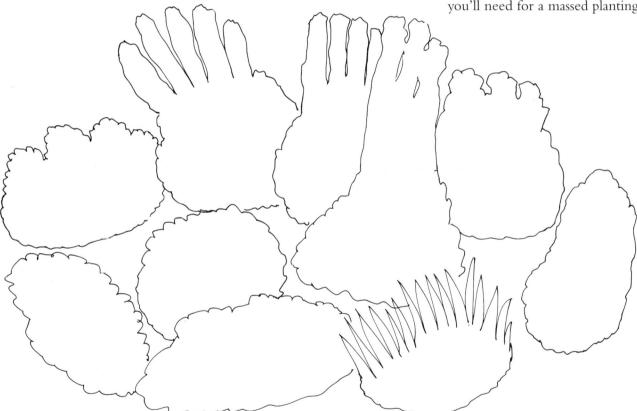

A side view of a plot plan shows the relative shapes and heights of the individual plants. A side-view sketch will help you visualize whether your planting is balanced and will reveal any "holes" in your design.

214

First, calculate the total square footage of your site (multiply length times width; an estimate is fine for odd-shaped gardens. Then, figure out how many square feet each plant will require and divide that number into the total square footage. The result is the number of plants you'll need.

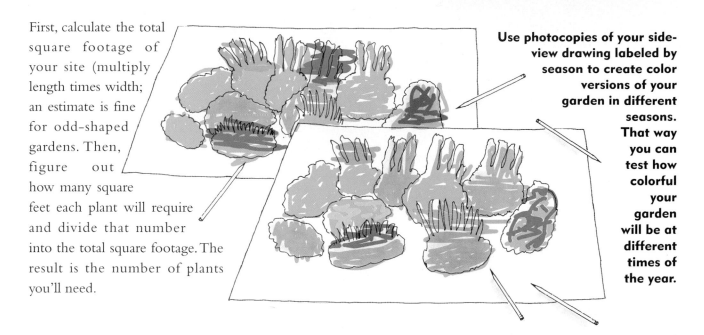

Use photocopies of your side-view drawing labeled by season to create color versions of your garden in different seasons. That way you can test how colorful your garden will be at different times of the year.

Even a small garden benefits from thoughtful plant choices. A dwarf pine, fountain grass (*Pennisetum alopecuroides*), allium (*Allium thunbergii* 'Ozawa'), and sweet alyssum (*Lobularia maritima*) all will thrive in sunny, well-drained conditions.

Carrying Out Your Landscape Plan

By Jean M. A. Nick

After the planning is done, the planting begins! Putting in new plantings is one of the most exciting and satisfying parts of gardening. And one of the best things about perennial gardens is the long-term rewards they give for your efforts. With careful planting and proper care, perennial gardens will bloom and thrive for years, offering ever-changing combinations of colors, shapes, and textures. In this section, you'll find clear instructions and illustrations that show you how to prepare garden sites, including "hardscape" features like paths and arbors. You'll also learn how to produce your own stock of perennials by dividing, taking cuttings, and starting seeds. An illustrated care calendar guides you from season to season through the perennial gardening year.

Chapter 9

Preparing and Planting Your Garden

Preparing for Perennials • Getting Rid of Weeds • Improving Your Soil • Edgings

• Paths • Stone Retaining Walls • Trellises and Arbors •

Lighting Your Landscape • Water Features • Planting

Perennials • Growing into a New Landscape

Preparing for Perennials

Perennials are like houseguests: Give them a comfortable bed and tasty meals, and chances are they'll return to your garden year after year. And to ensure years of perennial pleasure, prepare those beds *before* the plants arrive. Once they're planted, it can be very frustrating to remove problem weeds, loosen the soil, or work in soil amendments around them.

One of the best times to start preparing a new site is late summer, after the hottest days are past. This gives you enough time to spread out heavy tasks—such as digging up persistent thistle roots—so you won't exhaust yourself trying to do it all in one weekend. By fall, you'll be ready to plant perennials that prefer fall planting. Come spring, long be-

fore the soil is dry enough to prepare from scratch, you can slip in any remaining perennials that call for spring planting.

You can also prepare a site in spring, once the soil dries out, and plant later that same season. Just don't shortchange your perennials by skimping on digging or weed removal because you're in a rush to get them into the ground.

Steps to Success

Whatever time of year you choose to start a new site, there are certain steps you should follow to create the best possible home for your new perennials.

Here's an overview of the steps you'll need to follow to achieve a top-quality perennial planting.

1. Evaluate the existing plants and soil on your site. Transplant

all of the plants that are worth keeping into a holding bed.

2. Remove unwanted weeds, debris, and plants, then compost or discard them.

3. Loosen the soil.

4. Amend the soil as needed.

5. Install edgings, paths, walls, or other hard features.

6. Plant correctly and strategically, and mulch all your new plantings.

You'll find detailed how-to instructions for each of these steps in this chapter. Of course, every site has its unique features and problems. In some cases, you may skip steps that don't apply to your site. For example, if you're creating a perennial bed on a site that's currently a thriving annual flowerbed, you may not need to loosen the soil or install an edging. You'll skip straight to amending the soil, and then planting.

Evaluating Your Site

Some potential garden sites are easy to prepare. Your preparation work may be to simply enrich the soil and plant. Other sites may be candidates for major root eradication, double digging, or soil relocation.

Outline the site. Start by marking the outline of your planned garden on the soil surface using small stakes, white powdered limestone, or a length of flexible hose.

Study the surface. Look closely at the plants, weeds, rocks, and other objects on the site. Sometimes your mental picture of a site omits patches of noxious weeds, exposed tree roots, a wet spot, or large rocks. A long stare will bring you back to reality.

Move "keeper" plants. Now is the time to relocate plants you want to save to a holding bed. See page 252 for information on holding beds.

If your site includes very large perennials, grasses, or shrubs, you may want to work around the plants rather than move them. Mark them with colorful flagging tape to make them more visible. Lift and gather together the branches of bushy plants and tie them up snugly with twine so they'll be easier to work around.

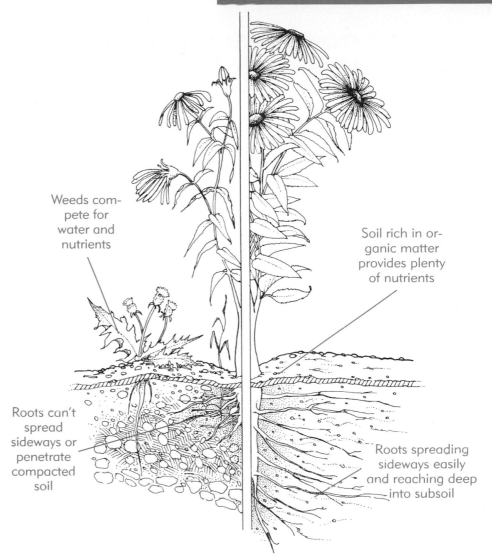

Weeds compete for water and nutrients

Soil rich in organic matter provides plenty of nutrients

Roots can't spread sideways or penetrate compacted soil

Roots spreading sideways easily and reaching deep into subsoil

A view below ground level explains why perennials planted in poorly prepared soil (*left*) often languish. When soil isn't loosened and improved before planting, roots just can't do their job, sentencing the plants to a slow death.

Look underground. The most important part of a site evaluation is sizing up the soil. To do this, dig an 18-inch-deep hole in the middle of the site. If a shovel won't get through the tough soil on your site, try a pickax. You'll discover whether your soil is rocky, or filled with stubborn tree roots, or has a compacted layer below the topsoil. Refill the hole when you're done.

Make an action plan. After evaluating your site and soil, you may know from experience what kind of clearing and soil improvement your site needs. If you're not sure how to proceed, turn to "Deciding on a Site Preparation Action Plan" on page 220.

Deciding on a Site Preparation Action Plan

Current Condition of Your Site	Evaluation of the Work Ahead
Existing garden; no major problems below the soil surface.	Lucky you! Much of your work is already done.
Lawn; no major problems below the soil surface.	No sweat! It's easy to convert lawn into garden.
Weeds and brush; no major problems below the soil surface.	Woody brush can't be cleared in a rush! Long-neglected sites will be the hardest to reclaim.
Rocks, debris, or branches littering soil surface; more rocks and debris below ground.	Heavy lifting ahead—but at least rocks and trash don't have roots.
A moderate to steep slope; no major problems below the soil surface.	Coping with a slope can be hard work, depending on how steep it is and the type of plant cover.
Sparse, wilting plants, hard-baked soil surface; below the surface, soil is sandy, gravelly, or forms sticky clods.	More water needed! Adding organic matter is a must, as is choosing plants that tolerate dry conditions.
Lush vegetation, puddles on surface after a rain; layers of yellow or gray soil below the surface.	A drainage dilemma. Either improve drainage or create a bog garden.
Sparse vegetation; a thin layer of topsoil, or soil too hard to penetrate with shovel.	This soil needs help! But organic soil improvement builds topsoil.

Steps in Preparing Your Site

Step 1	Step 2	Step 3	Step 4
Remove all weeds and plants you don't want to keep (222).	Loosen soil as needed (224).	Test soil and amend as needed (225).	
Dig out taprooted weeds like dandelions.	Roll up and remove the sod (224).	Loosen soil as needed (224). If soil is compacted, double-dig.	Test soil and amend as needed (225).
Dig out unwanted plants and any roots more than $1/2$ inch thick or try thick mulching (222).	Loosen soil as needed (224).	Test soil and amend as needed (225).	
Remove all weeds and plants you don't want to keep (222).	Remove large objects—consider making huge rocks part of your design (68).	Loosen soil as needed (224). Remove all debris and large chunks of rocks, brick, or concrete.	Test soil and amend as needed (225).
If you plan to walk on the slope, install retaining walls (232) and level paths (230).	Remove all weeds and plants you don't want to keep (222).	Loosen soil as needed (224).	Test soil and amend as needed (225). Consider planting a mix of groundcovers on a slope (80).
Remove all weeds and plants you don't want to keep (222).	Loosen soil as needed (224).	Test soil and amend as needed (225). Work in lots of organic matter.	Consider installing drip irrigation. This is especially important if the site is under the eaves of a building.
Find the source of the water; divert it elsewhere if possible. Or, build a raised planting area (76).	Remove all weeds and plants you don't want to keep (222).	Loosen soil as needed (224).	Test soil and amend as needed (225). Work in lots of organic matter, especially if the soil is smooth and sticky.
Remove all weeds (222).	Loosen soil as needed (224). If compacted, double-dig. If the soil has a hard subsurface layer, break it up, or punch drain holes with a pickax and build a raised planting area (76).	Test soil and amend as needed (225). Add as much compost as you have available.	

Note: The page numbers in parentheses will lead you to detailed how-to information for the techniques suggested.

Clearing Weeds and Debris

Ask any group of gardeners what their biggest problem is and you'll hear a resounding chorus of "Weeds!" Well, it doesn't have to be that way. You *can* win the weed war, but you must do it before you plant a single perennial in your new site.

Start by examining your opponents. Every location seems to have more than its share of weeds; most likely there are some you can't identify by name.

However, every single weed growing in your prospective site falls into one of three weed types.

- Mildly troublesome annual weeds with weak roots. These spread only by seed.
- Annoying taprooted weeds with long, fleshy roots that live for more than one year. These spread only by seed.
- Downright infuriating weeds with fleshy roots, stems, or bulbs. These spread both by creeping roots and by seed.

Check "Strategies for Beating Weeds" on the opposite page to find out which control techniques will work for your weeds.

Mowing weeds. If you mow weeds that have begun to set seed, remove and dispose of

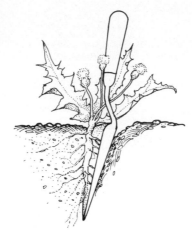

Water the area well the day before you plan to dig weeds out by hand.

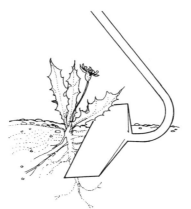

Use a hoe to slice off annual weeds just below the soil.

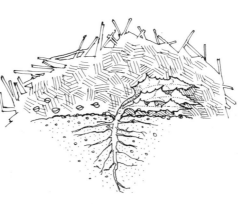

To smother weeds, cover the area with a 4- to 6-inch layer of organic mulch.

the seedy tops in the garbage or burn them; don't compost them.

Hand-digging. Digging weeds by hand is tedious but ultimately very effective. If you are digging out weeds that have spreading roots, do one major digging session, then dig out every shoot that appears for the following month or so.

Smothering weeds. You can kill weeds by spreading a dense layer of organic mulch over them. Flatten or remove the weed tops before you mulch. Or you can cover the weedy area with black plastic, sealing the edges of the plastic with soil. If the weeds you're mulching have spreading roots, watch out for new shoots popping up outside the mulched area.

Clearing large areas. If you have a large area that's infested with weeds, the least labor-intensive way to prepare it is to plant a series of dense cover crops on the site for a year. See "Preparing a Site with Green Magic" on page 227 for instructions.

While dealing with weed problems is the most important part of clearing your site, you should also clear away logs, rocks, and other debris. Remember, if you can't lift it without hurting yourself—don't. Get help, cut or smash it into smaller sections, or adapt your design to include it.

Strategies for Beating Weeds

Types of Weeds	Cut Off or Kill the Tops	Remove the Roots	Smother with Mulch
 **Annual Weeds (and young seedlings of all types of weeds)**	**Excellent control; fast and easy** Mow weeds. Hoe. Pour boiling water on tops. Spray organically acceptable herbicide such as Superfast.	**Excellent control; fast and easy** If your weeds are less than 1' tall, go straight to loosening the soil with a rotary tiller or spading fork. Rake off any weeds lying on the surface after loosening the soil.	**Excellent control; takes 1 month** Cover annual weeds and young weed seedlings with organic or black plastic mulch; the weeds will die within one month.
 **Taprooted Weeds**	**Temporary control only** Mow weeds that are more than 1' tall to make digging them up or mulching over them easier. Mow flowering weeds to prevent them from setting seed and spreading to new areas.	**Excellent control; requires some work** Hand-pull or dig up taprooted weeds before rotary tilling for best results.	**Excellent control; takes 1 year** Mulch over taprooted weeds and they'll die in a year or so. Check next year for signs of life, and remulch if you find any.
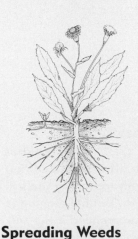 **Spreading Weeds**	**Temporary control only** Mow weeds that are more than 1' tall to make digging them up or mulching over them easier. Mow flowering weeds to prevent them from setting seed and spreading to new areas.	**Moderate to excellent control; lots of work** Carefully dig down and remove every bit of sideways-reaching root. *Never* rotary-till weeds with spreading roots. You will chop the roots into little bits—every one of which will grow into a new plant!	**Excellent control; takes 2 years or more** Cover the weeds with a thick layer of cardboard, including a 3' margin out from the edges of the infested area. Overlap the edges of the cardboard by at least 1'. Cover with at least 6" of organic mulch. Lift and check after a year, replace cover if pale living weed shoots are visible.

Loosening Your Soil

After you've cleared your site of existing weeds and other obstructions, it's time to loosen the soil. This task has a major effect on how well your perennials will perform. Guarantee the best results possible by loosening the top 12 to 18 inches of the soil.

If your site is covered with sod, strip off the sod before digging, as shown in the illustration on this page. If you till or dig the sod directly into the bed, you'll end up with a terrible weed problem as the grass resprouts among your perennials. Use the stripped sod to patch your lawn elsewhere, or just add it to your compost pile.

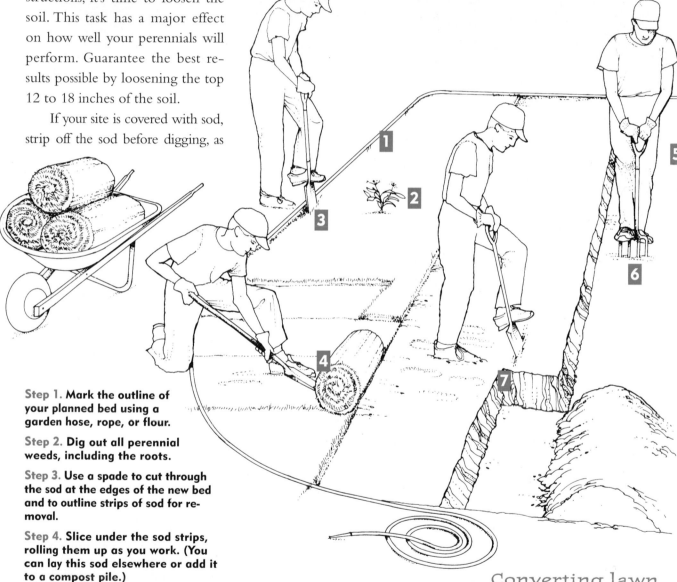

Step 1. Mark the outline of your planned bed using a garden hose, rope, or flour.

Step 2. Dig out all perennial weeds, including the roots.

Step 3. Use a spade to cut through the sod at the edges of the new bed and to outline strips of sod for removal.

Step 4. Slice under the sod strips, rolling them up as you work. (You can lay this sod elsewhere or add it to a compost pile.)

Step 5. Dig a trench along one end of the bed. Pile the soil on a tarp or in a garden cart. You will use this soil to fill the final trench.

Step 6. Insert a garden fork deeply, and rock it back and forth to loosen and aerate the soil.

Step 7. Make a second trench by pushing the soil into the first trench. Loosen the soil in the bottom of the second trench. Continue making trenches until the bed is finished.

Converting lawn to garden requires stripping off the sod and thoroughly loosening the soil beneath. Double-digging is recommended if the soil is heavy or compacted.

You can choose between single digging and double digging to loosen the soil. Single digging loosens the soil to one shovel or spading fork's depth. To single-dig a bed, insert a spade as deeply as you can into the soil, and rock the handle backward to loosen a chunk of soil. Then lift and flip the soil. After you've repeated this process over the bed, use a digging fork to go back over the surface and break up any large soil clods.

If you need the heavy artillery (pickax, digging bar, or jackhammer) to dig at your site, double digging is highly recommended. This process, which is shown in the illustration on the opposite page, fully loosens the top foot or so of soil and breaks up harder subsoil layers, too. It is more work than single digging, but you'll only need to do it once, and the results are more than worth the sweat invested.

The key to successful double digging is pacing. Don't try do double-dig your whole yard in one weekend. Between 25 and 50 square feet is plenty to tackle for one session. Divide your site into manageable sections— 4-foot-wide strips work well. While hand digging is shown here, you can also use a rotary tiller to single-dig your soil or to loosen the top layer of soil before double digging.

Improving Your Soil

Once your site is clear and the soil is loosened, you can add soil amendments and plants. However, if you plan to install any hardscape at your site—features such as edgings, walls, raised beds, or paths, it's best to do that first. See pages 228-237 for information on designing and installing hardscape features.

If you've been gardening a long time in your present yard, chances are you know your soil's approximate pH and fertility. If not, it's a good idea to check the soil's pH before you plant. If you want detailed information about your soil's fertility, collect a soil sample and send it to a soil-testing laboratory for analysis. (This is rarely necessary unless your plants show nutrient deficiency symptoms.) See page 277 for more information on troubleshooting deficiency problems.

Testing Your Soil

Plants make their own food out of sunshine and carbon dioxide. In order to do so, they need specific mineral nutrients— just as we need vitamins and minerals. The soil is the source of these nutrients for plants. A soil test will reveal how much of these nutrients are available in your soil.

Nutrient availability. Nutrient availability depends on soil pH. A pH less than 6.0 means your soil is fairly acidic. A pH higher than 7.0 means your soil is alkaline. Both conditions reduce nutrient availability. You can buy a do-it-yourself pH test kit at garden centers. Follow the directions in the kit to determine your soil's pH.

Nutrient levels. Plants need lots of nitrogen, phosphorus, and potassium (these three are the "N-P-K" you find on fertilizer bag labels) and much smaller amounts of other nutrients, including magnesium, calcium, iron, boron, and sulfur. If you adjust your soil's pH to between 6.0 and 7.0 and add compost or balanced organic fertilizer, your plants will be well nourished and should grow beautifully.

Adding Soil Amendments

If your soil's pH is less than 6.0, spread ground limestone or oystershell lime on the soil to raise the pH to between 6.0 and 7.0. To raise pH by roughly one pH point over 100 square feet of soil, spread 3 pounds for sandy soil, 8 pounds for loamy soil, or 11 pounds for clay soil.

If the pH is greater than 7.0, spread sulfur on the soil to lower the pH to between 6.0 and 7.0. To lower pH by roughly one pH point over 100 square feet of soil, spread 1 pound for sandy soil, 1½ pounds for loamy soil, or 2 pounds for clay soil.

Next, spread compost. Use 4 inches for poor, low fertility soil; 2 inches for good, high fertility soil. Compost is high in organic matter. It provides a slow-release source of nutrients while helping to make the nutrients already in the soil available to your plants.

Work the amendments into the top few inches of the soil with a spading fork. As a final step, rake the soil surface smooth.

Reducing Future Weed Problems

Every handful of soil in your landscape contains thousands of dormant weed seeds. When you dig, you wake up hundreds of seeds and signal them to sprout. Here are three ways to prevent

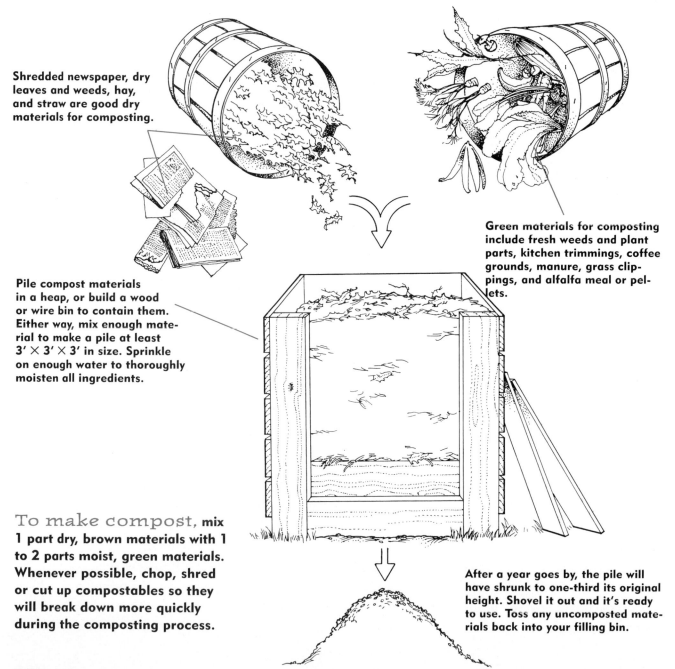

Shredded newspaper, dry leaves and weeds, hay, and straw are good dry materials for composting.

Green materials for composting include fresh weeds and plant parts, kitchen trimmings, coffee grounds, manure, grass clippings, and alfalfa meal or pellets.

Pile compost materials in a heap, or build a wood or wire bin to contain them. Either way, mix enough material to make a pile at least 3' × 3' × 3' in size. Sprinkle on enough water to thoroughly moisten all ingredients.

To make compost, mix 1 part dry, brown materials with 1 to 2 parts moist, green materials. Whenever possible, chop, shred or cut up compostables so they will break down more quickly during the composting process.

After a year goes by, the pile will have shrunk to one-third its original height. Shovel it out and it's ready to use. Toss any uncomposted materials back into your filling bin.

those seeds from turning your site into a carpet of weeds.

Smother them with mulch. Cover your newly prepared site immediately with 2 to 4 inches of organic mulch. Carefully plant through the mulch without uncovering the soil any more than necessary.

Encourage them to germinate—then kill them. Water your newly prepared site frequently. Cultivate it very shallowly (no more than 1 inch deep) once a week to dislodge and kill the weed seedlings. In a month or so you'll have exhausted the supply of weed seeds near the surface and be ready to plant. You can also use a cover crop to outcompete the weed seedlings, as explained in "Preparing a Site with Green Magic" on this page.

Cook them with sunshine. If it's midsummer and you live in an area with ample summer sunshine, try a process called solarization to kill weed seeds and reduce future soilborne disease problems. Water your newly prepared site and dig a 3-inch-deep trench around it, piling the soil to the outside. Stretch a single sheet of clear, 1- to 4-mil-thick plastic over the area. Anchor the edges with the soil dug from the trench. After 4 to 6 weeks, remove the plastic and you'll be ready to plant.

Preparing a Site with Green Magic

If you're looking for a magic way to weed, dig, and enrich a planting site without doing much physical labor, you'll be delighted by the green magic of cover crops (also called green manure crops). A cover crop is a grass (like rye) or a legume (like alfalfa) that you plant and grow specifically to add back into the soil. As cover crops grow, they outcompete weeds, and their roots aerate and loosen the soil. When you till the cover crop into the soil, it adds rich organic matter.

Planting and tilling in a cover crop is much easier than double digging and hand-weeding a bed. The catch with cover crops is time—you need to plan a season in advance to get the most from them.

Before planting a cover crop, prepare the site by mowing down weeds and raking them away. Till the entire area or scratch the soil surface with a rake. Then sprinkle on cover crop seeds, rake again gently to cover the seeds, and water well. Try the following techniques for managing cover crops.

To loosen heavy soil. Plant alfalfa (⅛ cup seed per 100 square feet) or another deep-rooted cover crop as soon as the soil can be worked in spring. Mow the area with a scythe or string trimmer whenever the alfalfa starts to flower; add the trimmings to your compost. During the season, the roots will penetrate heavy or compacted soil up to 2 feet deep. The following spring, mow the alfalfa as short as possible and then till it to kill the roots. For even better results, let it grow through a second spring and summer before tilling it under.

To control weeds. Plant a quick-growing cover crop such as buckwheat (½ cup seed per 100 square feet) in spring or summer, or rye grain (1 cup seed per 100 square feet) in fall. After 8 to 10 weeks (or the next spring for late fall plantings), mow the cover crop with a scythe or string trimmer. Let it lie for a few days, then reseed the area. Repeat until few new weed shoots or seedlings appear with the cover crop.

To add organic matter. Plant buckwheat or annual rye grass (½ cup seed per 100 square feet) in spring and summer, or rye grain (1 cup seed per 100 square feet) in fall for overwintering. Mow and till under 1 week before planting.

Edgings

Edgings are picture frames for your landscape. They accent individual sections and help tie sections together into a unified whole. They also reduce mowing and trimming by preventing lawngrass from creeping into your perennials and by giving you a clean edge to trim up to.

Decorative edgings. Garden centers offer diminutive picket fencing, rustic log ends, terra-cotta tile roping, and other attractive edgings. Collectors may enjoy making their own edgings from large seashells, river pebbles, or salvaged bricks. If you're patient, try the timeless elegance of a miniature clipped box hedge. For a quicker version, try a hedge of tiny-leaved bush basil plants, or an edging made of willow shoots.

Hard-working edgings. For quick results, use a commercial black plastic edging made up of interlocking 8-inch-wide pound-in sections. It's easy to install, but you'll need to push it back in each spring because it tends to frost-heave. Roll edgings work well also. Spend a little extra when you buy plastic edging and get one guaranteed not to crack in heat or cold.

Cast-in-place concrete edging with a mowing strip and a decorative edge of brick or stone, like the one shown on the opposite page, is very convenient and durable. The concrete base prevents the bricks or stones from falling over and from frost-heaving. Choose bricks or pavers designed to be walked on. If your ground freezes in the winter, choose severe-weathering brick.

Mixing your own ready-mix concrete isn't hard; just follow the instructions on the bag. To decide how many bags you'll need, multiply the width of your edging by its depth and length. This will give you its volume in cubic inches. Each ½-cubic-foot bag of concrete mix will fill 864 cubic inches.

When you work with concrete, wear tough gloves. Wash off any concrete that gets on your skin right away to prevent chemical burns. Don't pour more concrete base at one time than you can finish before it hardens.

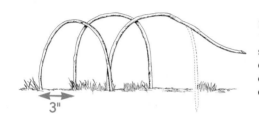

3"

Step 1. Push one end of an 18" willow branch into the soil. Insert the other end about 6" away. Repeat along entire edge, overlapping the arches.

Step 2. Weave 4 long twigs in and out around bases of arches; push ends into soil.

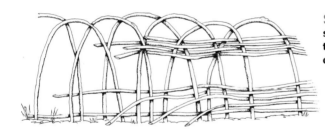

Step 3. Weave a second band of 4 twigs near top of arches.

A decorative willow edging **is fun to make and is also surprisingly durable. Choose green, flexible branches that are easy to bend and weave, and strip the bark off the ends to prevent them from sprouting.**

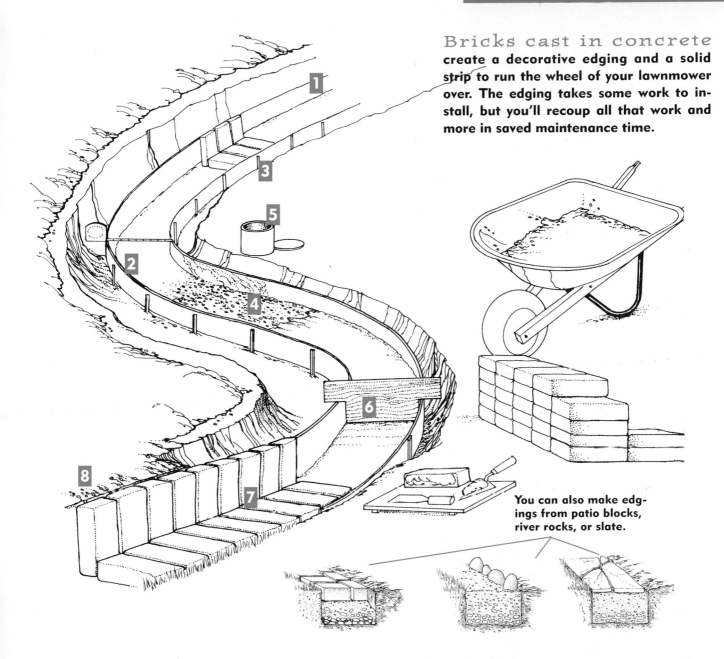

Bricks cast in concrete

create a decorative edging and a solid strip to run the wheel of your lawnmower over. The edging takes some work to install, but you'll recoup all that work and more in saved maintenance time.

You can also make edgings from patio blocks, river rocks, or slate.

Step 1. Dig a 9"-deep, flat-bottomed trench. The trench should be 8" wider than the width of the edging.

Step 2. Hammer in wooden stakes and fasten 8"-high hardboard strips to them to make a form for the edging. Check with a measuring tape as you work to be sure forms are parallel.

Step 3. Set a few loose bricks in place to check that the form is correct. Pack soil into low spots to level the bottom of the trench.

Step 4. Pour a 4" layer of fine gravel into the trench between the forms, and use your feet or the end of a 2 × 4 to pack it smooth.

Step 5. Grease inside edges of forms with vegetable shortening so they'll be easy to remove after edging is laid.

Step 6. Pour 2" of prepared ready-mix concrete over the gravel; smooth it with a leveler.

Step 7. Set bricks in still-soft concrete; slant flat bricks slightly outward to shed water. Coat the forward edge of each brick with a ¼"-thick layer of ready-mix mortar. Use a putty knife to remove excess mortar and to cut a groove in each joint.

Step 8. Wait a few hours once bricks are in place. Then take off forms, fill in soil, and replace turf. Wait a few days before putting weight on the edging.

Paths

The minimum width for a foot path is 18 inches. For a path that's used daily, 3 or 4 feet is a more suitable width. On a 5-foot path, two people can walk abreast even if plants drape romantically over the path's edges.

Choosing materials. Paths that will take daily use should be smooth, solid, and nonslip. Poured concrete, asphalt, or large slabs of quarried stone are your best choices. Firmly set bricks or pavers or wooden walkways will also do but are harder to keep free of snow.

Loose material such as gravel, crushed shells, or sand makes a fine path for more leisurely strolling. Wood chips, bark chips, sawdust, mown grass, stepping-stones, and even bare soil in some climates serve well for lightly traveled, informal paths and are easy on the budget.

A brick path set in sand, like the one shown on this page, is easy to build and will stand up to all climates. If you live in an area where the ground freezes in winter, use severe-weathering bricks.

In regions where the ground never freezes, you can skip the gravel layer as long as your soil drains well. Dig the trench 4 to 6 inches deep, spread landscape fabric over the soil base, and add 2 to 4 inches of sand. If your design involves cutting bricks, get the professionals at the building-supply center to show you what tools you'll need and how to make cuts safely.

Cut out — — Cut out

For better drainage, cut your leveler like this to give your walk a gentle, mounded shape.

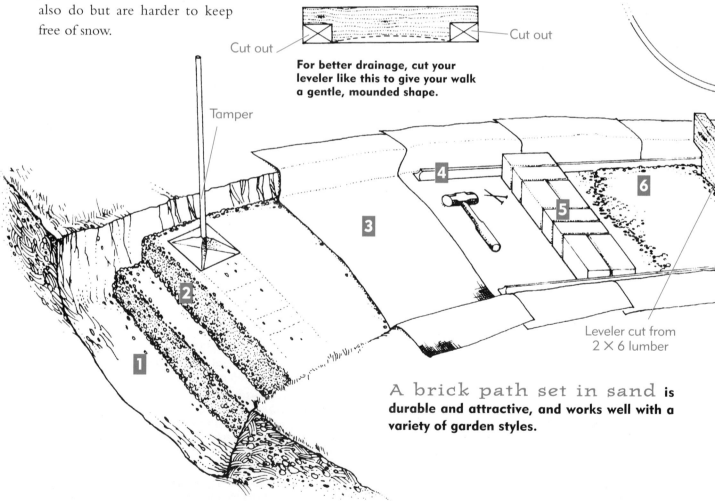

Tamper

Leveler cut from 2 × 6 lumber

A brick path set in sand is durable and attractive, and works well with a variety of garden styles.

Try making a brick "rug" in the center of a fragrant perennial planting for a seating area. Use the same techniques as you would for a brick path, but make an oval or rectangular frame instead.

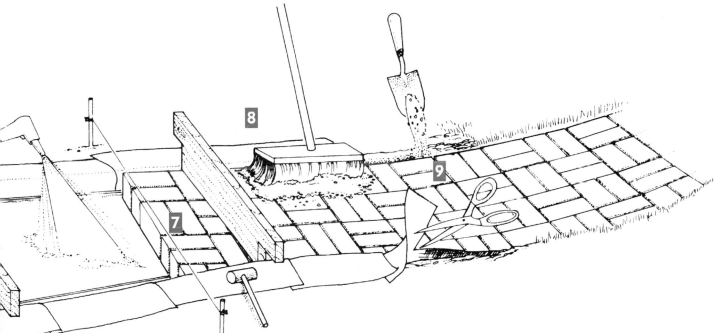

Step 1. Dig a flat-bottomed trench 12" deep and about 5' wide.

Step 2. Pack in a 5"-deep layer of compactable gravel. Then add and tamp more gravel to create a 9" compacted base.

Step 3. Spread landscape fabric over the gravel, overlapping the pieces.

Step 4. Lay two strips of rigid plastic edging along the sides of the trench, and use galvanized spikes to anchor one strip in place.

Step 5. Test-lay some bricks to determine exactly where to position the second edging strip. Anchor the second edging strip, keeping the two strips parallel.

Step 6. Spread 1" sand, water it well, and tamp it solid. Smooth out the surface with a leveler (a second person helps here). If the brick pattern involves straight lines, stretch a string guide now as a starting point.

Step 7. Begin laying bricks. Tap each brick sharply with a rubber mallet to set it firmly in place. Press bricks tightly against edging strips. Leave ⅛" gap between bricks.

Step 8. Use a leveler to check whether bricks are even. Tap down any high ones. Brush loose sand into the gaps until they are ¼" short of being full. Water with a fine spray. From this point on, you can walk on the bricks.

Step 9. Fold fabric over bricks and backfill the remaining gap with soil. Snip off the excess fabric ½" below the path surface.

Stone Retaining Walls

By building a stone retaining wall, you can turn a tough-to-maintain slope into a productive and beautiful garden. A dry-laid (mortarless) stone wall is an excellent project for a beginning wall builder.

It's best not to try building a wall more than 3 feet high. If you have a slope that would require a high wall, you have two options: Either split the slope and build two walls with a level planting terrace between them, or hire a professional to build one high stone wall.

Step-by-Step Wall Building

If you don't already have an abundance of stones on your property, you can buy natural and quarried stone, or even man-made interlocking building blocks. To find sources, look under "Stone" in the yellow pages of your telephone directory. If you have stone delivered, have it dumped as close to the worksite as possible, preferably with about half of the load on the uphill side of your wall and half downhill.

Take it easy when you're working. Always lift with your legs, not your back; and if you

can't lift a stone easily—*don't* lift it. Use a couple of stout iron bars to roll and pry stones that are too big to lift, and use sturdy wooden ramps to get them up onto the wall as you build.

Here's how to build a stone retaining wall like the one shown on the opposite page.

1. Use a spade or shovel to dig out a flat area at the base of the slope. Cut out a flat area equal to the thickness of the planned wall, plus 1 foot more.

Pile the excavated soil up slope, or somewhere else out of your way.

2. Mark the outline of the outside face of your wall in the dirt. (Keep in mind that there's no law that walls have to be straight.) Then mark a second line behind the first, one foot back from the rear edge of the wall. For example, if your wall will be 1½ feet thick, mark the second line 2½ feet back from the first. Two flexible hoses work well for marking out smoothly curving walls.

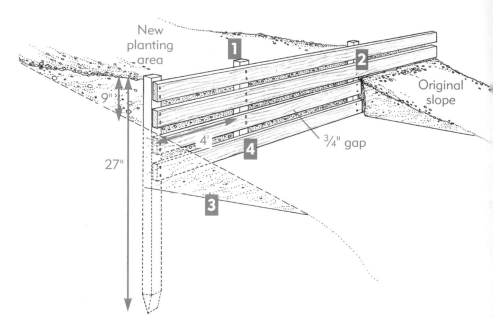

Step 1. Pound posts into the ground in a line along the area you want to terrace. Leave 9" exposed at the top.

Step 2. Nail two rows of 1 × 4 boards along the tops of the posts.

Step 3. Dig the soil out downslope and pile it above the wall to expose another 9" of post.

Step 4. Nail two rows of 1 × 4s to the newly exposed parts of the posts.

A simple wooden retaining wall **is a quick, temporary solution for controlling an unstable slope. It will hold the earth in place for at least three years.**

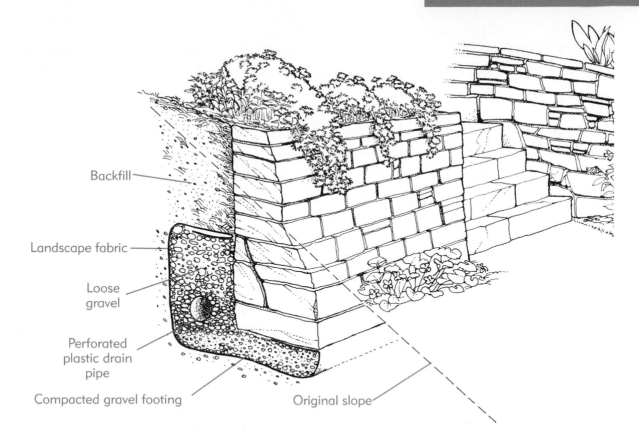

Backfill

Landscape fabric

Loose gravel

Perforated plastic drain pipe

Compacted gravel footing

Original slope

A dry-laid stone wall works well as a retaining wall at the bottom of a slope. Perforated plastic pipe positioned behind the wall promotes good drainage.

3. Dig a 12-inch-deep, flat-bottomed trench between the two guidelines you marked. Don't dig deeper than 12 inches your wall should be built on undisturbed soil.

4. Line the trench and 2½ feet up the exposed earth face with strips of landscape fabric, overlapping adjacent strips 6 inches. Anchor the fabric temporarily to keep it in place.

5. Pour a 6- to 8-inch layer of compactable gravel into the trench and tamp it down well. Fold the fabric in over the gravel at the outside edge of the trench.

6. Spread out all the stones so you can see what you have to work with. Then, start laying up your wall. Place the largest stones first, following the outer contour of the trench. Adjust the underlying gravel so the stones sit firmly.

7. Continue adding layers, choosing the stones carefully. Ideally, each stone should span the joints in the layer below it, from front to back and/or from side to side. Overlapping the stones strengthens the wall. Also, make sure the stones sit firmly. If necessary, slip small, flat stones under the larger ones to remove any wobble.

8. When the wall is about 1 foot high, lay a length of 4-inch-diameter perforated plastic pipe on the gravel behind it for drainage. The pipe will exit the wall at a corner. Or, if your wall will not have exposed corners, use an elbow to direct the pipe out through the front of the wall. Cover the pipe with 1 foot of loose, coarse gravel and fold the landscape fabric over the gravel toward the wall.

9. Lay more layers of stone, making the wall a little narrower with each layer (about 2 inches for every foot of height). Keep the back of the wall vertical, and taper the outside. Use large, flat stones for the top layer, then backfill in behind the wall with the soil you dug out of the slope.

Adding Height with Trellises and Arbors

A yard full of perennials can look like a flat sea of plants. To give your landscape depth, variety, and some soothing shade in the long term, you'll want to include shrubs and trees in your design. You can also use arbors, pillars, and other vertical features like those shown on this page.

A rustic arch. It's easy to add height with a rustic arch made from cut saplings, like the one illustrated on the opposite page. You can use hickory, oak, or maple saplings. Cedar or locust would be even better because they are more rot-resistant.

To build the arch, you'll need 4-inch-diameter saplings for the uprights and crossbars. Cut the four uprights 6½ feet long; cut two 18-inch crossbars and two 12-inch crossbars.

For the ridge pole and rafters, use 2½-inch-diameter saplings. The ridge pole is 18

A wooden arch is a lovely rustic feature for a perennial garden. You can build one in a single weekend, using only a saw, hammer, and drill. ➤

inches long; the four rafters are each 5 feet long.

Last, you'll need 1½-inch-diameter saplings for the lattice; cut 12, each 4 feet long.

The arch is held together with 8-, 10-, and 12-penny common nails.

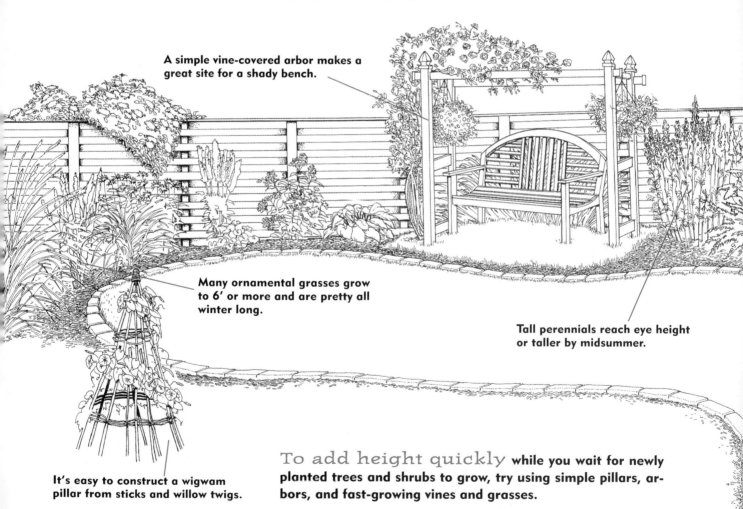

A simple vine-covered arbor makes a great site for a shady bench.

Many ornamental grasses grow to 6' or more and are pretty all winter long.

Tall perennials reach eye height or taller by midsummer.

It's easy to construct a wigwam pillar from sticks and willow twigs.

To add height quickly while you wait for newly planted trees and shrubs to grow, try using simple pillars, arbors, and fast-growing vines and grasses.

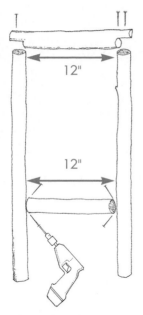

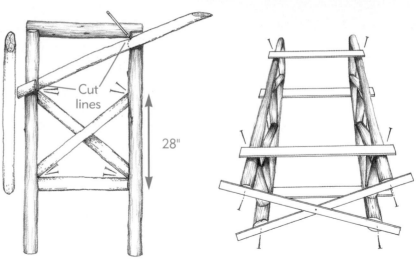

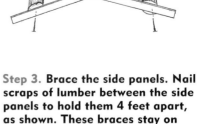

12"

12"

Cut lines

28"

Step 1. Assemble the two side panels. Drill two holes through the uprights at each joint, insert 12d nails, and hammer them firmly into the crossbars.

Step 2. Add lattice braces. Lay a lattice piece across the panel. Mark where to cut and trim with a saw. Drill two holes through each end, insert 10d nails, and hammer them firmly into the uprights.

Step 3. Brace the side panels. Nail scraps of lumber between the side panels to hold them 4 feet apart, as shown. These braces stay on until the arch is installed.

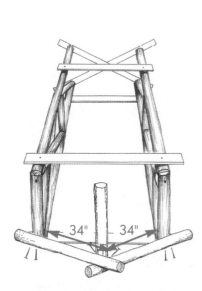

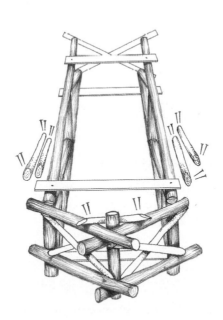

34"   34"

Step 4. Add the rafters and ridge pole. Drill and nail two rafters to the uprights and each other. Position the ridge pole, and drill and nail it firmly to the rafters. Then attach the second pair of rafters.

Step 5. Attach the roof lattices. Use the same procedure as for the side lattices. Use the scrap ends of the lattice pieces to reinforce the arch joints. Drill and nail them on firmly with 8d nails.

Step 6. Set the arch on concrete pavers (to keep the wood dry and prevent rot). Anchor the arch with 4' metal fenceposts driven into the ground next to each of the uprights.

235

Lighting Your Landscape

If you have a busy lifestyle, you may rarely see your perennials during the workweek. Wouldn't it be nice to sit outside and enjoy your flowers long after the sun sets? You can do it by adding lighting to your perennial plantings. You can position lights to illuminate a bed from either the front (spotlighting) or above (downlighting), or you can create special, subtle effects by backlighting or lighting them from below (uplighting).

With a simple do-it-yourself 12-volt lighting system, it's surprisingly easy and affordable to light up your landscape. You can buy simple kits with a transformer that plugs into a regular household outlet. In some systems the lights even snap on or off the wire with no tools, so you can move them around to create different effects.

Spotlighting shows plants in color, though they're more pastel than they are by daylight. Use a row of spotlights to illuminate a planting of perennials so that you can enjoy a view of them from inside after dark.

Uplighting behind spotlighted plants softens their harsh shadows. For a glowing effect, try uplighting ornamental grasses or a perennial with loose, feathery flower clusters.

Backlighting gives you dark silhouettes against a lighted background. Backlighting against a fence or wall works well behind plants that sway in the breeze, such as ornamental grasses or tall ferns.

Downlighting allows you to enjoy the flowers and walk safely at night.

Water Features

Water is a wonderful garden accent, and a water garden surrounded with perennials can be the centerpiece of your landscape. It's easy to construct a small pool in your yard from a kit available at garden centers or from mail-order suppliers.

To frame a small pool, plant tall perennials such as hollyhocks (*Alcea* spp.) beside and behind it. Or build a low mound around the back edge of the pond and plant it with hostas and astilbes. Plants with nodding stems, such as daylilies, blue fescue (*Festuca cinerea*), and fountain grass (*Pennisetum* spp.), reflect prettily in the water and the arching leaves give an illusion of cascading water.

Tie the pool to the surrounding plantings by setting moisture-loving plants such as primroses (*Primula* spp.), Japanese iris (*Iris ensata*), yellow flag (*I. pseudacorus*), Siberian iris (*I. sibirica*), and cardinal flower (*Lobelia cardinalis*) in the moist soil around the edge and in pots set in the shallows.

To keep the water clean, stock your pool with one aquatic snail and one bunch of underwater plant for every square foot of surface. Decorate the surface of the pool and keep the water cool with small floating plants (one for every 3 to 6 square feet of surface) and water lilies (one for every 10 to 20 square feet). Adding fish will help keep your pool free of mosquito larvae. Use 1 inch of fish per square foot of water surface; for example, ten 2-inch fish or five 4-inch fish for a pool with 20 square feet of surface.

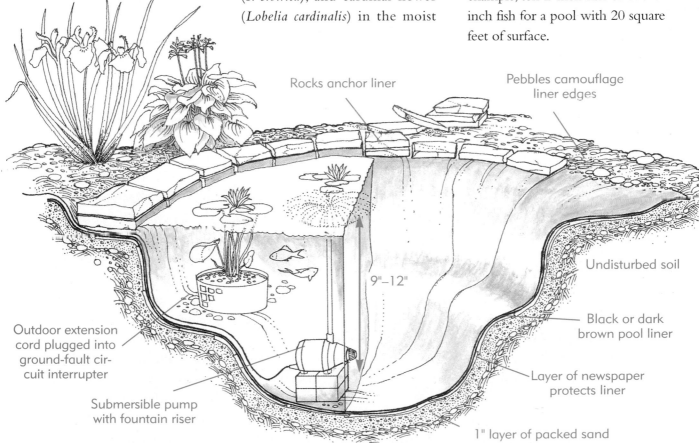

Rocks anchor liner

Pebbles camouflage liner edges

9"–12"

Undisturbed soil

Outdoor extension cord plugged into ground-fault circuit interrupter

Submersible pump with fountain riser

Black or dark brown pool liner

Layer of newspaper protects liner

1" layer of packed sand

A cross-section of a water garden reveals the plastic liner that holds the water in, and a submersible pump that creates the fountain at the water's surface.

Planting Perennials

Planting perennials in well-prepared soil is a simple matter of digging a hole, slipping the plant in, and giving it a good drink. If at all possible, take the time to thoroughly cultivate and improve the soil before planting (see pages 222-227 for guidance). But, if you're set on planting right now, at least use a spading fork to loosen the soil 9 to 12 inches deep before digging the actual planting hole.

Perennial plants are sold either in pots (or pot-shaped chunks of potting medium) or with their roots washed clean of soil (bareroot). Both types will give you good results, and you plant them in much the same way. For both types, be sure to keep the roots moist until you are ready to plant them. Store dormant plants in a cool, dark place. Put growing plants in a cool, shady spot.

Planting Technique

On planting day, you will need a shovel or trowel, a watering can or hose, extra mulch, and the written planting plan that shows where to position your plants. If you're planting more than a few plants, use a measuring tape and marking stakes to measure and mark where each new plant should be set before you start. If it's a cloudy day, you can use the plants themselves as markers— just set them where they will go. But if it's hot and sunny, keep the plants cool and shaded until just before you plant them.

Set the roots free. Each planting hole needs to be large enough for the roots to be spread out without cramping, so take a look at your plant's roots before digging. Carefully knock a container plant out of its pot and use your fingers (not a knife) to tease loose the roots and knock free as much of the potting mix as possible. It may help to slosh the rootball around in a bucket of water or squirt it with a hose.

This may strike you as cruel and unnecessary treatment. Keep in mind that potting mix is usually lighter and better-draining that natural soil. Container plants that are planted with the rootball intact often suffer (and may die) even when the surrounding soil is moist because the potting mix drains so readily. By "bare-rooting" container plants, you allow their roots to make contact with the real soil right away.

Once you've liberated the roots, see how wide they stretch. For plants that arrive bareroot, just open up the bundle and see how long the roots are. Then cover the plant's roots back up so they don't dry out. (Try throwing an old wet terry towel over them.)

Dig a planting hole. Scrape away any surface mulch and dig a hole. The hole should be large enough so you can spread the roots in all directions at about a 45 degree angle. (If you're planting a group of plants, you may want to dig one large flat-bottomed hole, as shown on the opposite page.) Pile a small heap of soil in the bottom of the hole and drape the roots over the heap. The plant should sit at the same level as it grew at the nursery. If it doesn't, adjust the height of the soil heap. Then arrange the roots gently over the heap and fill the hole with soil. Wiggle the plant a little as you fill the hole to help the soil settle around the roots. Use your fingers to push the soil between the roots and under the crown of the plant.

Quench the plant's thirst. When the hole is almost full, pour in a good drink of water or compost tea and let it soak in. (See page 275 for a recipe for compost tea.) This will help settle the soil. Then finish filling in the hole with soil, and give the roots another drink. Finally, redistribute the mulch or add new mulch to cover the bare ground around the new plant.

Fill out a name tag. Label your new plant. You may get a plastic name tag when you buy the plant—it will last a few seasons. Metal labels last longer. Be sure the pen you use to write on the label will stand up to the elements. Some so-called permanent markers fade to invisibility after just a few weeks of exposure. Buy a marker designed for outdoor use, or use a lead pencil.

If you don't like the looks of plastic or metal labels, use your creativity. One clever gardener collects smooth, round, cream-colored river pebbles, writes the plant names on them with a horticultural marking pen, and then applies varnish. The resulting labels look quite charming.

Aftercare

If you're planting an actively growing plant rather than a dormant one, it's a good idea to give it some shade for a few days. Put a lawn chair or an old storage crate over the plant to make great instant shade.

You'll need to keep your new plants watered until they are well established. For a dormant plant, you may only need to water every few days for the first two weeks after planting. Actively growing plants will use more water and may need watering every day for a few weeks and occasional watering thereafter.

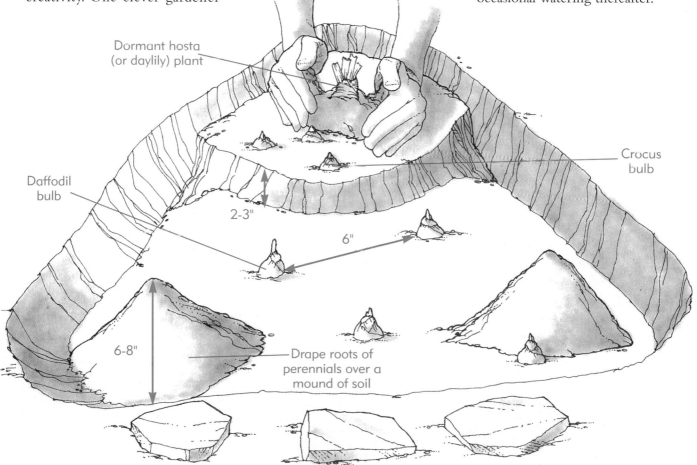

Dormant hosta
(or daylily) plant

Crocus bulb

Daffodil bulb

2-3"

6"

6-8"

Drape roots of perennials over a mound of soil

Late-sprouting perennials like hostas **are perfect bedmates for spring-flowering bulbs. Save yourself time by planting a group of perennials and bulbs in one large excavated site. Combine crocuses and daffodils with hostas for a shady site, or with daylilies for a sunny site.**

Growing into a New Landscape

When compared to the quick, colorful display you can achieve with annuals, a new perennial planting can be disappointing at first. Newly planted perennials often take a year or two to fill out into attractive, blooming plants that give you the lush landscape of your dreams. Take heart—there are some tricks you can use to make the growing-in years more palatable.

Fill the Holes

Fill the empty spaces between your new perennials with colorful annual flowers, vegetables, shrubs, or with sculpture or driftwood. Be sure to leave enough space around your perennials so they have room to grow. Choose filler plants with a similar color scheme to the perennials near them so you can enjoy a finished effect right away.

Annuals. Some great tall annuals for adding height and substance include ornamental sunflowers, tall zinnias, and airy cosmos. Frilly redleaf and greenleaf lettuce, red and yellow peppers, and stately okra with its showy flowers are also interesting additions. And of course, petunias, impatiens, and marigolds make good space fillers.

Bulbs. Groups of lilies and alliums (*Allium* spp.) are a great permanent addition to any planting and help give a finished look from year one. Spring bulbs get the season off to an early, colorful start and are perfect companion plants for slow-to-sprout perennials. Plant bulbs in groups or clusters, rather than individually. For fast summer flower power, it's hard to beat showy frost-tender bulbs like gladiolus, dahlias, and cannas (*Canna* spp.). Frost-tender caladiums (*Caladium hortulanum*) are great foliage plants for sun or shade. In colder zones, treat them as annuals or dig up the bulbs in fall and store them in a cool room during winter for replanting the following spring.

Vines and grasses. Don't overlook vines for adding height and interest. Train them up temporary or permanent trellises, chicken-wire pillars, and fences. Ornamental grasses are also good plants for adding height and interest throughout the life of your landscape. When choosing ornamental grasses, be sure to select clump formers rather than running grasses, unless you want a grass that spreads rampantly across the landscape.

For more suggested plants to complement your perennials, see pages 242–247.

Phase It In

The easiest way to phase in a garden is to divide your proposed planting into two or more parts, then prepare and plant one part each year. This spreads the cost and work out over time.

One of the easiest ways to make your new perennial planting look less sparse is to fill in between the perennials with colorful annual flowers and summer-blooming bulbs like lilies, gladiolus, and dahlias.

For a filled appearance right away, plant the area you've prepared with large plants that will bloom in the first season. The following season, prepare the second section of the bed, and buy large plants to fill it as well.

An alternate strategy is to buy small plants, and buy all the plants needed to complete the entire garden. You'll plant these at close spacings in half the bed. By the following season, you can prepare the other half of the bed and transplant the appropriate plants into it.

With a little forethought, you can use divisions taken from perennials planted in the first year to fill the sections you'll prepare in subsequent years. This approach does require patience

For a finished look right away, plant just a portion of a planned bed. In a year or two, when the plants have grown larger, prepare the balance of the area and transplant the plants to their final locations.

because you may need to wait more than one year for your original plants to become big enough to divide.

You can also fill spaces in beds with perennials that are available free from friends or from an inexpensive source.

While they're not part of your planned design, they will give you a finished-looking bed. As time goes on and you can afford to buy more of the perennials you need for the design, you can dig out the "filler" perennials and replace them.

New perennial plantings will look less sparse when attractive mulch surrounds them. Garden sculpture and pots of bright annuals add interest. Hanging baskets on poles add height and draw the eye away from the sometimes puny perennials.

Companions for Perennial Gardens

Flowering perennials aren't the only plants you'll want to use in your gardens. Ornamental grasses, shrubs, annuals, vines, and bulbs all have important roles in the home landscape.

In the tables that follow, you'll find suggested plants that will provide quick color while new perennial gardens are growing in. You'll also find great plants for adding early and late (or evergreen) color to give your landscape four-season interest. In addition, many of the shrubs, grasses, and vines listed are excellent choices when you want to add height and structure to perennial beds and borders.

For each grass, shrub, annual, vine, and bulb named, you'll also find suggestions for a perennial companion plant that will grow well in the same light and soil conditions.

Grass Companions for Perennial Gardens

Common and Botanical Name	Description	Culture and Plant Combinations
Reed grass *Calamagrostis* spp.	Clumps of narrow, arching leaves and tall, upright flower spikes 4'–7' tall.	Sun or partial shade. Combines well with goldenrod (*Solidago* spp.). Adds vertical interest. Most species hardy from Zones 5–9.
Sedges *Carex* spp.	Clumps of narrow, arching leaves to 2' tall. *C. elata* 'Bowles Golden' has green-edged, yellow leaves and is hardy in Zones 5–9.	Sun or shade. Thrive in a wide range of soil moisture. Not all are frost hardy. Try black sedge (*C. nigra*) with columbines (*Aquilegia* spp.) to bring out the blue-gray leaves of both. Some species hardy from Zones 5–9, others only to Zone 7 or 8.
Blue fescue *Festuca cinerea*	Soft, fine-textured mounds of blue-green foliage. 'Elijah Blue' is 8" tall. 'Azurit' is 12"–16" tall.	Sun to partial shade. Use blue fescue to set off pinks (*Dianthus* spp.). Zones 4–9.
Maiden grass *Miscanthus* spp.	3'–15' clumping grasses with large, plumelike blooms. *M. sinensis* var. *strictus* grows to 6' and has green leaves with golden bands every few inches.	Sun. This is not a plant for small gardens. Try it with large swaths of orange coneflower (*Rudbeckia fulgida*). Zones 4–9.
Switch grass *Panicum virgatum*	Upright, clumping grass with dark green leaves and airy flowers. 'Heavy Metal' has blue-green foliage and airy flowers to 3½'.	Partial shade. Try reddish 'Haense Herms' with boltonia (*Boltonia asteroides*) for a fall display. Zones 5–9.
Fountain grass *Pennisetum* spp.	Arching clumps with white, yellow, or reddish bottlebrush flowers. *P. alopecuroides* 'Hameln' is 12"–20" tall with white flowers and green leaves.	Sun. Combine with purple coneflower (*Echinacea purpurea*) for an informal display. Some species Zones 6–9; others are less hardy but can be grown as annuals.

Shrub Companions for Perennial Gardens

Common and Botanical Name	Description	Culture and Plant Combinations
Bottlebrush buckeye *Aesculus parviflora*	Spreading 8'–10' shrub with 8"–12" upright clusters of white flowers in midsummer.	Sun to light shade. Much wider than it is tall—makes an imposing backdrop for a perennial planting. Try it behind a mass planting of mixed daylilies. Zones 4–8.
Butterfly bushes *Buddleia* spp.	Quick-growing shrubs with arching branches and long spikes of fragrant purple, pink, yellow, or white flowers from summer to early fall.	Sun. Prune at least one-third of the stems back to ground level each spring. Combine with butterfly weed (*Asclepias tuberosa*) to attract butterflies all summer. Zones 5–9.
Summersweet *Clethra alnifolia*	3'–8' shrub with spikes of small, fragrant pink or white flowers in late summer.	Sun. Spreads sideways to form a broad clump. Pair with the curious steel blue flowers of globe thistle (*Echinops ritro*). Zones 4–9.
Winterberry *Ilex verticillata*	Deciduous 6'–10' shrub with brilliant red or yellow berries in fall and winter.	Sun or partial shade. Tolerates poor drainage. The rich, green foliage is a fine foil for bee balm (*Monarda didyma*). Zones 4–8.
Shrubby cinquefoil *Potentilla fruticosa*	Spreading shrub to 4' with small leaves and covered with 1" yellow, orange, or white flowers from summer through frost.	Sun. Prune in late winter to keep small and neat if desired. Pair with summer-blooming cranesbills such as *Geranium* 'Johnson's Blue' and *G. endressii* 'Wargrave Pink'. Zones 2–8.
Roses *Rosa* spp.	Shrubs with large, often fragrant flowers, in all colors but blue. Try disease-resistant or old-fashioned types.	Sun. Some species will tolerate partial shade. Blue balloon flower (*Platycodon grandiflorus*) or peach-leaved bellflowers (*Campanula persicifolia*) are delightful with pink roses. Zones 4–10.
Bumald spirea *Spiraea bumalda*	Low, rounded shrub to 2' with small white to deep pink flowers in flat 4"–6" clusters in late spring.	Sun. Tolerates most types of soil. Prune before flowering. Combine with pink and white astilbes (*Astilbe* spp.). Zones 4–8.
Lilacs *Syringa* spp.	Arching shrubs with large, fragrant flower clusters in white, blue, wine red, and lavender. *S. microphylla* and *S. patula* 'Miss Kim' are small enough to blend well with perennials.	Sun. Prune the oldest one-third of the stems off at ground level every winter. Plant with purple rock cress (*Aubrieta deltoidea*) or yellow basket-of-gold (*Aurinia saxatilis*). Zones 3–8.
Blueberries *Vaccinium* spp.	2'–6' shrubs with small pink or white spring flowers, tasty blue fruit, and beautiful red fall color.	Sun or partial shade. Needs acid soil. Plant with woodland wildflowers such as trout lilies (*Erythronium* spp.), which also thrive in acid soil. Zones 4–8.
Viburnums *Viburnum* spp.	4'–15' shrubs with showy clusters of white or pink flowers in early spring to early summer; orange-red fall foliage.	Sun or partial shade. Prune after flowering. The later-flowering types are a great backdrop for bright, late-spring bloomers like peonies. Hardiness varies by species.

Annual Companions for Perennial Gardens

Common and Botanical Name	Description	Culture and Plant Combinations
Joseph's-coat *Amaranthus tricolor*	Upright 2' foliage plant with red, yellow, and green leaves.	Sun. Space plants 1½'–2' apart. Try this bold foliage plant with yellow daylilies.
Madagascar periwinkle *Catharanthus roseus*	Sprawling 1'–2' plant with numerous pink or white flowers.	Sun. Heat- and drought-tolerant. Never needs deadheading. Space plants 1' apart. For a bold splash of color, pair it with rose mallow (*Hibiscus moscheutos*).
Cleome *Cleome hasslerana*	Bushy 3'–5' plant with airy white, pink, or purple flower clusters.	Sun. Heat- and drought-tolerant. Space plants 1'–3' apart. These airy, spiderlike flowers go well with blue or purple delphiniums.
Coleus *Coleus × hybridus*	Brilliantly colored purple, red, yellow, and green leaves on 8"–18" plant. Leaves are often crinkled.	Shade. Pinch often for short, stocky plants. Grow from seed or cuttings. Space 6"–10" apart. Try coleus around the feet of cardinal flowers (*Lobelia cardinalis*) in dappled shade.
Cosmos *Cosmos bipinnatus*	Purple, pink, or white flowers with yellow centers on 2'–6' airy plant.	Sun. Tolerates poor, dry soil. Choose stocky cultivars to avoid staking. Space 1'–2' apart. Plant with blue catmint (*Nepeta × faassenii*) for a pretty, airy look.
Common sunflower *Helianthus annuus*	Large single or double orange, yellow, cream, or red-brown flowers on branches of 2'–10' plant.	Sun. Heat- and drought-tolerant. Space plants 2'–4' apart. Try planting sunflowers behind blanket flowers (*Gaillardia × grandiflora*) to echo their color and shape.
Sweet alyssum *Lobularia maritima*	Clusters of tiny white, pink, or purple honey-scented flowers on 6"-high mats.	Sun. Shear off faded flowers to encourage rebloom. Great for filling in large areas between young perennials. Space plants 6" apart.
Moss rose *Portulaca grandiflora*	Low-growing mats studded with white, pink, red, yellow, or orange single or double flowers.	Sun. Succulent plants that thrive in hot sites and poor soils. Space 12" apart. Try moss roses at the base of hollyhocks (*Alcea rosea*).
Castor bean *Ricinus communis*	Imposing 3'–6' plants with large, reddish leaves and fluffy red or cream ball-shaped flowers.	Sun. Repels moles from the area. Seeds are poisonous. Space 3' apart. Looks stunning behind the chartreuse flowers of lady's-mantle (*Alchemilla mollis*).
Mexican sunflower *Tithonia rotundifolia*	Orange daisylike flowers with yellow centers on 3'–6' plants.	Sun. Heat- and drought-tolerant. Space 2' apart. The orange flowers are a perfect echo for orange crocosmia (*Crocosmia × crocosmiiflora*) flowers.
Narrowleaf zinnia *Zinnia angustifolia* (also known as *Z. linearis*)	Single orange flowers on bushy 1' plants.	Sun. Mildew-resistant and tolerant of heat and humidity. Space 1' apart. Try these in front of common torch lilies (*Kniphofia uvaria*).
Pansy *Viola wittrockiana*	Showy flat blooms in a variety of solid colors or with mixed markings on 6"–12" tall plants.	Sun or shade. Thrive in cool weather in rich, moist soil. Space 6" apart. Pansies look great beside tall bearded hybrid irises.

Climbing Companions for Perennial Gardens

Common and Botanical Name	Description	Culture and Plant Combinations
Crimson starglory *Mina lobata* (also known as *Quamoclit lobata*)	Twining vine to 20' with long-stalked clusters of scarlet buds and creamy yellow-and-orange flowers throughout the summer.	Sun to light shade. Grows best in well-drained soil. Try behind hot-colored perennials like monbretias (*Crocosmia* spp.). Zones 8–10; grow as an annual in colder areas.
Hybrid clematis *Clematis* hybrids	Woody vines 6'–15' tall with purple, blue, red, pink, or white 3"–6" star-shaped flowers in summer.	Sun or light shade. Likes cool, moist roots, so plant in humus-rich soil and mulch well. Try a light blue clematis behind pink and white peonies. Zones 4–9.
Hyacinth bean *Dolichos lablab* (also known as *Lablab purpureus*)	Twining vine to 15' with showy clusters of lavender flowers and purple pods all season.	Sun. Tender perennial grown as an annual. You can eat the beans as snap, shell, or dry beans. The flowers, leaves, and fleshy roots are also edible. Pair this imposing plant with sunflower heliopsis (*Heliopsis helianthoides*).
Morning glory *Ipomoea tricolor*	Twining vines to 10' tall with large heart-shaped leaves and 4"–5" blue, lavender, pink, or white flowers all season.	Sun. Tolerates poor, dry soil. Plant seed in spring. Morning glories go well with garden phlox (*Phlox paniculata*). Hardy to Zone 8; in colder zones, grow as an annual.
Sweet pea *Lathyrus odoratus*	Tendrilled vine to 6' with clusters of fragrant flowers in all colors in summer. Nonvining dwarf cultivars also available.	Sun, or sun with afternoon shade in warm areas. Pick flowers to encourage continuous bloom. Annual; plant seed in early spring or in fall in warm areas. Try planting them near clustered bellflower (*Campanula glomerata*).
Scarlet runner bean *Phaseolus coccineus*	Twining vine to 8' with clusters of red or white flowers all season.	Sun. Tender perennial grown as annual. You can eat the beans as snap, shell, or dry beans. Flowers, young leaves, and fleshy roots are also edible. Try planting this to echo the vibrant color of Maltese cross (*Lychnis chalcedonica*).
Climbing roses *Rosa* spp.	Long, sturdy canes to 10' with 3"–4" flowers in red, pink, white, or yellow in summer. Some rebloom later.	Sun. Can be trained up or along supports with ties. Remove spent flowers to encourage rebloom. Pink and white roses are beautiful companions for common foxgloves (*Digitalis purpurea*). Hardy to Zone 6.
Black-eyed Susan vine *Thunbergia alata*	Twining vine to 6' with 1"–2" dark-eyed orange, yellow, or white flowers all season.	Full sun and moist soil. Start seeds indoors 6–8 weeks before last frost for earlier display. Plant this near 'Palace Purple' heuchera (*Heuchera micrantha* var. 'Palace Purple'); the flower centers pick up the color of the heuchera leaves.
Canary creeper *Tropaeolum peregrinum*	Vine to 8' with deeply lobed leaves and yellow birdlike flowers all season.	Partial shade and moist soil. Annual. Try this with shasta daisies (*Chrysanthemum* × *superbum*) or threadleaf coreopsis (*Coreopsis verticillata*).

Bulb Companions for Perennial Gardens

Common and Botanical Name	Description	Culture and Plant Combinations
Allium *Allium* spp.	Dense balls of flowers on tall stalks (4" to 4' tall, depending on species) above clumps of foliage in spring, summer, or fall. *A. giganteum* sports 5" lilac balls on 3'–4' stems in early summer.	Sun. Plant in groups for best show. Plant the tall types among silvery-leaved artemisias whose leaves will hide the tired allium foliage. Zones 5–9, some to Zone 3.
Grecian windflower *Anemone blanda*	2"–3" white, pink, purple, or blue daisy-shaped blooms on 3"–6" stems in spring.	Partial shade. Foliage is quite attractive and lasts after flowers fade. Sprinkle drifts of them in shady gardens in front of Virginia bluebell (*Mertensia virginica*). Zones 6–8.
Caladium *Caladium hortulanum*	Arching bunches of 6"–12" arrowhead-shaped green, pink, and white leaves.	Partial to full shade. Zone 10 or annual. Dig after first frost and store the almost dry tubers at around 65°F in dry vermiculite. Try planting them with hostas or ferns.
Canna *Canna generalis*	4"–6" yellow, orange, pink, or red blooms on substantial clumps of 2'–8' stalks with broad green or bronze leaves.	Sun. These bold plants combine well with young daylilies. Zones 8–10 or grown as an annual. Start plants indoors 1 month before last frost. Dig after first frost and store tubers in barely moist vermiculite at 45°–50°F.
Glory-of-the-snow *Chionodoxa luciliae*	1" star-shaped flowers in white, pink, or blue in early spring.	Sun to light shade. Plant glory-of-the-snow along walkways where their early blooms will signal spring. Plant them with daffodils and irises for a color show that will start as snow melts and last throughout spring. Zones 5–9.
Autumn crocus *Colchicum autumnale*	2"–4" lavender-pink or white goblet or water-lily–shaped flowers spring up on 4"–12" leafless stems in fall.	Sun. Plant colchicums where their coarse spring and summer foliage will be concealed by other plants. The surprising fall flowers blend well with fall asters. Zones 5–9.
Crocuses *Crocus* spp.	1"–2" goblet-shaped white, yellow, or purple blooms on 4"–6" stems in very early to early spring.	Full sun to partial shade. Crocuses light up almost any garden before most perennials even start to sprout. Zones 4–8.
Dahlias *Dahlia* spp.	1"–12" daisy- or mum-shaped blooms in every color but blue on bushy, 2'–6' plants.	Sun. Stake all but dwarf types at planting time. Plant dahlias to provide showy color all season after peonies fade. Zones 8–11, or grow as an annual. Dig after first frost and store tubers in barely moist vermiculite at 45°–50°F.
Winter aconite *Eranthis hyemalis*	1" yellow blooms on 2"–3" stems in very early spring.	Sun to full shade. These early charmers look delightful sprinkled around hellebores (*Helleborus* spp.) or just on their own. Zones 4–9.

(continued)

Bulb Companions for Perennial Gardens—Continued

Common and Botanical Name	Description	Culture and Plant Combinations
Common snowdrop *Galanthus nivalis*	One 1"–1½" white-and-green bell-shaped flower on each 6" stalk in very early spring.	Full sun to partial shade. One of the first flowers to bloom every spring (late winter). Plant these with winter aconite or with sweet woodruff (*Galium odoratum*). They naturalize freely. Zones 3–8.
Gladiolus *Gladiolus hortulanus*	2"–5" triangular blooms in every color but blue on stiff, upright 1½'–5' stems in summer and fall.	Sun. Plant bulbs at 2-week intervals until midsummer for continuous bloom. Stake taller types. The showy flower spikes look nice near threadleaf coreopsis (*Coreopsis verticillata*). Zones 7–10 or annual. Dig after first frost, dry, and hang corms in mesh bags at about 45°F.
Spanish Bluebell *Hyacinthoides hispanicus* (also sold as *Scilla hispanica* or *Endymion hispanicus*)	Loose spikes of 1" blue, pink, or white flowers on 10"–15" stems in late spring.	Partial to full shade. Care-free, long-lived shade dwellers. Try these paired with Bethlehem sage (*Pulmonaria saccharata*) for a colorful spring shade garden. Zones 3–8.
Hyacinth *Hyacinthus orientalis*	Fat spikes of 1" star-shaped flowers in all colors on 8"–12" stems in spring.	Sun. Try combining colored hyacinths with white moss pink (*Phlox subulata*) or vice versa for an eye-popping display. Zones 4–8.
Lilies *Lilium* spp.	Clusters of 2"–8" trumpet-shaped flowers in every color but blue on 2'–8' stems in summer.	Lilies like their heads in the sun and their feet in the shade, so plant them with other, shorter plants. Try orange or yellow lilies with a bright blue speedwell (*Veronica* spp.). Zones 5–8; some to Zone 3.
Common grape hyacinths *Muscari* spp.	1"–2" spikes of tiny blue or white flowers on 6"–8" stems in spring.	Sun to partial shade. Try planting hostas and grape hyacinths together under a deciduous tree. The grape hyacinths will bloom and fill the space before the late-sprouting hostas get going. Zones 4–8.
Daffodils *Narcissus* spp.	White, yellow, or orange flowers up to 4" bloom on 6"–18" stalks in early spring.	Sun to partial shade. Combine with primroses (*Primula* spp.) for a delightful spring display. Zones 3–8.
Tuberose *Polianthes tuberosa*	Loose spikes of fragrant white blossoms on tall stems up to 36" from summer to early fall.	Sun. Plant after frost in rich, well-drained soil. Keep evenly moist. Combine with fragrant daylilies and other night-fragrant perennials. Hardy to Zone 8; in cooler areas, lift the tubers and overwinter them indoors.
Siberian squill *Scilla sibirica*	Clusters of ½"–1" star-shaped blue or white flowers on 4"–6" stems in spring.	Sun to partial shade. Squills naturalize well and self-seed freely. Sprinkle squills in patches of vinca (*Vinca minor*) to give the flowering season a sensational start. Zones 2–9.
Tulips *Tulipa* spp.	1"–4" star- or goblet-shaped flowers in every color but blue on 4"–36" stems in spring.	Sun to partial shade. Try pink and white tulips with bleeding heart (*Dicentra spectabilis*). Zones 3–8.

Chapter 10

Plant Swapping, Shopping, and Propagation

Plant Swapping and Shopping • Creating Your Own Plant Nursery •

Perennial Division and Multiplication • New Plants from Roots •

Starting from Stem Cuttings • Starting Perennials from Seed •

Multiplying Bulbs

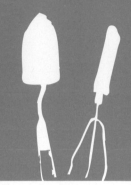

Plant Swapping and Shopping

Once your site is prepared, it's time for one of the most exciting parts of perennial gardening—getting the plants!

Shopping for perennials, whether at garden centers or through mail-order catalogs, can be almost intoxicating. There's such a range of gorgeous plants to try, and it's so tempting to try

them all. But while your first impulse may be to buy all your plants, don't overlook other sources. One of the delights of perennial gardening is swapping and sharing plants with other gardeners.

Sources of Free Plants

Gift plants. Gift plants can be a great way to enliven your landscape without spending a lot of cash. So if a plant you yearn for is growing in a friend or neighbor's garden, look it up and find out how it's propagated. Then ask boldly. Chances are she'll give you a stem cutting right now or a bit of the plant the next time it's divided.

Impassioned gardeners love to share the plants they care for. Some will whip a trowel out of their back pocket, separate a

healthy chunk of the plant, and bestow it on you with a radiant smile on the slightest provocation. A friend and mentor like this is a budding perennial gardener's dream. Of course, gift plants can also become a problem if they carry disease, insect, or weed problems. See "Be a Smart Plant Swapper" on the opposite page for some tips to help you prevent gift plants from creating a garden predicament.

Garden clubs. Local garden club swaps or sales are also good places to pick up great deals on plants that thrive in your area. To find them, check newspaper ads or bulletin boards at nurseries and your local extension office.

The woods? You may be tempted to look to local woodlands or wild areas for free plants. *Don't do it.* When you wild-collect, you may be disturbing or destroying rare or endangered plants. You may also be collecting the seeds or roots of invasive weeds or be collecting plants that are diseased.

Plant societies. As you gain experience with perennials, you may want to become a member of a local, national, or international plant society. Many focus on a specific kind of perennial, like the Iris Society. For a reasonable membership fee, members have access to meetings, workshops, lectures, newsletters, seed exchanges, plant swaps and sales, experienced members who share information and plants, and/or garden tours. For a list of plant societies, see "Resources" on page 283.

Buying Perennials

When you shop for perennials, always take a plant list with you. Think of plant shopping like grocery shopping—go by your list or you may not end up with the ingredients you need for the results you want. (Consult Chapter 8 for guidance on how to create a plant list.)

Once you have a plant list, you have more decisions to make. What size plants should you buy? And should you buy plants at local nurseries and garden centers, or via mail order from specialty nurseries? There are no universal

Be a Smart Plant Swapper

Some free (or even purchased) plants are more trouble than they are worth. If the plants or the soil around the roots contain disease organisms, weeds, or insects, they'll end up in your garden, where they could balloon into a serious pest problem. Inspect possible acquisitions carefully for the following symptoms.

• Check upper and lower leaf surfaces, stems, and crowns for insects or insect eggs.

• Reject plants that are malformed or off-color (a few spots on the leaves don't indicate a major problem).

• Plants pulled from weedy gardens or growing in weedy pots may have weed roots or seeds in the soil around their roots. Carefully wash all the soil off the roots and pick out any foreign roots before planting the specimen in your garden.

Decline possible problem plants that are offered to you by well-meaning fellow gardeners politely, or dispose of them clandestinely in a sealed trash bag. And certainly don't spend money for them!

Some quick-spreading perennials can become pests in their own right if space is tight and/or they really like the soil that you make their home. Some of these potential pests are well-loved plants, including bee balm (*Monarda didyma*), evening primrose (*Oenothera speciosa*), feverfew (*Chrysanthemum parthenium*), lamb's-ears (*Stachys byzantina*), obedient plants (*Physostegia* spp.), purple coneflower (*Echinacea purpurea*), tawny daylily (*Hemerocallis fulva*), and yarrows.

Be sure to look up all gift plants in a reliable perennial encyclopedia or catalog before you plant. If a plant is described as invasive or fast-spreading, plant it only in a site where you're sure you'll appreciate its aggresive characteristics.

answers to these two questions. But there are some guidelines that will help you make good choices.

Plant-buying strategies. Perennials are sold in three basic sizes: large, medium, and small. Price ranges tend to correspond to plant size. Check the chart on this page for a breakdown of the pros and cons of starting your garden with each size of plant.

Creating a new perennial bed or border from scratch can be an expensive proposition if you start with blooming-size plants, each

Large Plants

Large, actively growing, ready-to-bloom plants. Available in 1-gallon (or larger) pots from local garden centers, or dug-to-order field-grown plants from local grower. Rarely available by mail order.

PROS

• Ready-to-bloom plants; offer an instant finished look to your landscape

• Easy to see what the plant actually looks like

• Fresh-dug, field-grown plants usually establish themselves quickly after planting

CONS

• Large expense

• Plants are heavy to move and need large planting holes prepared

• Cultivar selection may be quite limited

• Container-grown plants may be rootbound

Midsize Plants

Small, blooming-size plants. Available either as dormant bareroot plants by mail order or as container-grown plants from garden centers and nurseries, in pots ranging in size from 4 inches up to 2 quarts.

PROS

• Huge cultivar selection via mail order

• Modest price

• Plants establish quickly; often equal in size with a larger container-grown plant within one season

CONS

• Can't see what you're getting when you order plants by mail.

• Cultivar selection may be limited at local garden centers

Small Plants

Small plants in 2- or 3-inch pots or multi-packs that are not ready to bloom. Available either from speciality mail-order catalogs or local suppliers.

PROS

• Largest selection of cultivars

• Least expensive route to starting a perennial garden

CONS

• Longer wait (possibly 2 years) for full display of flowers

• Plants need extra care to get started

of which can cost from $5 to $10 (or far more for certain desirable cultivars). You'll need to balance your need for immediate results or special cultivars against your need to stay within a budget. If you opt to start your new garden with small perennials that won't bloom or fill the garden the first year, refer to "Growing into a New Landscape" on page 240 for help in making new beds look more full and finished.

Shopping in person. Buying locally offers two advantages: You can look before you buy, and you can ask questions face to face. Choose a garden center or nursery where the plants look well cared for and are clearly labeled. The staff should have answers for your questions or find answers quickly.

When you buy a perennial, what you're really looking for is a great set of roots. Tops are nice, too, but without the roots, they're just window dressing.

When you select plants, start by taking an overall look at the plants you're considering. They should have good leaf color and be perky, not thirsty and wilted. Yellowed or missing lower leaves suggest the plants haven't been cared for properly and may not do well for you. Check the undersides of leaves for signs of disease or insects. Reject any plants that don't meet the grade.

Also look at the soil. It should be moist, not dry or soggy. Potted plants should not have a gap between the soil and the pot (a gap indicates the soil has been allowed to dry out too much in the past).

Carefully turn plants out of their pots to check the roots. The roots should be white and firm. They should hold the rootball together, but they should not be circling around. Reject plants with too few or overgrown roots.

When everything else has checked out favorably, choose plants with flowerbuds rather than open flowers, especially if the plant has a limited season of bloom.

Shopping by mail. You can catalog-shop no matter where you live. It does require a leap of faith to buy plants sight unseen, but the wealth of choices offered by mail order is nearly impossible to match with local sources. Not all suppliers are equally reliable. Here are some tips to help you evaluate potential suppliers by their catalogs.

- Plant descriptions should include the botanical name. Some plants have several common names. You need to mail-order by botanical name to ensure that you get the precise plants you want.
- Be suspect of photos with bright colors that don't look natural: They've probably been artificially enhanced. Also be wary

of catalogs with fanciful illustrations or grandiose claims.

- Outrageously cheap prices often mean small or poorly rooted plants—or no service.
- Check the replacement policy. Some nurseries will replace plants that die or do poorly for up to a year, perhaps asking you to pay the postage on the replacements. Others only guarantee that the plants are in good condition when shipped.

You'll find a list of perennial mail-order suppliers starting on page 283. Gardening magazines also carry advertisements from mail-order companies. Another good way to find reputable mail-order sources is to ask other gardeners who their favorites are.

Order early to avoid disappointment, or call and check availability before you order. Indicate whether you want substitutions or a refund if a particular plant isn't available.

Specify a shipping date that suits your climate and schedule. Have your plants arrive on Thursday or Friday if you plan to plant them on Saturday.

Open and examine your plants as soon as they arrive. Report to the supplier immediately. It's much easier to get replacements for plants that die a few months after planting if you've made your complaints promptly.

Creating a Plant Nursery

As you lay plans for perennial gardens, think about starting a mini perennial nursery in your yard. It's not hard to grow your own perennials from divisions ands cuttings—or even from seed for some types—and it can save you lots of money. As you get more involved in propagating perennials, you'll want a place where you can coddle small plants until they're ready to plant out in your landscape. You'll need a cold frame, a nursery bed, and a potted-plant holding area. An area just 4 × 16 feet can house all three.

Cold Frame

Perennial gardeners will find cold frames serve a purpose year-round—for overwintering tender plants or root cuttings, starting and hardening off seedlings, rooting cuttings, and giving dormant seeds a winter cold period. You can buy them commercially as kits or build your own, as shown on this page.

Build your cold frame on a sheltered site that faces south or east. It should get at least half a day of full sun.

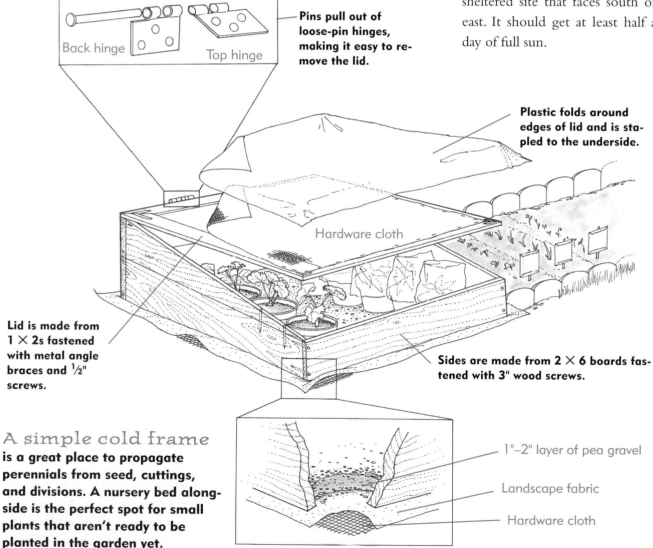

Back hinge

Top hinge

Pins pull out of loose-pin hinges, making it easy to remove the lid.

Plastic folds around edges of lid and is stapled to the underside.

Hardware cloth

Lid is made from 1 × 2s fastened with metal angle braces and ¹/₂" screws.

Sides are made from 2 × 6 boards fastened with 3" wood screws.

1"–2" layer of pea gravel

Landscape fabric

Hardware cloth

A simple cold frame is a great place to propagate perennials from seed, cuttings, and divisions. A nursery bed alongside is the perfect spot for small plants that aren't ready to be planted in the garden yet.

Fall. In mid-fall, load the cold frame with pots of seeds that need a cold period, potted perennials or rooted stem cuttings that won't survive the winter outside, and pots of root cuttings. Put the lid on the frame. On warm days, prop it open a few inches to prevent overheating. Once the average outdoor temperature drops to about 32°F, close the lid, and cover the frame with a tarp or blanket to keep out light for the winter.

Winter. Check inside every few weeks to make sure that no mice have set up housekeeping. Don't water anything unless it gets bone-dry, and then only very sparingly. In late winter, remove the tarp or blanket so that sunlight can start warming the frame. On warm days (50°F or warmer), prop the lid open. You can buy a temperature-activated

vent mechanism to open and close the lid automatically.

The warm, moist conditions in a cold frame can be a paradise for disease organisms. When you must water, do so early in the day on a day when it's likely to be sunny so the leaves will dry off as fast as possible.

Early spring. A month or so before you can plant outdoors, you can start seedlings directly in your cold frame. You can also move seedlings started indoors into the frame to harden off. On very cold nights, throw an old blanket over the cold frame to keep the day's heat in longer.

Early summer. Once the weather warms, remove the lid. The summer cold frame is a good place to start seeds unmolested and to root stem cuttings. If your cold frame is in full sun, you'll want to cover it with 50

percent shade cloth or a scrap of snow fence in the hottest months. Water pots generously early in the day during summer.

Nursery Bed

A nursery (or holding) bed is nothing more than a prepared bed where you can plant small or displaced plants in purely functional rows. Your nursery bed is also a good site to start seedlings outdoors.

A 4 × 8-foot bed is a good size to start with. Shelter from strong sun and wind is nice, and a nearby source of water is advisable. If you have no place for a full-size nursery bed, use inconspicuous spots here and there in your yard as mini holding beds.

Potted Plant Holding Area

A holding area for potted perennials is a frame made of 2 × 4s, lined with landscape fabric, with a few inches of pea gravel layered over the fabric. (A 4-foot-square area is a good size to start with.) Weeds don't grow in it, the pots drain readily after watering, and plants' roots tend not to sneak out the drainage holes and latch on. You can also sink the plants, pot and all, into your nursery bed, but don't leave them there too long because the roots are sure to wander out and into the surrounding soil.

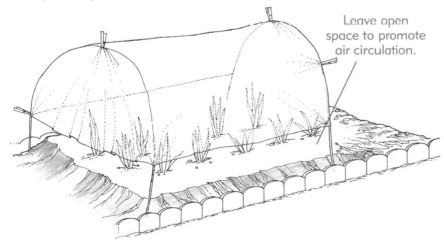

Leave open space to promote air circulation.

Shading a nursery bed will help young plants grow better. Use floating row cover and wire hoops to make a self-supporting shade structure.

Perennial Division and Multiplication

Even if math wasn't your best subject in school, you can be a straight-A student in plant division. Dividing, or separating your clumps of perennials into smaller sections, is easy and a great way to get more plants for free. Ripping your plants apart may sound like cruel and unusual punishment for them, but it really isn't. Loosening up crowded stems and roots and removing the older growth periodically will keep your perennials vigorous and blooming generously.

When to divide. Divide most perennials in fall when they are going dormant and the weather is cool. (Gardeners north of Zone 5 should wait until very early spring.)

Fall-blooming perennials should be divided in early spring. There are a few spring- and early-summer-blooming perennials, such as oriental poppies (*Papaver orientale*) and bearded irises, that go dormant or even disappear in midsummer. Divide these plants in early summer when you see their foliage starting to turn yellow.

Whatever the time of year, be sure the perennials you plan to divide are vigorous plants that will withstand the stress of being split apart. Water the plants thoroughly the day before you plan to divide them. If you can, choose a day when the weather will be cloudy and cool, so the plants will lose as little moisture as possible during the process. (If the weather is sunny or hot, your plants will do better if you wait until evening to divide them.)

How to divide. Perennials such as yarrow and bee balm (*Monarda didyma*) with shallow, spreading roots are easy to divide. Just plunge a shovel into the plant to sever the connecting roots around the section you wish to leave in place. Then use a trowel to work loose the outer portions of the plant. You can pot these up or transplant them immediately to another part of your garden.

Perennials that grow in a tight clump, such as astilbes, are a little harder to divide. It's usually easiest to dig up the whole clump and attack it above ground. Use a shovel to cut a circle around the plant, 4 to 12 inches out from the outermost stems. Insert the shovel straight down, as deeply as you can. Then work the shovel's blade under the plant to loosen and preserve as many of the roots as possible.

Hoist the rootball out and lay it on its side on a tarp next to the hole. Use your fingers or a strong spray of water to work the soil out of the roots so you can see them.

Separate the clump by pulling it apart with your fingers. If that won't work, try cutting through the roots with hand pruners, or even sawing with an old pruning saw.

If you're dividing a plant that you want to continue growing strongly, separate it into three or four good-size pieces. Replant one of the divided sections in the spot where you grew the original plant. Plant the others around your yard as desired, or give them away.

For maximum multiplication, split the plant into small sections with one or two stems each, and plant them in a nursery bed to grow and develop for a season.

Dividing an overgrown plant. One way to create a large group of new plants at low cost is to divide an overgrown potted perennial. You'll often find such overgrown plants discounted at nurseries or garden centers.

These plants tend to be pot-bound and suffering from lack of care. If you plant them in a garden bed, they just won't do well no matter how much effort you lavish on them. However, they can be a great source of material for division, and for root and stem cuttings as well. The illustration on the opposite page shows you how to take full advantage of a "propagation special."

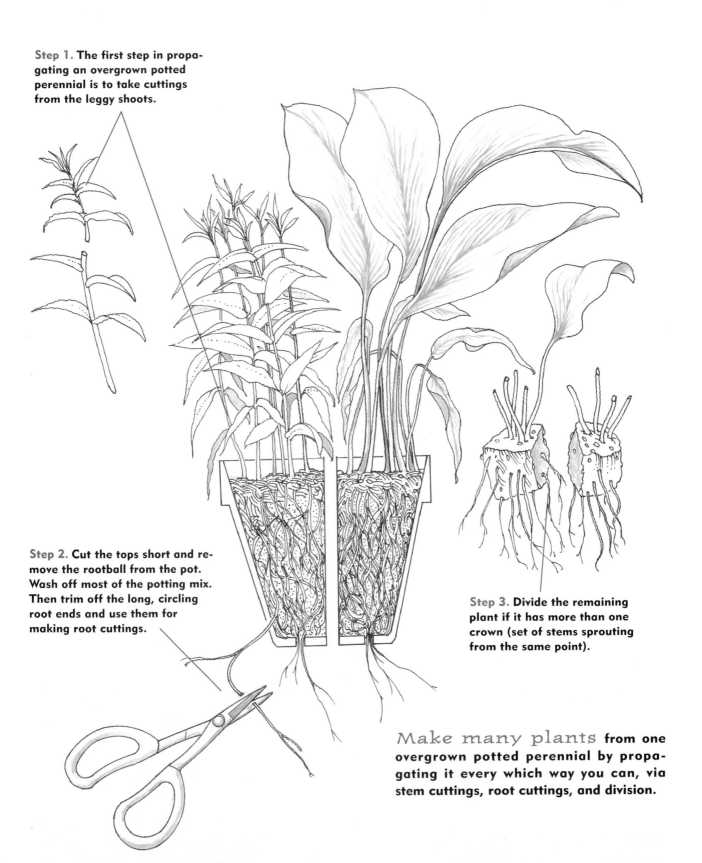

Step 1. The first step in propagating an overgrown potted perennial is to take cuttings from the leggy shoots.

Step 2. Cut the tops short and remove the rootball from the pot. Wash off most of the potting mix. Then trim off the long, circling root ends and use them for making root cuttings.

Step 3. Divide the remaining plant if it has more than one crown (set of stems sprouting from the same point).

Make many plants **from one overgrown potted perennial by propagating it every which way you can, via stem cuttings, root cuttings, and division.**

New Plants from Roots

Anyone who has ever cursed thistles, bindweed, or dandelions for regenerating tenfold from tiny bits of root has experienced the propagative power of root cuttings. Many cultivated perennials, such as orange coneflower (*Rudbeckia fulgida*) or blanket flowers (*Gaillardia* spp.) will sprout from pieces of root also.

Fall is the best time to take root cuttings. But for plants such as Oriental poppies (*Papaver orientale*) that go dormant early in the season, take root cuttings any time after flowering ends.

To take root cuttings from a plant growing in your garden, you can lift the entire plant, or just dig down and cut off a few roots. Rooting technique varies slightly depending on the type of roots the perennial has.

Thin, wiry roots. Blanket flowers (*Gaillardia* spp.), garden phlox (*Phlox paniculata*), mulleins (*Verbascum* spp.), sea hollies (*Eryngium* spp.), and violet sage (*Salvia* ✕ *superba*) all have thin roots. For these plants, cut the harvested roots into 1- to 2-inch-long sections. Fill 4-inch pots three-quarters full of moist potting mix and lay the root cuttings on the surface of the mix (6 to 8 per pot). Cover them with ½ inch of sand or vermiculite. Label the pots and water them well.

Thick, fleshy roots. Baby's-breath, bleeding hearts (*Dicentra* spp.), oriental poppies (*Papaver orientale*), and peonies are examples of perennials with thick roots. Cut the harvested roots into 2- to 3-inch-long sections, keeping track of which end is up. (Do so by using a flat cut at the top and a slanted cut at the bottom.) Stick the cuttings into 4-inch pots of moist potting mix, with the top ¼ inch sticking out of the mix. Label the pots and water them well.

Aftercare. Put the pots of root cuttings in a cold frame. Keep the soil moist (but never soggy) until you close the frame for the winter. Resume watering when you open the frame in late winter. New shoots will appear as spring advances. Transplant the new plants into separate pots or a nursery bed in early summer.

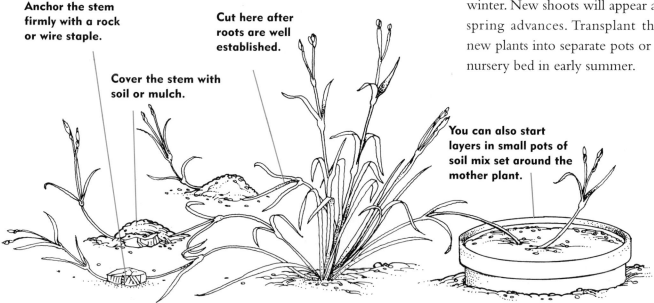

Anchor the stem firmly with a rock or wire staple.

Cut here after roots are well established.

Cover the stem with soil or mulch.

You can also start layers in small pots of soil mix set around the mother plant.

To start new plants by layering, **pinch off leaves along the stems of perennials that are growing in your garden. Press the stem area against the soil and anchor it in place. After the stem forms roots, cut it off the mother plant.**

Starting from Stem Cuttings

Taking stem cuttings lets you multiply your plants without digging them up. Friends are almost always willing to let you take a few stem cuttings from their plants, allowing you to expand your perennial pallette for free.

Most perennials will grow from stem-tip cuttings: Pinks (*Dianthus* spp.), coreopsis, lavender, asters, phlox, and chrysanthemums are easy to propagate this way. If you take stem-tip cuttings early in the season before flowerbuds form, the mother plant will go on to produce flowers later in the season.

Cuttings from some perennials—such as obedient plant (*Physostegia virginiana*), bee balm (*Monarda didyma*), and mint—root so easily that you can cut a stem into many small sections and get a new plant from each.

Put pots or flats of cuttings in a cold frame or a shady spot. Check the cuttings every few days and water them if the potting medium starts to dry out. Remove any cuttings that are brown or diseased. After two weeks give a few cuttings a gentle tug. If they don't resist being pulled from the soil mix, press them back in place. Wait a week, and test them again.

Once the cuttings resist the tugging (a sign they're forming roots), you can leave them uncovered. Give them a few more weeks and transplant them into individual pots.

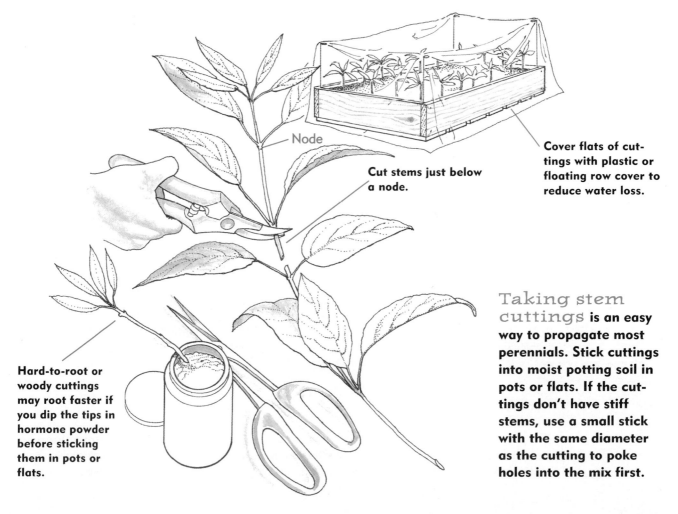

Node

Cut stems just below a node.

Cover flats of cuttings with plastic or floating row cover to reduce water loss.

Hard-to-root or woody cuttings may root faster if you dip the tips in hormone powder before sticking them in pots or flats.

Taking stem cuttings **is an easy way to propagate most perennials. Stick cuttings into moist potting soil in pots or flats. If the cuttings don't have stiff stems, use a small stick with the same diameter as the cutting to poke holes into the mix first.**

Starting Perennials from Seed

Starting perennials from seed is tops in the money-saving department. It does require more time and patience than buying plants, but a packet of seed (which will produce as many seedlings as most gardeners could possibly want) costs less than a single potted perennial!

"Flowers from Seed in One Season" on page 261 lists some perennials that flower the first year from seed. If you want a specific named cultivar, such as 'Moonbeam' coreopsis or 'Autumn Joy' sedum, you may find it isn't available from seed.

You can start perennials from seed indoors or outdoors, but starting seeds inside has advantages. First, you can start seeds in late winter and have transplants ready to plant outside as soon as the weather warms enough. Also, you can control the environment and lavish care on the little seedlings.

If you like having the winter off from gardening, outdoor seed starting may be the best choice for you. Starting seeds outdoors requires patience but very little hands-on labor.

Starting Seeds Indoors

Starting stocky seedlings indoors is easy if you have some basic inexpensive equipment.

Light. The main limiting factor for starting seeds indoors is light. Few gardeners have enough south-facing windows to start more than a handful of plants. And windowsill seedlings are often disappointingly leggy. So most gardeners resort to starting seedlings under lights.

The best place for a seed-starting setup has a temperature that stays between 60° and 65°F, is close to a water source, and has free air movement (a closet is not a good choice). If you have cats, a place that can be shut off from the rest of the house is also in order. Cats consider plant lights a

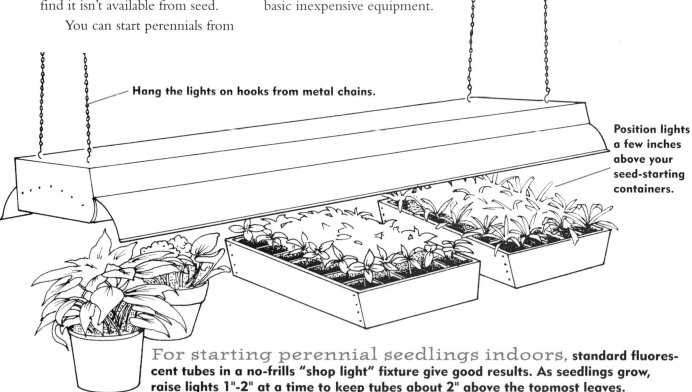

Hang the lights on hooks from metal chains.

Position lights a few inches above your seed-starting containers.

For starting perennial seedlings indoors, standard fluorescent tubes in a no-frills "shop light" fixture give good results. As seedlings grow, raise lights 1"-2" at a time to keep tubes about 2" above the topmost leaves.

delightful basking spot, and they may snatch a mouthful of greenery now and then. You can also build a hardware-cloth cage around your seed-starting setup to keep felines at a safe distance.

You can build an improvised plywood-and-sawhorse table in your basement for seed-starting season and put it away the rest of the year. Or, you could appropriate some countertop space in the kitchen—or a table in a family room or spare room—and protect the surface with large, watertight trays.

Seed-starting medium. A soil mix for seed-starting must be lightweight, drain quickly, but hold a lot of water. Buy a commercial mix designed for starting seeds—not a potting soil designed for houseplants—or mix your own custom blend. See "Mix Your Own Seed-Starting Medium" on this page for ideas.

Add water to your medium until it has the moistness of a wrung-out sponge. Mixes that contain lots of peat often resist wetting; try using hot water if this happens. Store the moist mix in a closed plastic bag.

Containers. You can start seeds in any container that you can fill at least 2 inches deep and that has drainage holes in the bottom. Many gardeners reuse the lightweight plastic six-packs that bedding plants come in. Soak reused containers in hot, soapy water and let them air-dry before you fill them with fresh premoistened mix.

Mix Your Own Seed-Starting Medium

To make your own seed-starting medium, combine equal parts vermiculite or perlite and one or more of the following: milled sphagnum moss, peat moss, screened and pasteurized garden soil, or screened compost.

Planting. Most perennial seedlings take 10 to 12 weeks to reach transplanting size. So, to find out when to sow seed, count back from your frost-free date (your local extension service can tell you when this is in your area) or from the time you want to have seedlings available for planting out.

The biggest mistake gardeners make when starting perennial seeds is planting the whole packet. If the seeds are fresh, chances are good that most of the seeds will grow. Do you really need hundreds of each type of plant? If you only want six plants, for example, plant seven or eight pots (one or two seeds per pot) and put the rest of the seed away. There's a good chance of getting at least one plant in each pot, plus a couple of extra pots for insurance.

Planting one or two seeds is quite easy if the seeds are big enough to handle. But what about dustlike ones you can barely see? Sow tiny seeds by moistening the very tip of a lead pencil and touching it into the seeds. A few will cling to the pencil momentarily, and you can deposit them on the soil where you want them.

Sow your seed in premoistened seed-starting mix. Cover seeds with a thin layer of fine mix or sand—usually about twice as thick as the diameter of the seed. Then mist the surface gently and cover the pots with a plastic bag or a clear plastic cover.

Set the planted pots in a warm location to encourage germination. You can buy commercial thermostatically controlled heat mats designed for seed starting. Some gardeners use an old waterbed heater as a seed-starting mat. Others have good luck putting flats on top of the refrigerator (but be sure to move the seedlings into light as soon as they break through the soil).

Germination Tricks

Most perennial seeds germinate readily when exposed to moisture and warmth, but some types need special treatment to get growing. Check the information on the seed packet or the catalog description for the plants you plan to start from seed; they should tell you what treatment is required.

Cold treatment. Some plants native to regions with cold winters have a built-in safety mechanism—no matter how nice the conditions are, they can't germinate until after they've had a cold period. Some common perennial seeds that need a cold treatment are bleeding hearts (*Dicentra* spp.), columbines (*Aquilegia* spp.), daylilies, hellebores (*Helleborus* spp.), and monkshoods (*Aconitum* spp.).

There are two simple techniques for mimicking this cold period (this is referred to as *stratification*). The quickest way is to put the seeds in moist peat moss in a plastic bag in the refrigerator before planting (the seed packet should state how long to expose the seeds to cold). Be sure to label the bag with the name of the seeds and the date you start the treatment. If you're not in a hurry, a second stratification technique is to plant the seeds in flats in fall and leave them in your cold frame during winter.

Breaking the seedcoat. A few types of perennial seeds have such a thick, hard seedcoat that the seedlings have a difficult time cracking through them. Try filing an area of the seedcoat with a nail file or shaking the seeds in a jar lined with sandpaper to create thin spots in the seedcoats (this is called *scarification*). Baptisias (*Baptisia* spp.) and lupines (*Lupinus* spp.) benefit from this technique.

Presprouting. Presprouting perennial seeds that are slow to germinate can save valuable indoor growing space (certain types take as long as three weeks to germinate). To presprout seeds, wet an unbleached coffee filter and spread the seeds on half of it (only seeds as big or bigger than a grain of sand are practical to handle this way). Fold the other half over the seeds, slip the filter into a resealable plastic bag, and put it in a warm place. One handy trick is to set the bag on a magazine on top of your plant lights. That way, they also get the benefit of bottom heat while germinating!

Check the seeds every couple of days. If the filter starts to dry, add just a few drops of water.

Once you see a root poking out of a seed, place it carefully, with the root pointing down, in a hole in a pot or six-pack cell filled with moist seed-starting mix. Cover the seed gently with the mix.

Caring for Seedlings

Once your seedlings poke out of the soil, you'll need to give them light. Turn the lights on for 12 to 18 hours a day. For a few dollars, you can buy a timer that will control the lights for you automatically.

The plants will soon reach the height of the plastic film covering the flats. Remove the plastic before the plants grow into it. Keep the soil moist at all times by misting it or by watering from the bottom. Make watering easier by setting the pots on capillary matting (available from garden suppliers) or carpet padding. One edge of the matting rests in a reservoir of water and the plants wick up water as they need it.

After the plants are a few weeks old, start watering them with a dilute liquid fertilizer such as half-strength fish emulsion and seaweed extract. If any of the pots have two seedlings, use scissors to snip off the less vigorous of the pair.

Transplanting. As a rule of thumb, if a plant's leaves spread wider than the edge of the container it's growing in, it needs more root space. Carefully squeeze the rootball of the seedling out of the six-pack and repot it in growing mix in a 4-inch pot.

Hardening off. Don't plant your seedlings outdoors without giving them a chance to slowly adjust to outdoor conditions. If you have a cold frame, move the seedlings out there a few weeks before you plan to plant in beds. Lacking a cold frame, move the plants outdoors to a sheltered spot each day for a few hours, then bring them back inside. Increase the time outdoors a few hours a day until they are out all day.

Starting Seeds Outdoors

Starting seeds outdoors is less fussy than starting them indoors. You can sow seeds in pots in the cold frame, in your nursery bed, or right in the garden where they will grow.

The cold frame. Sowing seeds in pots or flats and putting them in your cold frame is a good choice if animal pests are a concern. You can also start seeds in a cold frame about a month earlier than you could in the open soil. Keep in mind that you will have to water the seedlings as long as the cold frame is covered. In general, they'll need watering more often than plants in the ground do.

The nursery bed. Your nursery bed is a great site for starting large numbers of seedlings. You may get help with watering from Mother Nature. You will still need to transplant the seedlings to your garden beds once they reach the proper size.

The garden. Direct-seeding where you want the plants to grow eliminates transplanting. It also means that you'll have sparse spots in your garden while the plants grow. Usually the seedlings will also be less likely to get regular care. Despite these drawbacks, direct-seeding is the best choice for perennials that don't transplant well (the seed packet or catalog description will tell you which these are).

Flowers from Seed in One Season

Start these perennials indoors in winter and you'll enjoy blooms the following summer. This list includes expected time to germination in the conditions stated.

Butterfly weed (*Asclepias tuberosa*). 3–4 weeks at 68°–86°F. Fresh seed may need chilling.

Candle larkspur (*Delphinium elatum*). 18 days at 70°F. Be sure to use fresh seed.

Carpathian harebell (*Campanula carpatica*). 2–4 weeks at 65°–70°F.

Large-flowered tickseed (*Coreopsis grandiflora*). 3 weeks with light at 70°.

Maltese cross (*Lychnis chalcedonica*). 10 days with light at 68°F.

Purple coneflower (*Echinacea purpurea*). 10–21 days with light at 70°–75°F.

Red valerian (*Centranthus ruber*). 3 weeks with light at 65°F.

Shasta daisy (*Chrysanthemum × superbum*). 10–18 days with light at 60°–70°F.

Spike speedwell (*Veronica spicata*). 2–3 weeks at 65°–70°F.

Sunflower heliopsis (*Heliopsis helianthoides*). 1–2 weeks at 68°F.

Sweet violet (*Viola odorata*). 2–3 weeks at 54°–90°F.

Violet sage (*Salvia × superba*). 2–3 weeks at 68°–86°F.

Yarrows (*Achillea* spp.). 1–2 weeks with light at 70°F.

Multiplying Bulbs

Bulbs are a lovely addition to your perennial landscape, and many of them gradually propagate themselves naturally over the years. Here are some ways to give nature a hand.

True Bulbs

Bulbs that look like onions are "true" bulbs. Daffodils, grape hyacinths (*Muscari* spp.), and snowdrops (*Galanthus* spp.) are common examples of true bulbs that multiply rapidly. The easiest way to help them spread is to divide the clumps every few years.

Wait until the foliage starts to turn yellow, then dig them carefully and separate the clump. Replant them immediately at the same depth or a little bit deeper. If it's more convenient, you can store the extra bulbs in a cool, dry, rodentproof area until fall and plant them then.

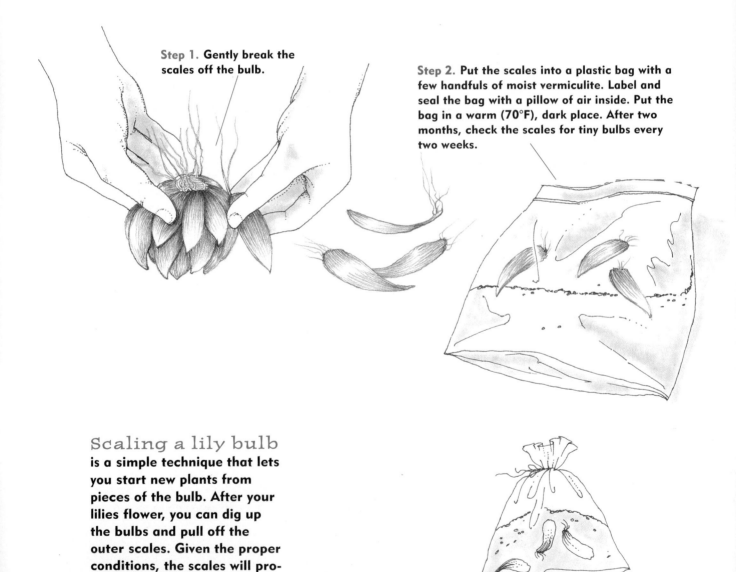

Step 1. Gently break the scales off the bulb.

Step 2. Put the scales into a plastic bag with a few handfuls of moist vermiculite. Label and seal the bag with a pillow of air inside. Put the bag in a warm (70°F), dark place. After two months, check the scales for tiny bulbs every two weeks.

Scaling a lily bulb

is a simple technique that lets you start new plants from pieces of the bulb. After your lilies flower, you can dig up the bulbs and pull off the outer scales. Given the proper conditions, the scales will produce new tiny bulbs that you can pot up.

Lilies

Lilies are the crowning glory of the summer garden, but the bulbs aren't cheap. They do multiply themselves slowly, but if you want to increase your lily display more quickly, there are two easy ways to go about it.

Lily bulbs aren't true bulbs: They look like a globe artichoke, with layers of scales. You can harvest scales from new bulbs before you plant them, as shown on the opposite page. A healthy bulb can donate up to six scales without any setback to its growth. If you find any small bulbs near the existing bulbs, harvest those, too. It will take about three years for each scale to grow into a blooming-size bulb. Let the potted scales grow for one year in a cold frame, transplant them into a nursery bed for a year or two, and then move them to their final home in your landscape.

Some lilies, including tiger lilies (*Lilium lancifolium*), make bulblets (tiny bulblike structures) cradled above each leaf along the stem. You can pot these up or poke them about an inch deep in your nursery bed in late summer. Within a few years, each bulblet will produce a blooming-size bulb to plant in your garden.

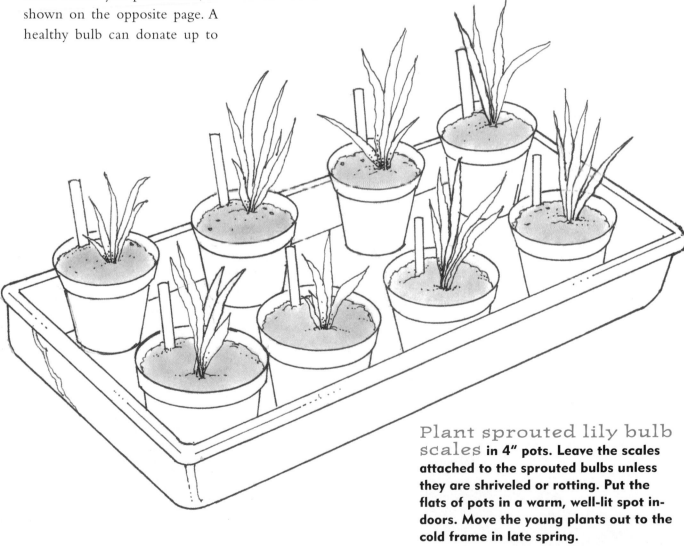

Plant sprouted lily bulb scales in 4" pots. Leave the scales attached to the sprouted bulbs unless they are shriveled or rotting. Put the flats of pots in a warm, well-lit spot indoors. Move the young plants out to the cold frame in late spring.

Chapter 11

Keeping Your Perennials at Their Best

Care through the Seasons • Insects and Other Problems • Managing

Animal Pests

In this chapter, we've prepared special illustrations for the tasks that will keep your perennials looking at your best. In the illustration on this page and the following pages, you'll find information on what to do in your garden as the seasons progress.

We've broken up tasks by seasons rather than month-by-month so that these illustrations will be useful to gardeners throughout our large, climatically diverse country. For example, daffodils are a classic herald of springtime. But daffodils may bloom in January in Georgia, while in Pennsylvania, the first daffodils appear in March. In northern New York, gardeners may have to wait until

Caring for Perennials in Late Winter and Early Spring

Remove the protective mulch you spread the previous fall. (Leave any marginally hardy plants covered a few weeks longer.) Leave the remains of last year's weed-suppressing mulch in place.

Now is the perfect time to pull winter-growing weeds, most of which are small annuals. Wear a pair of heavy-duty dishwashing gloves over polypropylene glove liners when weeding to keep your hands from getting wet and cold.

Be careful not to damage the cheerful green "noses" of spring bulb foliage that are appearing now.

mid- to late April for daffodils.

To use these illustrations, match the season named to the weather in your area, and follow the instructions for that season. If the first springlike weather occurs in your area in February, then February is the time to begin removing protective mulch from your perennials. However, if you live up in Zone 3, where spring may not stir until April, then April is your month to remove mulch.

Starting the Garden Year

The garden year starts in winter, inside the house and garage. Here's a rundown of indoor garden chores you can do to prepare for warmer days ahead.

• Start a new garden journal now, while you have time.

• Whittle down your wish lists from those armchair-gardening sessions of midwinter (oh, how tempting catalogues are!), and send off your orders for seeds, plants, and summer-blooming bulbs to plant once spring is here.

• Inspect your tools. Repair or replace any that won't do the job this year. Sharpen blades and coat them with vegetable oil.

• If you start seedlings indoors, start planting those seeds now!

• Do some stretching every day for a few weeks to limber up those gardening muscles (you know, the ones that got so sore last spring) before you spend a whole weekend raking and bending.

• Bundle up and head outside to check on any plants overwintering in your cold frame. Take off the lightproof cover and give the plants a little water if they seem dry. Be sure to vent the frame on warm, sunny days, too.

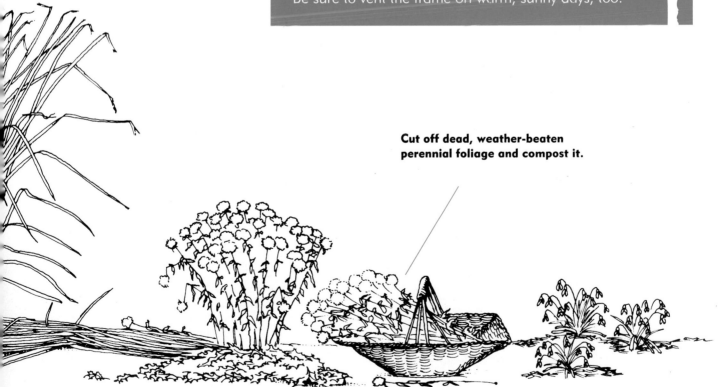

Cut off dead, weather-beaten perennial foliage and compost it.

Spring Reminders

• Get your compost pile going by turning it and working in some green weeds, grass clippings, or dry alfalfa.

• Transplant volunteer seedlings where they will suit your design.

• Plant dormant plants. Be sure to label them or put them on your master map.

• Start moving hardy seedlings outside into your cold frame to harden off.

• Plant tender bulbs two weeks before your last expected frost or when the tulips are in full bloom.

• Remember where late-sprouting perennials are planted so you won't dig into them by mistake as you work.

Caring for Perennials in Spring

Divide fall-blooming perennials when the new shoots are 2"–3" tall. If the plant is dying off in the center, lift the entire clump, discard the center, and replant about one-third of the vigorous outer growth.

Sprinkle a blended organic fertilizer over your entire planting.

Remove the protective mulch from marginally hardy perennials once the chance of hard frost is past. But be ready to throw a blanket over new, tender growth if a late frost threatens.

Custom-Blended Organic Fertilizer

You can buy commercial organic fertilizer blends, or you can make your own mix. Making your own gives you the freedom to mix just enough to suit your needs and to adjust the richness of the blend to match your soil fertility. The following recipe makes enough to fertilize 100 square feet of low-fertility soil or 200 square feet of high-fertility soil.

50 pounds alfalfa meal OR 30 pounds fish meal

6 pounds rock phosphate

1 pound kelp meal

3 pounds greensand

If you've tested your soil and test results show that phosphorus is much lower than potassium, double the rock phosphate in the mix. If potassium is much lower than phosphorus, double the greensand.

Brush cut from shrubs makes a good support for bushy perennials like baby's-breath. The plant will grow quickly around the brush and hide it from view. Choose brush with many small side branches for the best support.

Don't braid, twist, or clip spring bulb foliage to make it look tidy. The leaves need to make food to supply energy for next year's blossoms. Once bulb foliage turns yellow and comes away with a gentle tug, you can remove it from the garden.

Thin some shoots out of crowded clumps of perennials to allow the remaining shoots to produce bigger flowers. This also lets more air and sunshine into the plants, which helps prevent disease problems. Remove small, non-vigorous shoots first.

Put supports up now while your plants are small. You can buy commercial products or make a plant support by twisting a handful of dropped weeping willow branchlets into a skinny wreath and resting it on 3 forked twigs.

Early Summer Reminders

- Check for plants that didn't survive the winter and decide what to replace them with.

- Plant out tender seedlings after the weather has settled and there is no chance of frost.

- Plant annuals in bare spots to add quick color.

- While your spring gardens are still fresh in your mind, make a list of spring-blooming bulbs and perennials to add. (Send off your orders as soon as the catalogs come in so you'll get your shipments in time to plant in fall.)

- Take a stroll in your garden once a week, and bring along your garden journal. Make notes about what's coming into flower and check for pest and disease problems.

- Nip weed problems in the bud. Mow any wild areas near your plantings whenever you see them flowering to prevent weed seeds from blowing or falling into your garden.

Caring for Perennials from Early Summer to Midsummer

Support stately regal lilies with a 6' bamboo stake pushed into the ground about 1'. Add figure eights of green twine 1' apart as the plant grows.

Snip off and compost faded flowers from your peonies and other large-flowered perennials once or twice a week. Be especially careful to remove rotting flowers or browned, drying buds to help prevent brown-rot fungus from spreading.

Leafminers sometimes make tunnels in leaves of columbines (*Aquilegia* spp.), delphiniums, and other perennials. The damage is more cosmetic than life-threatening. Pinch off and destroy infested leaves if you wish.

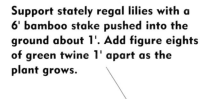

Wearing Out Weeds Step by Step

You can get rid of taprooted and spreading perennial weeds by cutting the shoots off at or just below ground level. Of course they will send up new shoots right away, but that burns up stored food. If you chop the tops off repeatedly, the roots will eventually run out of stored food and die. Here's how to starve weeds out as quickly as possible.

1. Cut off every weed shoot at or below the soil line. A sharpened long-handled trowel works well for this: It does the job with one quick, no-stoop motion. Using this tool barely disturbs the soil, so you don't bring new weed seeds to the surface to sprout.

2. Wait for new shoots to sprout up, then *let them grow* for another week. During that week, the new shoots are using up food stored in the roots.

3. Within the next week, cut off the new crop of shoots. (You can wait until the weekend if necessary because the shoots don't begin replenishing the food supply in the roots until about day 15 of their life.)

4. Repeat the chopping cycle every two weeks until no new shoots appear. It may take all summer or possibly even longer, but you can eliminate almost any kind of weed if you're dedicated.

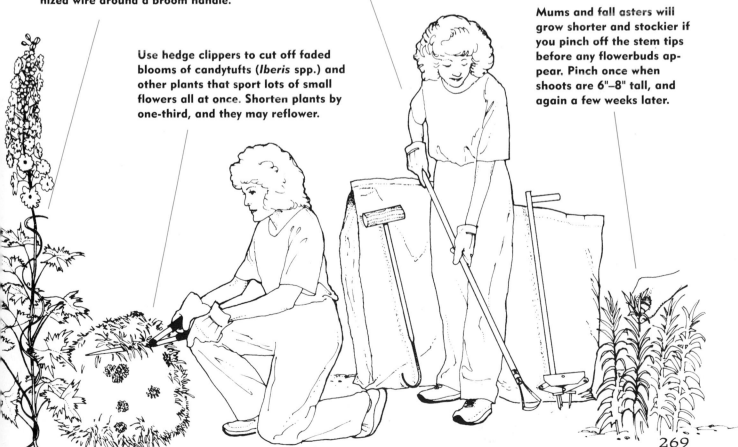

Use a spiral-shaped wire stake to support plants with upright stems like delphiniums. Make your own by twisting lengths of #9 galvanized wire around a broom handle.

Weeds pop through at times, even in well-mulched beds. Pull them out ruthlessly when they're young. A long-handled tool makes removing weeds easier.

Mums and fall asters will grow shorter and stockier if you pinch off the stem tips before any flowerbuds appear. Pinch once when shoots are 6"–8" tall, and again a few weeks later.

Use hedge clippers to cut off faded blooms of candytufts (*Iberis* spp.) and other plants that sport lots of small flowers all at once. Shorten plants by one-third, and they may reflower.

Late Summer Reminders

- Cut flowers for drying.

- Order plants and bulbs now for fall planting, if you haven't already.

- Take cuttings from plants you'd like more of next year and put them in a cold frame covered with shade cloth.

- Mark out proposed planting areas so you'll be ready to prepare them when the weather cools down.

- When all else fails, lie in the shade with your dog or a good book.

Caring for Perennials from Midsummer to Late Summer

Water newly transplanted specimens by hand. Use a rose attachment to break the water into a fine shower, and water the soil, not the plant's leaves.

Just because it's hot, don't expect pests and diseases to take time off. Like everything else, they'll be hiding in the shade or, like slugs, working at night. Take your weekly scouting walks in the early morning or late afternoon to escape the worst of the heat. To keep your garden looking its best, snip off spent flowerstalks and diseased or chewed leaves.

Gardeners with large spaces are often partial to perennials such as orange coneflowers (*Rudbeckia fulgida*) that spread by self-seeding. However, if you don't want an increased supply of a self-seeding perennial next year, snip off the spent blossoms once a week until the bloom season for that plant ends.

To save time on watering, install a drip irrigation system. It's the most efficient way to get extra water to your plants right where they need it.

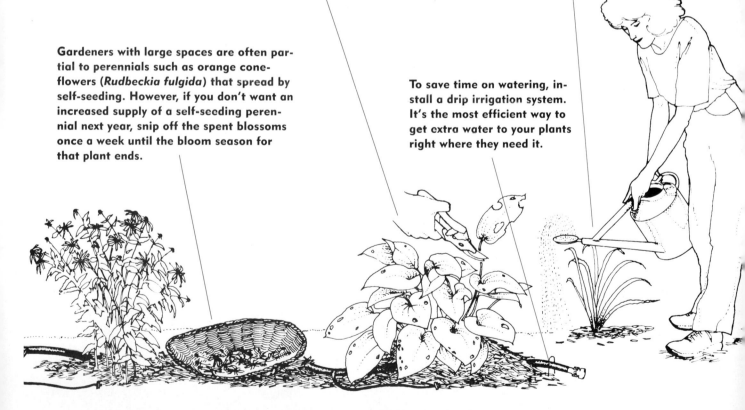

Watering Wisdom

When it's really hot, your garden can lose 2 to 3 inches of water per week—even when the relative humidity is above 90 percent.

If your landscape has only native and drought-tolerant perennials, you may get by on natural rainfall. But if your garden includes plants that need more water than the local natives, you'll need to plan for their needs. Your first line of defense is to add organic matter to the soil when you prepare a new planting area and mulch the surface of the soil. When you water, use a soaker hose or set up a drip irrigation line in your perennial beds. These deliver water efficiently directly to the root zone.

You can buy a mechanical timer for between $10 and $30 to attach directly to your water line. That way, you can set up the irrigation system and forget it, with no need to remember to turn off the water later in the day.

A few spring- and early-summer-blooming perennials, such as Virginia bluebells (*Mertensia virginica*), Oriental poppies, and bearded irises, go dormant and disappear long before fall. Divide them now, after their foliage starts to yellow but while you can still find them.

In the cool of early morning, go outside and cut some perennial flowers for indoor bouquets. That way you can enjoy your garden even when it's too hot to spend the day outdoors.

Organic mulch tends to break down and disappear as the season wears on. Find time to renew the mulch under your perennials now, when they need the protection the most.

Fall Reminders

- Be ready with blankets, row cover, or card-board boxes to throw over still-flowering specimens when frost threatens.

- Plant hardy bulbs to complement your perennials next year.

- Collect, clean, and store stakes, hoses, and other garden paraphernalia.

- Update your landscape plan while the growing season is still fresh in your mind. Make a list of the things you want to add or change in your landscape.

- Make a gift wish list of gardening items you'd like for the holidays and pass it around.

- Close your cold frame completely for the year once the temperature averages about 32°F.

- Check your seed-starting supplies and order seeds early if you plan to start plants indoors.

- Cut your new plant lists ruthlessly back to reality and order early to avoid disappointment.

Caring for Perennials in Fall

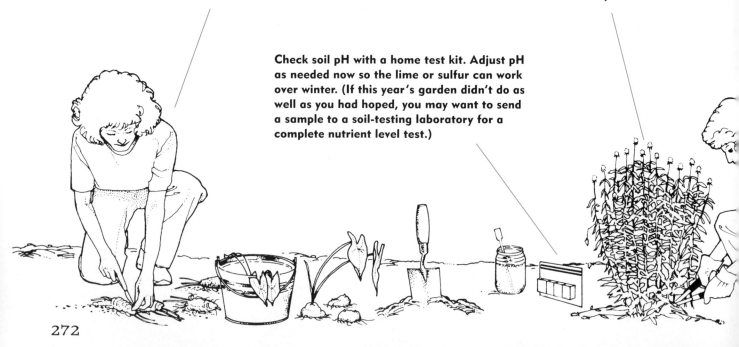

Dig and store caladiums and any other tender bulbs that you want for next season's garden before the ground freezes. Also, before your first frost, pot up tender plants you want to carry through winter. Store them in a cool basement or cold frame.

As fall advances and your perennials stop blooming, it's time to cut off and compost the tattered tops.

Check soil pH with a home test kit. Adjust pH as needed now so the lime or sulfur can work over winter. (If this year's garden didn't do as well as you had hoped, you may want to send a sample to a soil-testing laboratory for a complete nutrient level test.)

Mulching Precautions

Although fall is one of the best times to add organic mulch to the garden, there are some special situations when you should be careful about mulching. If your garden includes any extra-early spring bulbs or winter-flowering perennials, don't smother those areas with heavy mulch.

If you've had trouble with voles in the past, wait until late fall to add mulch. By then the voles will have found nests elsewhere. When you do mulch, leave a 4-inch unmulched space around tree and shrub trunks to prevent voles from nibbling the tender bark.

After winter storms, check your beds to see if any mulch has blown off. Settle frost-heaved plants back into the soil and replace the mulch covering.

Once the ground freezes, it's a good idea to add a thick layer of coarse mulch, such as evergreen branches or burlap bags of leaves, over perennials to keep them from frost heaving. (If your area gets snow cover that lasts all winter, the snow will protect your perennials for you.)

Leave ornamental grasses and perennials with long-lasting attractive foliage uncut to add interest in the winter landscape.

Insects and Other Problems

Avoiding pest problems usually isn't difficult in perennial gardens. The best insurance against problems is a good offense: Feed your soil regularly with plenty of organic matter, make sure the drainage is good before you plant, avoid planting problem-susceptible cultivars and species, and space and thin plants to increase air movement.

Once a week, take a walk in your yard and look for potential problems. Be especially watchful for holes in leaves, spots on leaves, or discolored or distorted growth. If you find symptoms on any of your plants, read through the symptom descriptions in "Solving Problems on Your Perennials" on pages 277–279 to identify the problems and learn about what to do to reduce or eliminate them. It's also a good idea to keep records from year to year so you'll be able to predict when problems are likely to happen.

Manual Controls

Many disease and insect pests of perennials cause a cosmetic problem but don't threaten the actual health of the plant. In these cases, simple hands-on controls like picking off damaged leaves are often sufficient.

Handpicking. Using your fingers to pluck insect pests off your plants is a tried-and-true method that can be highly effective in small gardens. If you don't like touching insects, wear rubber gloves when you go on pest patrol. You can squash the insects or drop them into soapy water to drown. Hand picking will often reduce an outbreak long enough for beneficial insects to move in and attack the population of pest insects. Removing diseased plants or plant parts by hand can also slow a disease outbreak. (Get rid of the diseased plant parts by burning them or putting them out for disposal with household trash.)

Cutworm collars. Use stiff paper collars to protect transplants from these soil-dwelling caterpillars. Cut cardboard strips 2 × 6 inches. Wrap one around the stem of each plant at planting time. Fasten the overlapped ends with a paper clip, and press the collar into the soil around the stem about ½ inch deep.

Copper barriers. Slugs and snails devour the leaves of a wide range of perennials. The best way to prevent them from reaching your plants is to encircle your garden beds with a strip of copper. Scientists have posed several theories as to why slugs and snails won't pass over the copper strip. While no one knows for certain why this control works, it has repeatedly proved its effectiveness. Press the copper strip upright into the soil or nail it to the outside of raised beds. Be sure there are no gaps or "bridges" over the copper.

Diatomaceous earth. Also called DE, this mineral dust is the fossilized shells of microscopic creatures. Its razor-sharp edges pierce soft-bodied pests who then die from dehydration. Buy natural-grade DE from a garden center; the kind meant for pool filters won't work on pests. Wear a dust mask when using DE since it can irritate the human respiratory system, too.

Water. A strong spray of water will knock many pests off your plants. It also deters spider mites because they thrive only in hot, dry places.

Soil solarization. The heat of the sun can be harnessed to kill organisms in the top few inches of the soil. See "Cook Them with Sunshine" on page 227 for details.

Biological Controls

It's an eat-or-be-eaten world out there, so take advantage of it. Using organic practices, such as growing a diverse range of plants and avoiding the use of pesticides, will encourage native predatory and parasitic insects and other organisms to keep pest populations in bounds. There are also several biological control products you can buy to help control pests.

BT. *Bacillus thuringiensis* (BT for short) is a bacterium that causes a fatal caterpillar disease. It is harmless to all other living things. Spray plants every few days with freshly mixed BT to kill caterpillars that feed on the plants. Don't spray it unless you have a serious caterpillar problem—some caterpillars grow up to be beautiful butterflies.

Beneficial nematodes. These microscopic organisms don't hurt plants, they go after soil-dwelling pests. Mix them according to the package directions and water them into the soil or inject them into borer tunnels.

Compost tea. Compost is full of beneficial organisms, by-products, and nutrients. It can help prevent harmful organisms from getting a foothold in your plants by feeding the plants and possibly by out-competing the bad guys. Dump a shovelful of finished compost into a bucket of water and let it brew for a few days. Then use the tea to water your plants, or strain it and spray the leaves.

Pest-Control Sprays

When a pest or disease problem is severe, you may need to pull out an organic control. The products below are reason-ably harmless to humans and animals and break down rapidly after application.

Soap. Soap repels or kills certain insect pests. Mix commercial insecticidal soap according to the label instructions, or use 1 to 3 teaspoons of liquid household soap per gallon of water. Test your spray on a few leaves of the plants you intend to treat, then wait a day to see if it causes any leaf damage. If it doesn't, go ahead and spray the entire plant. If it does cause damage, dilute the solution and test again. One word of caution: Insecticidal soap can kill beneficial insects, so don't spray it unless you need to, and only spray plants that have pest problems.

Oil. Oil kills insect eggs and immature insects by smothering them. Prepare a commercial summer oil spray according to the label instructions, or mix 1 tablespoon vegetable oil and ¼ teaspoon liquid soap into 1 quart of water to make a spray. Don't use oil and sulfur on the same plant within 30 days—the combination will burn the leaves.

Be Safe When You Spray

Natural sprays and botanical pesticides are considered organic, but that doesn't mean they are harmless. Handle these substances carefully and protect your body when you spray. Otherwise, you may end up with skin, eye, or lung irritations. Follow these tips for safe spraying.

- Store products in their original containers and away from food-preparation areas and children.
- Read and follow all label instructions and cautions.
- Use a dust mask and rubber gloves while mixing sprays or applying dusts.
- Wear rubber gloves, long sleeves, long pants, and eye protection while spraying. Wash everything when you're done, especially exposed skin.
- Strain spray solutions through cheesecloth or old panty hose to prevent clogging your sprayer's nozzle.
- Mix only as much spray as you need and wash the sprayer out after use.
- Don't touch treated plants until they are dry.

Garlic and hot pepper. Organic gardeners have long relied on homemade sprays of garlic and hot peppers to repel pests. Garlic also has antibiotic and antifungal properties. While it's important not to get garlic or hot pepper spray in your eyes, they are otherwise quite safe to use and safe for the environment.

To make a garlic spray, mince the cloves from one large garlic bulb and add 2 teaspoons of mineral oil. Let the garlic and oil soak for 24 hours. Stir in 1 pint of water and ¼ ounce of dishwashing liquid. Strain the mixture into a glass jar for storage.

When you want to apply the spray, combine 1 to 2 tablespoons of the mixture and 1 pint of water. Test the spray on a few leaves, and then wait two to three days to see if the leaves suffer any damage. If not, spray plants thoroughly.

Baking soda. Baking soda (that's right, the same stuff you use for baking and household cleaning) is a mild but quite effective preventive fungicide. Mix 1 teaspoon baking soda and ¼ teaspoon liquid soap into 1 quart of water and spray plants every few days.

Sulfur. Sulfur is a natural mineral. It burns fungal spores and prevents them from gaining a foothold on your plants. Dust plants when they are wet with dew, or prepare a spray of wettable sulfur according to the package directions. Apply sulfur every 10 days or after each rain that occurs in warm, humid weather. But don't apply sulfur when it's over 80°F—it will scorch the plants.

Bordeaux mix. This copper sulfate–hydrated lime mixture is quite a strong fungicide. Use it only when more gentle methods have failed because it can burn plants. It's reasonably safe for plants just before they sprout in spring. Mix and apply according to label instructions.

Botanical Pesticides

Some plants produce natural substances that repel pests or prevent disease organisms from gaining a foothold. Gardeners have harnessed the power of some of these botanical substances as pesticides. But while botanical pesticides come from natural sources, some are quite toxic to humans and other living creatures.

Rotenone, ryania, and sabadilla. In the past, most organic pest control recommendations have included spraying the botanical pesticides rotenone, ryania, and sabadilla. All three of these pesticides are still considered organically acceptable by many authorities. While they break down quickly after application, these substances are initially quite toxic and pose significant risk to the applicator (you), to animals, and to beneficial organisms.

In light of increased awareness of the potential harm from using these substances, *Organic Gardening* magazine no longer recommends them for use in organic home gardens.

So what sprays should gardeners use when a pest problem gets out of hand? Two that pose minimal hazards are neem and pyrethrins.

Neem. Neem (or its active ingredient azadirachtin) is a valuable botanical pesticide that kills certain insects by preventing them from maturing normally. It's effective against beetles, caterpillars, scales, thrips, and whiteflies, but reasonably harmless to most beneficials and animals. Use according to package instructions, spraying infested plants weekly. You can get it at some garden centers or from mail-order organic gardening supply companies.

Pyrethrins. Dried and ground pyrethrum daisies (*Chrysanthemum cinerarifolium* and *C. coccineum*) contain a botanical pesticide that is effective against a wide range of insects. Spray or dust in the early evening; two applications spaced two hours apart are most effective. Keep pyrethrins away from pets and fish, and be aware they may harm beneficial as well as damaging insects.

Solving Problems on Your Perennials

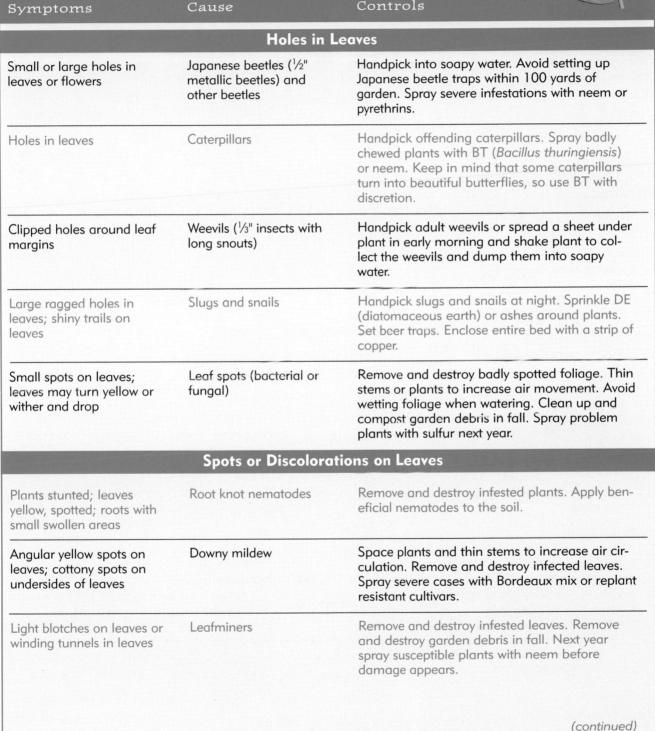

Symptoms	Cause	Controls
Holes in Leaves		
Small or large holes in leaves or flowers	Japanese beetles (½" metallic beetles) and other beetles	Handpick into soapy water. Avoid setting up Japanese beetle traps within 100 yards of garden. Spray severe infestations with neem or pyrethrins.
Holes in leaves	Caterpillars	Handpick offending caterpillars. Spray badly chewed plants with BT (*Bacillus thuringiensis*) or neem. Keep in mind that some caterpillars turn into beautiful butterflies, so use BT with discretion.
Clipped holes around leaf margins	Weevils (⅓" insects with long snouts)	Handpick adult weevils or spread a sheet under plant in early morning and shake plant to collect the weevils and dump them into soapy water.
Large ragged holes in leaves; shiny trails on leaves	Slugs and snails	Handpick slugs and snails at night. Sprinkle DE (diatomaceous earth) or ashes around plants. Set beer traps. Enclose entire bed with a strip of copper.
Small spots on leaves; leaves may turn yellow or wither and drop	Leaf spots (bacterial or fungal)	Remove and destroy badly spotted foliage. Thin stems or plants to increase air movement. Avoid wetting foliage when watering. Clean up and compost garden debris in fall. Spray problem plants with sulfur next year.
Spots or Discolorations on Leaves		
Plants stunted; leaves yellow, spotted; roots with small swollen areas	Root knot nematodes	Remove and destroy infested plants. Apply beneficial nematodes to the soil.
Angular yellow spots on leaves; cottony spots on undersides of leaves	Downy mildew	Space plants and thin stems to increase air circulation. Remove and destroy infected leaves. Spray severe cases with Bordeaux mix or replant resistant cultivars.
Light blotches on leaves or winding tunnels in leaves	Leafminers	Remove and destroy infested leaves. Remove and destroy garden debris in fall. Next year spray susceptible plants with neem before damage appears.

(continued)

Symptoms	Cause	Controls
Spots or Discolorations on Leaves—Continued		
Edges of oldest leaves turn dry and brown; young leaves crinkled and curled; plants stunted	Potassium deficiency	Spray plants with compost tea or kelp extract. Check soil pH and adjust to 7.0. Sprinkle greensand on soil.
Leaves, stems, or buds distorted, with sticky blackish coating	Aphids (1/12"–1/5" sucking insects)	Wash pests off with strong spray of water. Spray insecticidal soap for severe infestations.
Sticky, yellow leaves; plants stunted	Whiteflies (tiny white insects fly about when disturbed)	Spray plants with insecticidal soap. Remove infested weeds.
White powdery coating on leaves	Powdery mildew	Space plants and thin stems to increase air circulation. Spray highly susceptible plants with baking soda or sulfur every 10 days during warm, humid weather; plant where the foliage won't show, or choose resistant cultivars.
Leaves stippled, pale, reddish or yellowed; fine webbing beneath	Spider mites (specklike insects with 8 legs)	Spray plants with water daily. Spray plants with soap or oil if water doesn't solve the problem. Neem can be used as a last resort.
Leaves pale with powdery orange spots beneath	Rust	Thin stems and space plants to encourage air movement. Remove and destroy infected parts. Spray plants with sulfur.
Leaves yellow; small, green flowers; witches'-brooms at base of plant	Aster yellows	Remove and destroy infected plants. Control leafhoppers (which can spread the disease) with soap or oil.
Yellow leaves; plants may die; small bumps on leaves and stems	Scales (small hard or cottony stationary insects)	Prune off and destroy infested parts. Spray plants with soap, oil, or neem.
Leaves, flowers, and plants greenish yellow, distorted, mottled, streaked, stunted	Viruses	Remove and destroy infected plants. Control aphids and leafhoppers with soap or neem to prevent them from spreading viral diseases.
New leaves small, yellow-green; older leaves yellow and drop	Nitrogen deficiency	Spray plants with compost tea or fish emulsion; check soil pH and adjust to 7.0.

(continued)

Solving Problems on Your Perennials—Continued

Symptoms	Cause	Controls
New leaves small, undersides reddish purple; stems slender and stunted	Phosphorus deficiency	Spray plants with compost tea or liquid seaweed; check soil pH and adjust to 7.0. Sprinkle rock phosphate on soil.
New leaves yellow but normal size; old leaves remain green	Iron deficiency	Spray plants with kelp extract, compost tea, or chelated iron; check soil pH and adjust to 7.0.

Plants Wilting or Dying

Symptoms	Cause	Controls
Seedlings or young plants cut off at soil line	Cutworms	Treat soil with beneficial nematodes or drench with neem before replanting. Protect new transplants with collars of stiff paper.
Leaves or stems wilt, turn yellow, and die; stems firmly attached to roots	Fusarium or verticillium wilt	Remove and destroy infected plants. Clean up all debris in fall. Plant resistant cultivars and species.
Leaves or shoots wilt and die; stems exude sawdust-like material, may break off	Borers	Crush borers at once and spray base of affected plants with BT (*Bacillus thuringiensis*) every few days or neem once a week. Start control next spring before damage occurs.
Shoots wilt suddenly; stem bases blacken and rot; flowers and leaves brown	Bacterial blight (Botrytis blight, gray mold)	Remove and destroy infected parts. Remove faded flowers. Pull mulch away from crowns in spring to let soil dry. Thin plants to increase air movement.
Stems blacken and rot at base; foliage yellows and wilts; crowns may mold	Crown or root rot	Plant in well-drained sites; avoid damaging roots by digging/cultivating near plants. Keep mulch away from crowns. Remove and destroy infected plants.

Plants Develop Abnormally

Symptoms	Cause	Controls
Plants appear green and healthy but don't form flowers	Nitrogen excess	Plants will eventually use up the excess. Avoid adding any soil amendment containing nitrogen.
Flowerbuds wither and die; petals distorted or discolored; growth stunted	Thrips (specklike flying insects)	Remove and destroy affected parts. Spray plants with insecticidal soap or neem.
Deformed or dwarfed buds or leaves	Plant bugs ($\frac{1}{16}$"–$\frac{1}{2}$" shield-shaped insects)	Handpick adults into a can of soapy water. Spray severe infestations with insecticidal soap or neem.

Managing Animal Pests

Nothing short of gardening in a cage provides complete protection against animal pests. However, there are a few strategies that can help you stay friends with the local wild and domestic animals without sacrificing your garden to them.

Domestic Intruders

Dogs and cats often take a keen interest in your gardening efforts. Try some of these tactics for protecting your plants from investigation by dogs and cats.

- Cover new beds or plantings with wire mesh to keep cats from digging.
- Put up temporary fencing to keep out dogs until new plants are established.
- If your dogs are a serious problem in your gardens, you can install invisible fencing (an underground wire that sets off a shock collar when the pet gets too close) to keep the dogs out of garden areas (as well as on your property).
- A low fence around your property may keep neighborhood dogs out of your garden.
- Arrange your garden with mulched or mown paths so your dogs can run without trampling your plantings.
- Thorny clippings from roses or raspberry bushes may deter cats bent on parading through, sleeping on, or digging in your garden. But be careful not to prick yourself on the clippings!

Rabbits

Bunnies are cute on your lawn, but they can be a real problem when they start nibbling your perennials. They are mostly a problem in early spring when there are new, tender shoots and in winter when food is scarce.

- In early spring, try spreading the thorny clippings from your roses or brambles around the plants that rabbits favor. Gather and dispose of the clippings in early summer when the bunny threat is past. If rabbit damage is a severe problem in your area, you may need to use low fencing around your perennial beds for season-long protection.
- If winter nibbling is a problem, cover tasty plants with wire mesh cages in fall. Remove the cages in spring once the new growth is well started.
- Various smells are repellent to some rabbits some of the time. Experiment with hot pepper, dirty socks, dried blood, used cat litter, or fox lure (available at hunting-supply stores) to see what will repel your rabbits.
- Having cats and dogs around may make rabbits leave.

Small Rodents

Moles, voles, shrews, mice, and gophers chew on crowns and roots and/or dig tunnels in the soil. Try these ideas for making your yard less habitable for them.

- Keep mulch pulled away from plants until cold weather settles in so rodents will find winter homes away from your plants.
- Try drenching the soil with a product based on castor oil, or grow castor beans (*Ricinus communis*) to repel burrowing

critters. (Keep in mind all parts of the plant are poisonous.)

- A cat with a taste for hunting can put a dent in the rodent population. It's an individual choice whether to allow or encourage your cats to hunt around your yard.

Deer

To a frustrated gardener, a deer is an eating machine on springs. They effortlessly hop over 4-foot fences and have been known to eat just about any plant they can reach. Short of an ugly and horrendously expensive fence, there is no guaranteed way to banish deer altogether, but you may have success with some of these repellents and techniques.

Deodorant soap (the smelliest brand you can find). Drill holes through bars of deodorant soap (don't remove the wrapper), insert wire through the holes, and hang the bars about 3 feet off the ground around your garden.

Egg yolks. Whip a few egg yolks, mix them with a gallon of water, and spray your plants generously (you won't be able to smell them, but the deer will). Repeat as necessary. (Now you know what to do with all those leftover yolks from low-fat recipes.)

Human scent. Hanging old sweaty socks and tee shirts discreetly around your garden might do the trick if you can stand it. Cloth bags of hair clippings also repel deer—and they're easier to blend into a garden design.

Deer-resistant plants. Only plastic plants and a few cacti are truly deerproof. Among perennials, there are some that are less favored by deer—but if a deer population is stressed for food, they may eat any and all of your perennials. In general, deer are less likely to eat aromatic or medicinal plants, including baby's-breath, bee balm (*Monarda didyma*), blanket flowers (*Gaillardia* spp.), catmint (*Nepeta* × *faassenii*), cranesbills (*Geranium* spp.), daylilies, evening primroses (*Oenothera* spp.), false indigo (*Baptisia* spp.), gayfeathers (*Liatris* spp.), hosta, lamb's ears (*Stachys byzantina*), lavender (*Lavandula angustifolia*), orange coneflower (*Rudbeckia fulgida*), poppy, purple coneflower (*Echinacea purpurea*), Russian sage (*Perovskia atriplicifolia*), salvias (*Salvia* spp.), tickseed (*Coreopsis* spp.), and yarrow. It's impossible to predict which plants will be the favorites for a local deer population. Experimentation is the best way to find out which plants are deer-resistant in your area.

A dog. Keeping a dog on your property will deter deer somewhat. However, if your dog likes to chase deer, you may end up with another problem: *how* to keep the dog on your property. Training the dog to obey an invisible fence installed around the perimeter of your property may be the best approach.

Fencing. If all else fails, you may want to resort to installing electric fencing or a special polypropylene mesh fencing.

A single strand of electrified wire about 2½ feet off the ground will slow some deer. Look for earth-tone components to reduce its visual impact. It will work even better if you install it 3 feet outside another 4-foot fence. The combination makes a wide barrier deer don't want to leap over—especially if they can't see where they would land.

Black polypropylene mesh fencing that is virtually invisible from 20 feet away can be hung from trees or posts. Once the deer know it's there, they won't break through it. (An address for a supplier is on page 286.)

USDA Plant Hardiness Zone Map

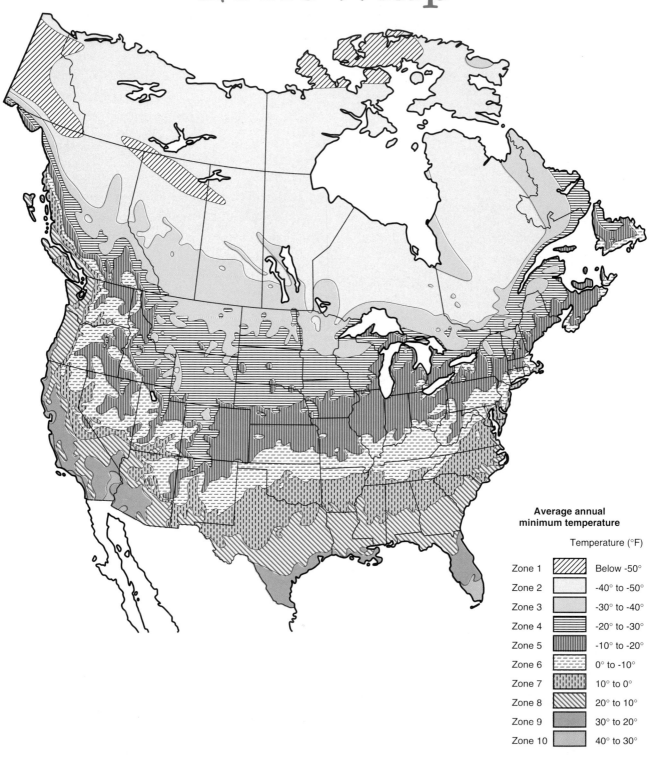

Average annual minimum temperature

Temperature (°F)

Zone		Temperature
Zone 1		Below -50°
Zone 2		-40° to -50°
Zone 3		-30° to -40°
Zone 4		-20° to -30°
Zone 5		-10° to -20°
Zone 6		0° to -10°
Zone 7		10° to 0°
Zone 8		20° to 10°
Zone 9		30° to 20°
Zone 10		40° to 30°

RESOURCES

One of the delights of perennial gardening is the feast of plants from which you can choose. There are so many kinds of perennials—plus new cultivars appearing each year—that you'll always have possibilities for new plantings and combinations.

As you continue to enrich your landscape with perennials, you may find you want more variety than your local garden centers offer. Mail-order shopping offers almost unlimited choices, delivered right to your doorstep or mailbox, often at very reasonable prices. Catalog browsing is also an enjoyable and inspirational pastime for those long winter evenings.

This list includes mail-order sources of plants, seeds, tools, supplies, and information. Some mail-order companies charge a small fee for their catalogs; the fee is often credited toward your first order. Plant societies and smaller companies would appreciate a self-addressed, stamped business envelope enclosed with your inquiry.

Some nurseries offer plants that have been collected from the wild, which may contribute to the near or total extinction of a species. Make sure bulbs, wildflowers, and native plants are nursery-propagated before you buy them.

Perennials and Ornamental Grasses

Ambergate Gardens
8015 Krey Avenue
Waconia, MN 55387-9616

Perennials and ornamental grasses; many new cultivars. Catalog divided into plants for sun and plants for shade; includes descriptions and some color photos.

Kurt Bluemel, Inc.
2740 Greene Lane
Baldwin, MD 21013

Specializes in ornamental grasses, including sedges and rushes for bogs; also carries perennials, bamboos, and ferns. Catalog includes short descriptions, hardiness zones, and some color photos.

Bluestone Perennials
7211 Middle Ridge Road
Madison, OH 44057

Perennials, most available in economy 3-packs, some in larger pots. Also shrubs. Short descriptions and color photos throughout catalog.

W. Atlee Burpee and Co.
300 Park Avenue
Warminster, PA 18974

Perennials; also annuals, bulbs, herbs, and shrubs. Descriptions, cultural information, hardiness zones, and color photos throughout catalog.

Busse Gardens
5873 Oliver Avenue SW
Cokato, MN 55321

Large selection of perennials and cultivars, some economy collections; also native plants. Short descriptions and line drawings throughout catalog.

Carroll Gardens
P.O. Box 310
Westminster, MD 21158

Perennials, roses, herbs, shrubs, and trees. Catalog includes descriptions, hardiness zones, cultural information, and some line drawings.

The Crownsville Nursery
P.O. Box 797
Crownsville, MD 21032

Perennials in 4½-inch containers. Catalog includes detailed descriptions and hardiness zones; no illustrations.

Daisy Fields
12635 Southwest Brighton Lane
Hillsboro, OR 97123

Old-fashioned perennials, most in 4-inch containers. Catalog includes descriptions, hardiness zones, and some illustrations.

Daylily Discounters
Route 2, Box 24
Alachua, FL 32615

Many cultivars of daylilies. Catalog includes complete descriptions, cultural information, color section with photos of most cultivars, and suggestions for cooking with daylilies.

Greer Gardens
1280 Goodpasture Island Road
Eugene, OR 97401

Perennials, plus a wide selection of ornamental trees and flowering shrubs. Also bonsai plants and tools. Catalog includes descriptions, some cultural information, and a limited number of color photos.

J. L. Hudson, Seedsman
P.O. Box 1058
Redwood City, CA 94064

Wide selection of seeds for perennials and native plants from around the world. Catalog includes descriptions and growing information; very few illustrations.

Klehm Nursery
Box 197, Route 5
South Barrington, IL 60010

Specializes in peonies, hostas, and daylilies; also sells other perennials, ornamental grasses, and ferns. Catalog includes descriptions, hardiness zones, and color photos of many selections.

Mellinger's, Inc.
2310 West South Range Road
North Lima, OH 44452

Large selection of perennials; also trees and shrubs (many available in inexpensive starter sizes). Catalog includes descriptions, hardiness zones, and some color photos.

Milaeger's Gardens
4838 Douglas Avenue
Racine, WI 53402-2498

Large selection of perennials, many shipped in pots. Catalog includes descriptions, hardiness zones, and color photos throughout.

Park Seed Co.
Cokesbury Road
P.O. Box 31
Greenwood, SC 29647

Perennial seeds and some plants; also annuals, herbs, bulbs, and shrubs. Catalog includes descriptions, hardiness zones, and color photos throughout.

Plant Delights Nursery
9241 Sauls Road
Raleigh, NC 27603

Specializes in hostas; also sells other perennials and conifers. Catalog includes descriptions, hardiness zones, and a sense of humor; no illustrations.

Roslyn Nursery
211 Burrs Lane
Dix Hills, NY 11746

Wide selection of rhododendrons and azaleas; also sells other flowering and ornamental shrubs, conifers, perennials, and ferns. Catalog includes short descriptions, hardiness zones, and a few color photos.

Thompson & Morgan, Inc.
P.O. Box 1308
Jackson, NJ 08527

Large selection of perennial seeds; also annuals and shrubs. Catalog includes descriptions, hardiness zones, some germination information, and color photos throughout.

Andre Viette Farm and Nursery
Rt. 1, Box 16
Fishersville, VA 22939

Large selection of perennials. Catalog organized by plants for sun and plants for shade; list of plants for bogs; includes short descriptions, hardiness zones, and a few color photos.

Wayside Gardens
1 Garden Lane
Hodges, SC 29695

Perennials, bulbs, ferns, groundcovers, ornamental grasses, shrubs, and roses. Catalog includes descriptions, hardiness zones, and color photos throughout.

White Flower Farm
Litchfield, CT 06759

Perennials, bulbs, ferns, ground-covers, ornamental grasses, roses, and shrubs. Catalog includes enthusiastic and informed commentary, detailed descriptions, hardiness zones, and color photos throughout.

Bulbs

The Daffodil Mart
Route 3, Box 794
7463 Heath Trail
Gloucester, VA 23061

Wide selection of bulbs, specializing in daffodils and tulips. Catalogs includes descriptions and some cultural information.

Dutch Gardens
P.O. Box 200
Adelphia, NJ 07710

Wide selection of Holland bulbs; some perennials. Catalog includes descriptions, cultural information, hardiness zones, and color photos.

McClure & Zimmerman
108 West Winnebago Street
P.O. Box 368
Friesland, WI 53935

Wide selection of bulbs, including many unusual species. Catalog includes descriptions, cultural information, hardiness zones, and some line drawings.

John Scheepers, Inc.
P.O. Box 700
Bantam, CT 06750

Wide selection of bulbs, including many unusual bulbs; also some perennials. Catalog includes descriptions, cultural and forcing information, and color photos.

Van Bourgondien
245 Farmingdale Road
P.O. Box A
Babylon, NY 11702

Imported and domestic bulbs and perennials; also some ferns and wildflowers. Catalog includes descriptions, some cultural information, hardiness zones, and color photos.

Herbs

Nichols Garden Nursery
1190 North Pacific Highway
Albany, OR 97321

Herb seeds and plants, many unusual and imported varieties of ornamentals, everlastings, and wildflowers; also sells garden supplies.

Richters
357 Highway #47
Goodwood, Ontario, Canada
L0C 1A0

Specializes in herbs; also sells wildflower and perennial plants and seeds. Catalog includes descriptions, uses, some germination information, and some color photos.

Sandy Mush Herb Nursery
316 Surrett Cove Road
Leicester, NC 28748

Wide variety of herbs; also flowering perennials and seeds. Catalog includes descriptions, cultural and use information, recipes, and a few line drawings.

Well-Sweep Herb Farm
317 Mt. Bethel Road
Port Murray, NJ 07865

Wide selection of herbs in 3-inch pots or quart containers. Catalog includes flower color, some cultural and use information. No photos or illustrations.

Water Garden Plants

Lilypons Water Gardens
6800 Lilypons Road
P.O. Box 10
Buckeystown, MD 21717

Hardy and tropical water lilies; bog and water garden plants; snails and fish; pond building and maintenance information and supplies. Catalog includes descriptions, hardiness zones, planting and care instructions, and color photos throughout.

Van Ness Water Gardens
2460 North Euclid Avenue
Upland, CA 91784-1199

Bog and water garden plants; snails and fish; pond building and maintenance information and supplies. Catalog includes descriptions, planting and care instructions, and color photos throughout.

Woodland Plants, Native Plants, and Wildflowers

Arrowhead Alpines
P. O. Box 857
Fowlerville, MI 48836

Extensive selection of woodland wildflowers, shrubs, perennials, and rock plants. Two catalogs: one for plants, the other for seeds; short descriptions, no illustrations.

Forestfarm
990 Tetherow Road
Williams, OR 97544

Perennials, western native plants, plants for wildlife, unusual ornamentals and conifers. Catalog includes descriptions and hardiness zones; few illustrations.

Niche Gardens
1111 Dawson Road
Chapel Hill, NC 27516

Specializes in nursery-propagated wildflowers and native plants, perennials, ornamental grasses, and unusual trees and shrubs.

Plants of the Southwest
Route 6, Box 11-A
Santa Fe, NM 87501

Specializes in native wildflower seeds; also sells perennial, ornamental grass, herb, and shrub plants and seeds. Plant list includes photos and descriptions.

Prairie Nursery
P.O. Box 306
Westfield, WI 53964

Seeds and plants of prairie wildflowers and grasses, including selections for moist areas and woodlands. Catalog includes detailed descriptions, line drawings and color photos, and cultural information on establishing and maintaining meadow gardens.

We-Du Nurseries
Route 5, Box 724
Marion, NC 28752

Specializes in nursery-propagated wildflowers and perennials. Catalog includes descriptions and some line drawings.

Woodlanders, Inc.
1128 Colleton Avenue
Aiken, SC 29801

Specializes in southeastern native perennials, shrubs, and trees and new exotic plants. Catalog includes short descriptions, hardiness zones; no illustrations.

Garden Tools, Supplies, and Accessories

Agri Drain Corp
1491 340th Street
Adair, Iowa 50002

In-ground drainage system supplies for wet areas.

Audubon Workshop
1501 Paddock Drive
Northbrook, IL 60062

Bird houses, feeders, food, and baths; bat houses; butterfly feeders; and hummingbird feeders.

Benner's Garden, Inc.
6974 Upper York Road
New Hope, PA 18938

Black polypropylene mesh deer fencing.

286

Brookstone Co.
17 Riverside Street
Nashua, NH 03062

Request the "Hard-To-Find Tools" catalog. A broad range of supplies for irrigation, composting, pest control, and weeding.

Brudy's Exotics
P.O. Box 820874
Houston, TX 77282-0874

Seeds for butterfly-attracting plants, kits for growing butterflies and making butterfly houses and butterfly feeders.

DripWorks
380 Maple Street
Willits, CA 95490

Drip irrigation supplies and pond liners.

Duncraft
102 Fisherville Road
Penacook, NH 03303-9020

Bird baths, feeders, food, and houses; hummingbird feeders.

Gardener's Supply Co.
128 Intervale Road
Burlington, VT 05401

A broad range of supplies including irrigation (request their irrigation sourcebook as well as the general catalog), composting, pest controls, fencing, edgings, and tools.

Gardens Alive!
5100 Schenley Place
Lawrenceburg, IN 47025

Organic pest, disease, and weed control supplies, including deer and rabbit repellent and mole repellent; bat houses and bird houses.

Hydro-Gardens, Inc.
P.O. Box 25845
Colorado Springs, CO 80936

Animal repellents/traps, drip irrigation, insect control, meters and instruments, row covers, hydroponics, and greenhouses and supplies.

Intermatic, Inc.
Intermatic Plaza
Spring Grove, IL 60081-9698

Outdoor 12-volt lighting systems with snap-on lights.

Johnny's Selected Seeds
310 Foss Hill Road
Albion, ME 04910

Cold frame and automatic opener, seed-starting supplies, soil-testing kits, labeling supplies, sprayers, watering supplies, and some perennial flower seeds.

The Kinsman Co., Inc.
River Road
Point Pleasant, PA 18950

Specializes in tools, garden ornaments, plant supports. Also offers composting equipment, cold frames and automatic opener, watering supplies, and bird and bat houses.

Landscape Lighting by Outdoor Gardens, Inc.
1961 NE 147th Terrace
North Miami, FL 33181

Outdoor lighting systems.

Langenbach
P.O. Box 453
Blairstown, NJ 07825

Garden tools, cold frame, arches, arbors, plant supports, watering supplies, and labeling supplies.

A. M. Leonard, Inc.
241 Fox Drive
P.O. Box 816
Piqua, OH 45356

Wide variety of professional tools and supplies, including composting equipment, irrigation, insect control, sprayers, stakes and ties, garden carts, and lawn edgings.

Mellinger's, Inc.
2310 West South Range Road
North Lima, OH 44452

Insect and disease control supplies, composting equipment, irrigation, seed-starting supplies, cold frames and automatic openers, and tools.

Walt Nicke Co.
36 McLeod Lane
P.O. Box 433
Topsfield, MA 01983

Specializes in tools; also offers cold frames, seed-starting supplies, labeling supplies, watering supplies, plant supports and staking supplies, trellises, and bird feeders and houses.

Peaceful Valley Farm Supply
P.O. Box 2209
Grass Valley, CA 95945

Offers a broad range of products, including cover crop seed, organic pest and disease control supplies, tools, seed-starting supplies, labeling supplies, irrigation supplies, cold frames, soil testing kits, and soil amendments.

Vista Landscape Lighting
8611 Kewen Avenue
Sun Valley, CA 91352

Outdoor lighting systems. Write for information on local distributors of their products.

Wind & Weather
P.O. Box 2320
Mendocino, CA 95460

Garden ornaments, including sundials, gazing balls, and weathervanes; weather stations.

Plant Societies

American Hemerocallis Society
Elly Launius
1454 Rebel Drive
Jackson, MS 39211

Offers a source list, slide library, and plants; publishes the Daylily Journal *and regional newsletters.*

American Horticultural Society
7931 East Boulevard Drive
Alexandria, VA 22308

Offers a seed service, horticultural inquiry service, books, seeds, plants; publishes American Horticulturist.

American Hosta Society
Robyn Duback
7802 Northeast 63rd Street
Vancouver, WA 98662

Publishes the Hosta Journal.

American Iris Society
Jeanne Clay Plank
8426 Vine Valley Drive
Sun Valley, CA 91352

Offers plants; has test gardens and publishes a bulletin.

American Rock Garden Society
P.O. Box 67
Millwood, NY 10546

Has many local chapters. Offers winter study weekends, an annual spring meeting, books, seeds, plants. Publishes a bulletin.

Hardy Plant Society— Mid-Atlantic Group
512 West Wayne Avenue
Wayne, PA 19087

Offers books, seeds, plants, and publishes a newsletter.

Hardy Plant Society of Oregon
33530 Southeast Bluff Road
Boring, OR 97009

Offers an annual study weekend, as well as books, seeds, and plants. Publishes a bulletin.

National Wildflower Research Center
4801 La Crosse Avenue
Austin, TX 78739

Publishes regional information packets with recommended wildflower species, bibliographies and fact sheets.

The New England Wildflower Society, Inc.
Garden in the Woods
Hemenway Road
Framingham, MA 01701-2699

Publishes Nursery Sources: Native Plants and Wildflowers, *a list of nurseries that only offer propagated, not wild-collected, plants.*

Perennial Plant Association
Attn.: Dr. Steven M. Still
3383 Schirtzinger Road
Hilliard, OH 43026

Primarily an organization for people with a professional interest in horticulture; publishes a quarterly newsletter and offers a yearly national meeting with speakers and garden tours.

SUGGESTED READING

Perennials

Armitage, Allan M. *Herbaceous Perennial Plants.* Athens, Ga.: Varsity Press, 1989.

Clausen, Ruth Rogers, and Nicolas H. Ekstrom. *Perennials for American Gardens.* New York: Random House, 1989.

Harper, Pamela, and Frederick McGourty. *Perennials: How to Select, Grow, and Enjoy.* Los Angeles: Price Stern Sloan, Inc., 1985.

Lima, Patrick. *The Harrowsmith Perennial Garden.* Camden East, Ontario: Camden House Publishing, 1987.

Landscaping

Brookes, John. *The Garden Book.* Edited by Marjorie J. Dietz. New York: Crown Publishers, 1984.

Cox, Jeff. *Landscaping With Nature.* Emmaus, Pa.: Rodale Press, 1991.

Harper, Pamela J. *Color Echoes.* New York: MacMillan Publishing Co., 1994.

Harper, Pamela J. *Designing with Perennials.* New York: MacMillan Publishing Co., 1991.

Hayward, Gordon. *Garden Paths.* Charlotte, Vt.: Camden House Publishing, 1993.

Hériteau, Jacqueline, and Charles B. Thomas. *Water Gardens.* New York: Houghton Mifflin Company, 1994.

Hobhouse, Penelope. *Color in Your Garden.* Boston: Little, Brown and Co., 1985.

Hynes, Erin, and Susan McClure. *Rodale's Successful Organic Gardening: Low-Maintenance Landscaping.* Emmaus, Pa.: Rodale Press, 1994.
Roth, Susan A. *The Four-Season Landscape.* Emmaus, Pa.: Rodale Press, 1994.

Squire, David. *The Complete Guide to Using Color in Your Garden.* Emmaus, Pa.: Rodale Press, 1991.

Taylor's Guide to Garden Design. (Taylor's Gardening Guides). Boston: Houghton Mifflin Co., 1988.

General Gardening

Ball, Jeff, and Liz Ball. *Rodale's Landscape Problem Solver.* Emmaus, Pa.: Rodale Press, 1989.

Benjamin, Joan, and Barbara W. Ellis, eds. *Rodale's No-Fail Flower Garden.* Emmaus, Pa.: Rodale Press, 1994.

Damrosch, Barbara. *The Garden Primer.* New York: Workman Publishing, 1988.

Ellis, Barbara W., and Fern Marshall Bradley, eds. *The Organic Gardener's Handbook of Natural Insect and Disease Control.* Emmaus, Pa.: Rodale Press, 1992.

Ellis, Barbara W., and Fern Marshall Bradley, eds. *Rodale's All-New Encyclopedia of Organic Gardening.* Emmaus, Pa: Rodale Press, 1992.

Hériteau, Jacqueline, and Andre Viette. *The American Horticultural Society Flower Finder.* New York: Simon and Schuster, 1992.

McClure, Susan, and C. Colston Burrell. *Rodale's Successful Organic Gardening: Perennials.* Emmaus, Pa.: Rodale Press, 1993.

Phillips, Ellen, and C. Colston Burrell. *Rodale's Illustrated Encyclopedia of Perennials.* Emmaus, Pa.: Rodale Press, 1993.

Phillips, Roger, and Martyn Rix. *The Random House Book of Perennials.* 2 vols. New York: Random House, 1991.

Taylor's Guide Staff. *Taylor's Guide to Perennials.* Rev. ed. Boston: Houghton Mifflin Co., 1986.

Woods, Christopher. *Encyclopedia of Perennials: A Gardener's Guide.* New York: Facts on File, 1992.

Other Landscape Plants

Appleton, Bonnie Lee, and Alfred F. Scheider. *Rodale's Successful Organic Gardening: Trees, Shrubs, and Vines.* Emmaus, Pa.: Rodale Press, 1993.

Gardner, Jo Ann. *The Heirloom Garden: Selecting and Growing over 300 Old-Fashioned Ornamentals.* Pownal, Vt.: Storey Communications, 1992.

Greenlee, John. *The Encyclopedia of Ornamental Grasses.* Emmaus, Pa.: Rodale Press, 1992.

McKeon, Judith C. *The Encyclopedia of Roses.* Emmaus, Pa.: Rodale Press, 1995.

Proctor, Rob and Nancy J. Ondra. *Rodale's Successful Organic Gardening: Annuals and Bulbs.* Emmaus, Pa.: Rodale Press, 1995.

Taylor, Norman. *Taylor's Guide to Annuals.* Rev. ed. Boston: Houghton Mifflin Co., 1986.

Taylor's Guide Staff. *Taylor's Guide to Ground Covers, Vines, and Grasses.* Boston: Houghton Mifflin Co., 1987.

Taylor's Guide Staff. *Taylor's Guide to Shrubs.* Boston: Houghton Mifflin Co., 1987.

Taylor's Guide to Trees. (Taylor's Gardening Guides). Boston: Houghton Mifflin Co., 1988.

Periodicals

Fine Gardening, The Taunton Press, Inc., Newtown, CT 06470.

Horticulture, Horticulture, Inc., 98 North Washington Street, Boston, MA 02114.

Organic Gardening, Rodale Press, Inc., 33 East Minor Street, Emmaus, PA 18098.

Other Books from Rodale Press

If you've enjoyed *Gardening with Perennials,* you may be interested in these other garden books from Rodale Press.

Rodale's Illustrated Encyclopedia of Perennials

Ellen Phillips and
C. Colston Burrell

Here's a perennial encyclopedia you can really use—not just look at. It presents 161 major perennial entries, plus hundreds of species and cultivars, all described in detail in the encyclopedia sections with complete growing and landscaping information.

The Four-Season Landscape

Easy-Care Plants and Plans for Year-Round Color
Susan A. Roth

An information-packed guide to selecting plants that add color to the landscape all year long, plus an encyclopedia of the best four-season trees, shrubs, groundcovers, grasses, and perennials.

The Encyclopedia of Ornamental Grasses

How to Grow and Use over 250 Beautiful and Versatile Plants
John Greenlee

Grasses are exciting plants with four-season landscape interest. This book is a complete reference to identifying grasses and using them in your yard and gardens.

The Encyclopedia of Roses

An Organic Guide to Growing and Enjoying America's Favorite Flower
Judith C. McKeon

Here is the only organic rose encyclopedia available that offers extensive and accurate rose information, written by a professional American rosarian.

Landscaping with Nature

Using Nature's Designs to Plan Your Yard
Jeff Cox

You'll find detailed instructions in this book for using nature's patterns and color schemes in garden design. Plus, you'll find practical instructions about gardening for wildlife, using water in the garden, landscaping with stone, and using native plants.

Rodale's Successful Organic Gardening: Perennials

Susan McClure and
C. Colston Burrell

A full-color guide to choosing and using over 110 perennials to beautify the home landscape.

Rodale's Successful Organic Gardening: Low-Maintenance Landscaping

Erin Hynes and
Susan McClure

Time-saving tips for creating a beautiful, easy-care yard and garden, including solutions to tough landscaping problems like slopes and shade, and converting your existing yard into a low-maintenance landscape.

PHOTO CREDITS

C. Colston Burrell: pages vii, 47, 62, 75, 96, 98, 103, 112 *(bottom)*, 119, 120 *(bottom)*, 124 *(bottom)*, 133 *(top)*, 174, 189, 212.

Les Campbell/Positive Images: page 30 *(top and middle)*.

R. Todd Davis: pages 87 *(top)*, 126 *(bottom)*, 132 *(top)*, 134 *(top)*, 173.

©Alan L. Detrick: pages 15, 61, 105, 110 *(bottom)*, 115 *(bottom)*, 116 *(bottom)*, 117 *(bottom)*, 125 *(top)*, 130 *(bottom)*, 136 *(top)*, 138 *(bottom)*, 140 *(top)*, 143 *(top)*, 149.

Barbara W. Ellis: pages 39 *(top)*, 85, 162, 172.

Derek Fell: pages 97, 109 *(top)*, 137 *(top)*.

T. L. Gettings/Rodale Stock Images: pages i, 22, 84, 91 *(top)*, 108 *(top)*, 121 *(bottom)*, 130 *(top)*, 152 *(top)*, 164 *(top)*, 179, 188, 193, 197, 205.

Joe Griffin/Rodale Stock Images: page 72 *(top)*.

Jerry Howard/Positive Images: page 38.

Balthazar Korab: pages 42, 46, 74.

Dwight R. Kuhn: pages 23, 26.

Ed Landrock/Rodale Stock Images: pages iv, 123 *(bottom)*, 210.

Ed Landrock/Rodale Stock Images; Joanne Kostecky Garden Design: page 202.

Mitch Mandel/Rodale Stock Images: pages 57, 113 *(bottom)*.

Alison Miksch/Rodale Stock Images: pages 54, 99, 142 *(top)*.

Nancy J. Ondra: pages 11, 63, 68, 110 *(top)*, 141 *(top)*, 153 *(bottom)*, 217.

Jerry Pavia: pages 19 *(right)*, 33, 43, 69, 76, 87 *(bottom)*, 100, 101, 106, 107, 111, 116 *(top)*, 118, 122 *(top)*, 127 *(bottom)*, 129 *(bottom)*, 132 *(bottom)*, 136 *(bottom)*, 138 *(top)*, 142 *(bottom)*, 143 *(bottom)*, 157, 166, 176 *(bottom)*, 196, 198, 201, 203.

Joanne Pavia: pages 95, 102, 123 *(top)*, 125 *(bottom)*, 127 *(top)*, 139 *(top)*, 206.

PhotoSynthesis™: pages ii, 3, 10, 14, 16, 20, 21, 31, 32, 39 *(bottom)*, 40, 50, 51, 60, 67, 73, 89, 90, 108 *(bottom)*, 109 *(bottom)*, 112 *(top)*, 113 *(top)*, 114 *(bottom)*, 115 *(top)*, 117 *(top)*, 120 *(top)*, 121 *(top)*, 122 *(bottom)*, 124 *(top)*, 126 *(top)*, 128 *(bottom)*, 129 *(top)*, 131 *(top)*, 135, 139 *(bottom)*, 141 *(bottom)*, 160, 161 *(bottom)*, 163, 165, 176 *(top)*, 177 *(top)*, 182, 183, 190, 191, 200, 204, 207, 209, 215.

John Pinca/Rodale Stock Images: page 27.

Diane A. Pratt/Rodale Stock Images: pages 1, 80 *(bottom)*.

Rodale Stock Images: pages 128 *(top)*, 170.

Susan A. Roth: pages 59, 72 *(bottom)*, 151, 152 *(bottom)*, 158, 159, 164 *(bottom)*, 167, 177 *(bottom)*, 184, 192, 194, 199.

Marilyn Stouffer/Rodale Stock Images: pages 30 *(bottom)*, 114 *(top)*, 133 *(bottom)*, 156.

Patricia A. Taylor: page 19 *(left)*, 66, 131 *(bottom)*, 153 *(top)*.

©judywhite: pages 18, 41, 56, 80 *(top)*, 91 *(bottom)*, 93, 134 *(bottom)*, 137 *(bottom)*, 140 *(bottom)*, 161 *(top)*, 195.

INDEX

Note: Page references in *italic* indicate illustrations. **Boldface** references indicate photographs.